The Wisdom of

Astronumerology

Volume 1

Discover your true nature and life purpose
with the ancient power of Astronumerology

Samantha I. Samuels

Published by Malavya Books

First Edition

ISBN-13: 978-0-9949131-0-4

Cover art by Gregory Rozek
Cover design by Arthur Sciberras

CONTENTS

PREFACE

Astronumerology is my lifelong passion and sharing its immense value with the world has been a dream of mine for many years. At the ripe old age of 11, this profound art and science came into my life and forever changed my world. At that time, no one in my family had this interest, nor did anyone around me. One could say I was remembering many lifetimes worth of study and the time had come once again to be introduced to my life purpose.

The horoscope column in the Toronto Star in spring of 1998 initially sparked my interest. The forecast written for my Sun sign Gemini uncannily unfolded as the weeks went by. Now from the perspective of having studied astrology for many years and writing a numerology forecast *Your Destiny in Numbers,* I know that the forecasts are meant for general guidance. I believe the specific accuracy I experienced was the guiding hand of God bringing me to fulfill my karmic purpose.

I was intrigued by the daily horoscope and I began reading information online, talking about it to whoever would listen. My first formal book came from a friend for Christmas that year. It was Sydney Omarr's annual day-by-day guide book for Gemini. I obtained a copy of my natal chart, celebrity charts, and the charts of family and friends, and began comparing their chart to their personalities.

Not too long after that, there was another important synchronicity. I was browsing through a bookstore and I came across a book called *Astronumerology, Your Stars are Numbered*. I picked this up and the rest is history! I was introduced to the power of numbers in shaping our lives and how it is intricately combined with astrology in coming to a more comprehensive understanding of personality. Throughout the next several years, I spent most of my spare time in pursuit of gaining knowledge of how this ancient knowledge held the key for unlocking deeper and deeper levels of awareness of who we really are. I feel so much joy immersing myself into this vast sea of knowledge, although one can never master the breadth and depth of all there is to learn in one lifetime.

In Western astrology I'm a Gemini with a Sagittarius Moon so my über curious and analytical mind loves to learn and teach. In Vedic astrology, my ascendant ruler Moon is tightly conjunct with Saturn, ruler of the 8th house of investigation and research. In numerology, my personality number 7 enhances the love of research and discovery, in addition to giving me the desire to share my knowledge via the written word. Learning about theories are intriguing but the real magic happens when you can see how people are living representations of their charts. Facts are verified by you just as easily as they are by me so I hope to make the theory come to life with numerous celebrity case studies. Seeing how other people embody their natal blueprint is an ongoing discovery process for me and I hope to ignite your interest in the same way mine was ignited many years ago.

My promise to you as a reader is that you will understand your personality, strengths, and talents on a deeper level, which will give you more courage in pursuing your passions in life. You will gain confidence in stepping into your personal power and maximizing your potential for success. By understanding the nature of those around you on a deeper level, greater tolerance and forgiveness in relationships can be cultivated.

To get the best value from this book, you should obtain a free copy of your natal chart at http://www.astro.com/cgi/genchart.cgi before you start chapter 1. This way you can apply the concepts being discussed as you go along. If you are new to astrology or numerology, don't be worried about not understanding all the technical terms. There is no need for you to understand every term in this book to understand the central messages and themes. A more intuitive understanding of the unique language comes with progressively deeper levels of study.

There is a time for everything. The key is to identify, and then act on, the dominant energies at the right time. Life flows more naturally when you align with the river than try to swim upstream. When you choose to consciously learn the lessons represented by the planets and numbers energy in your life, you will gradually gain more inner peace and equanimity.

Samantha I. Samuels

September 2015

CHAPTER 1

WHAT IS ASTRONUMEROLOGY?

"Character is Destiny"
- Heraclitus, *Fragments*

Birthdays are wonderful occasions when our family and friends have the opportunity to show us how special we are to them by giving us their blessings for the year ahead. As the Sun returns to the place it was when we were born, we feel increased vitality and happiness as we seize the day!

For many people, their birthday is just an opportunity to have fun and create good memories. As my birthday comes around every June 11th, I cherish the opportunity to celebrate, but to me birthdays have come to take on a much deeper level of meaning. As an Astronumerologist, I have observed that birthdays shape character in meaningful ways. People born under the same Sun sign/ birth date combination share similarities that will influence their behaviour.

I want to start with a powerful example that will give you some food for thought. In deciding what group of people to profile, I wanted to select a small group that is publicly recognizable and who share the same specialized career that is rare to attain. Most of the presidents in the world are male because throughout history that has been the norm. In 2015, there were 28 female world heads of state (excluding monarchs and governors-generals) who had publicly listed birthdays, and who had political power in office at some point in the year. The women I have chosen to profile are a group of extraordinarily intelligent trailblazers who had the stamina to shatter the highest glass ceiling.

There are 108 Sun sign/ birth date combinations and in a sample of 28, there can be a maximum of 28 of those combinations represented. In the female leaders, **7/28 or 25%** of the Sun/sign birthday combinations **comprise double that amount at 14/28 or 50%** of the sample.

If you break down the sample by astrological sign, these are the most popular signs:

1. Pisces (6)

2. Sagittarius (5)

3. Taurus (4) and Libra (4)

They account for 19/28 or 67.9% of the sample. In other words, 4/12 signs or 33.3% account for more than double that percentage in the sample. Even more symbolic is that Venus rules Taurus and Libra, and is exalted in Pisces. Venus is the Roman goddess of love, beauty and prosperity. She powerfully epitomizes the female essence.

The number 2 was by far the most popular birth date (from 1-9), at 8/28 or 28.6% of the sample[1]. In astronumerology, the Moon corresponds to the number 2. The Moon is the female luminary that is reflective of the yin principle. This is the gentle, sensitive, intuitive, emotional, receptive, and nurturing energy. These are the same characteristics that describe the number 2. In astrology, we commonly refer to the Sun and Moon as planets for the sake of convenience, although we recognize that astronomically they are luminaries. Therefore, out of all the ten planets, Venus and the Moon are the only two that are considered female.

1 Please see Appendix 1 for calculations

I also wanted to study the history of female world presidents since the mid-20th century (1940-present) to see if the results in 2015 would be similar to the patterns observed through history[2]. There are a total of 107 female heads of state (and acting heads of state). Out of these, there were 99 who have publicly listed birthdays and 97 whose astrological sign could be verified (not born on a cusp). My only criteria for inclusion was that she had to be in office for at least 180 days, this could be 180 days straight or it could be split over multiple terms.

The results in this sample were the same as the 2015 sample: an astrological sign that was most powerful for Venus was most popular, and number 2 was the most popular birth date. Specifically, out of 97 the sign Libra came out on top, appearing 14 times. Aries came in second at 13 times, and Sagittarius tied with Cancer for third place at 11 times each. In terms of birth dates, number 2 was most popular, appearing 18 times. Number 6 came in second at 15 times.[3] Number 6 is the number that vibrates to Venus and shares many of its characteristics. Among other things, number 6 is a magnetic number that represents beauty, harmony, peace, balance, empathy, compassion, and love.

The signs Libra, Aries, Sagittarius, and Taurus were within the top five signs both in the 2015 sample and in the presidents since the mid-20th century.

In terms of the astronumerology combinations, Aries 2, Cancer 8, and Taurus 11/2 were most popular, each combination appearing four times in the sample. Out of these three combinations, two of them are number 2 birthdates, and two of them (Cancer and Taurus) relate to the female planets (Moon and Venus).

The results in these samples of female world leaders indicate noteworthy symbolism and significance, so can there really be a deeper meaning behind the day you were born?

2 Please see Appendix 2 for the complete table
3 Please see Appendix 2 for calculations

Female Head of State in 2015	Birthday	Country	Sun sign/ birth date combination
Angela Merkel	July 17th	Germany	Cancer 8
Catherine Samba-Panza	June 26th	Central African Republic	Cancer 8
Ellen Johnson-Sirleaf	October 29th	Liberia	Scorpio 2
Tatiana Turanskaya	November 20th	Transnistria	Scorpio 2
Cristina Fernández de Kirchner	February 19th	Argentina	Pisces 1
Dalia Grybauskaite	March 1st	Lithuania	Pisces 1
Erna Solberg	February 24th	Norway	Pisces 6
Laimdota Straujuma	February 24th	Latvia	Pisces 6
Dilma Rousseff	December 14th	Brazil	Sagittarius 5
Helle Thorning-Schmidt	December 14th	Denmark	Sagittarius 5
Portia Simpson Miller	December 12th	Jamaica	Sagittarius 3
Ewa Kopacz	December 3rd	Poland	Sagittarius 3
Kolinda Grabar-Kitarović	April 29th	Croatia	Taurus 2
Ana Jara	May 11th	Peru	Taurus 11/2
Park Geun-hye	February 2nd	South Korea	Aquarius 2
Marie Louise Coleiro Preca	December 7th	Malta	Sagittarius 7
Simonetta Sommaruga	May 14th	Switzerland	Taurus 5
Kamla Persad-Bissessar	April 22nd	Trinidad and Tobago	Taurus 22/4
Saara Kuugongelwa-Amadhila	October 12th	Namibia	Libra 3
Ameenah Gurib	October 17th	Mauritius	Libra 8
Sheikh Hasina Wajed	September 28th	Bangladesh	Libra 1
Michelle Bachelet	September 29th	Chile	Libra 2

Atifete Jahjaga	April 20th	Kosovo	Aries 2
Doris Leuthard	April 10th	Switzerland	Aries 1
Andrea Belluzzi	March 23rd	San Marino	Aries 5
Lorella Stefanelli	February 20th	San Marino	Pisces 2
Eveline Widmer-Schlumpf	March 16th	Switzerland	Pisces 7
Camilla Gunell	September 7th	Aland Islands	Virgo 7

If this example captured your interest, I am delighted to tell you more about this wonderful art and science. Astronumerology--the combination of astrology and numerology--helps us gain a comprehensive understanding of an individual's personality, karma, and life trends. Separately, both astrology and numerology provide excellent tools that reveal this information, but when combined they add up to an unsurpassed level of accuracy. By using both astrology and numerology, the Astronumerologist is able to see how the planets, signs and numbers work together in shaping character.

This book combines western astrological Sun signs with numbers. The Sun, the core of who we are--our basic essence--represents our fundamental individuality and describes that on which we focus our attention. The 12 signs of the zodiac and nine base numbers total 108 combinations (12 x 9) that reveal specific information about one's personality. For example, people born on May 24th, June 6th, and June 15th are termed "Gemini Number 6" people. These particular individuals possess a mixture of personality traits reflective of the sign Gemini combined with the personality traits associated with the number six.

DIFFERENCES WITHIN ASTROLOGICAL SUN SIGNS

Regardless of your level of familiarity with astrology, you've probably noticed that two people born under the same Sun sign may display very different characteristics. For example, let's assume you have two friends who are Sagittarians. The sign of

Sagittarius is traditionally known for its optimism, good sense of humour, philosophical bent, and need for freedom. Nevertheless, you observe that only one of your friends fits this description. The other one is more mysterious, passionate, and intense. You may wonder, **why are there differences between people of the same Sun sign?**

Each sign hails from a different element (fire, air, earth, or water) and modality (cardinal, mutable, or fixed), which gives it a unique flavour. In addition, the Moon, Mercury, Venus, Mars, Jupiter, Saturn, Uranus, Neptune, and Pluto may have been moving through different zodiacal signs than our Sun at the time of our birth.

Each sign and planet has a different meaning. And each planet behaves differently in a different sign. A person with his or her Sun, Moon, and Jupiter in Sagittarius will be more conventionally Sagittarian than someone with simply her Sun in Sagittarius and all her other planets in different signs.

Signs

Aries ♈ keywords: desire, ambition, straightforward, self-centred thought, assertiveness, pushy, motivating, action-orientation, sports, competitiveness, leadership, impulsive, active mind, courage, bravery, impatience, and independence.

Taurus ♉ keywords: stability, security, comfort, stubbornness, tradition, love of material possessions and sense pleasures, musical, sensuality, resistance to change, steadfast, devotion, family orientation, dependability, conservative, practical, affectionate, possessive, and passion.

Gemini ♊ keywords: dual nature, intellect, curiosity, flexibility, changeability, versatility, diverse interests, restlessness, flighty, communication, quick-witted, fast learning, logic, detachment, mental activeness, speech, and love of knowledge.

Cancer ♋ keywords: attachment to home and family, security, emotional expressiveness, intuition, nurturing, shy, sentimentality, tradition, love of the past, sensitiveness, hospitality, peace loving, hoarding, subjectivity, excellent memory, and moodiness.

Leo ♌ keywords: creativity, drama, generosity, attention loving, fun-loving, pride, warmth, leadership, enthusiasm, uplifting, energy, nobility, grandness, confidence, showing off, bossy, vanity, idealism, inspiring, and vitality.

Virgo ♍ keywords: service, helpfulness, attention to detail, hard work, logical thinking, objectivity, humble, perfectionism, discerning, critical view, health consciousness, purity, cleanliness, objective analysis, responsible, methodical, practicality, conscientiousness, productivity, and intellect.

Libra ♎ keywords: harmony, diplomacy, tact, sociability, indecision, fairness, peace-loving, sophistication, need for partnership, supportive, charm, procrastination, gentleness, beauty, and excellent aesthetic sense.

Scorpio ♏ keywords: power, determination, investigation, mystery, secretive, depth, research activity, probing, passion, possessiveness, resourcefulness, intensity, strategic thinking, transformation, penetrating, extremes, obsessive, strength, love of truth, skepticism, suspicious, and survival instincts.

Sagittarius ♐ keywords: humour, truth, bluntness, joviality, enthusiasm, optimism, philosophies, outdoor activity, sports, independence, adventure, foreign travel, exploration, friendliness, generosity, idealism, freedom, love of knowledge and learning, and persuasiveness.

Capricorn ♑ keywords: order, hierarchy, authority, serious, discipline, perseverance, ambition, competition, good business sense, status oriented, responsible, conservative, realistic thinking, practicality, frugality, reserved, tradition, steadiness, and efficiency.

Aquarius ♒keywords: originality, uniqueness, eccentricity, revolution, friendship, group affiliations, humanitarian efforts, independence, detachment, rebelliousness, stubbornness, service orientation, visionary, unconventional, social activism, and freedom.

Pisces ♓ keywords: compassion, devotion, understanding, intuition, sensitive, dreamy, subjectivity, gentleness, empathy, impressionable, indirect, helpful, open-mind, transcendence, spirituality, imaginative, other-worldliness, fantasy, and creativity.

ASTROLOGICAL ELEMENTS

The 12 signs are divided into four groups based on their element: water, air, earth and fire. These signs share similar characteristics and ways of approaching the world. Signs in the same element are in a trine aspect (see section on aspects) therefore they get along best with each other. If your planet makes a trine with another's person's planet you will have an easy time relating to them in those planets' domains. Fire signs have good compatibility with air signs and water signs have good compatibility with earth signs.

Fire signs are Aries, Leo, and Sagittarius. These signs are passionate, optimistic, inspirational, intense, honest, vibrant, enthusiastic, assertive, action-oriented, confident, and energetic. They make excellent leaders and are excellent at motivating people. Their tendency to act without thinking about their actions first, and their proclivity towards having an explosive temper can get them into trouble.

Air signs are Gemini, Libra, and Aquarius. These signs are abstract, freedom-loving, friendly, curious, imaginative, intellectual, detached, talkative, logical, and objective. They are excellent communicators and thrive on exchange of ideas. They can appear cold because they don't like to get bogged down in heavy feelings, and they may have a tendency to talk about feelings than experience them.

Earth signs are Taurus, Virgo, and Capricorn. These signs are practical, businesslike, stable, productive, dependable, sensible, hardworking, pragmatic, conservative, and enjoy material pleasures. They are excellent at following through on ideas with concrete action. Their negative tendencies are that they can become materialistic, lack imagination, and not take enough risks.

Water signs are Cancer, Scorpio, and Pisces. These signs are sensitive, emotionally intense, intuitive, impressionable, subjective, sentimental, artistic, and express themselves best nonverbally. They have very accurate hunches and can easily and accurately feel what other people are feeling. At times, others can be overwhelmed by their intensity of emotions, and frustrated by their lack of logical reasoning.

ASTROLOGICAL QUALITIES

The 12 astrological signs are divided into three groups based on quality. These quality groups are cardinal, fixed, and mutable. Signs in the same group form a square aspect (see section on aspects) which means that they have to exert considerable effort to get along. The exception to this rule is that you will generally get along with members of the opposite sex in the opposite sign to yours. For example, if you are a Leo woman, you would probably get along well with an Aquarius man.

Cardinal signs are Aries, Cancer, Libra and Capricorn. These signs are action- oriented, enthusiastic, and entrepreneurial. They have the energy to initiate and lead projects, and can be trendsetters. However, they can get bossy and not consider other people's opinions.

Fixed signs are Taurus, Scorpio, Aquarius and Leo. These signs are stubborn, persistent, resistant to change, determined, and willful. They persist and exert all their energy until they accomplish their goal, one at a time. However, they are slow to change their opinions even if presented with facts to the contrary.

Mutable signs are Gemini, Virgo, Sagittarius and Pisces. These signs are adaptable, changeable, restless, and versatile. They can make the best of any situation because they quickly change their thinking to accommodate new circumstances. However, they can take on too many projects at once and not spend sufficient time in mastering any one project.

Opposite signs are: Aries ----- Libra

Taurus --- Scorpio

Gemini -- Sagittarius

Cancer --- Capricorn

Leo ------- Aquarius

Virgo ----- Pisces

Keep in mind that many couples who are in fulfilling and long-lasting relationships have their Sun signs in a square aspect and many couples who fight a lot have their Sun signs in a trine aspect. To accurately analyze the level of compatibility between two people, it is critical to do a holistic analysis of all the planets in each sign and house in one partner's chart, and consider where they are placed in relation to the other partner's chart- this is called a **synastry chart**. The **composite chart** is combining both people's charts to create one new chart. This is symbolic of the relationship itself, and may take on an entirely different energy than either person on their own. The relationship dynamics, areas of karmic focus, and overall purpose of the relationship can be gleaned from studying these charts in great detail.

PLANETS AND LUMINARIES

The **Sun** ☉ represents creativity, individuality, life force, essence, ego, confidence, power, the father, pride, and basic nature. The Sun is always center stage. The Sun rules Leo and is exalted in Aries. It is in detriment in Aquarius and in fall in Libra.

The **Moon** ☾ represents feelings, instinctual responses, habits, adaptability, comfort, security, protection, the mother, hunches, intuition, and imagination. The Moon rules Cancer and is exalted in Taurus. It is in detriment in Capricorn and fall in Scorpio.

Mercury ☿ represents thoughts, logic, idea exchange, reasoning, rationality, communications, writing, broadcasting, expression, curiosity, adaptability, objective analysis, intellect, and sense of humour. Mercury rules Gemini and Virgo and is also exalted in Virgo. It is in detriment in Sagittarius and in fall in Pisces.

Venus ♀ represents love and romance, happiness, beauty, music, art, sensuality, material comforts, sense pleasures, money, and entertainment. Venus is the lesser benefic in astrology. Venus rules Taurus and Libra and is exalted in Pisces. It is in detriment in Scorpio and Aries and in fall in Virgo.

Mars ♂ represents ambition, action, vitality, drive, energy, desire, assertion, and aggression, expressions of anger, sexual attraction, impulsiveness, and enthusiasm. Mars is the lesser malefic in astrology because its energy on the negative side can cause accidents (including travel-related), burns, cuts, violence, and antisocial and criminal behaviour. Mars rules Aries and Scorpio and is exalted in Capricorn. It is in detriment in Libra and Taurus and is in fall in Cancer.

Jupiter ♃ represents luck, optimism, goodwill, philosophies, religion, higher education, teaching, wisdom, law, morals and ethics, excess, expansion, and generosity. Jupiter is the greater benefic in astrology. Jupiter rules Sagittarius and Pisces and is exalted in Cancer. It is in detriment in Gemini and Virgo and in fall in Capricorn.

Saturn ♄ represents restrictions, hard work, discipline, perseverance, obstacles, isolation, responsibilities, authority figures, senior citizens, and challenges. Saturn is the greater malefic in astrology because its energy on the negative side can cause excess restrictions, poverty, intense deprivation, paralyzing doubt and fear, major depression, long-lasting trials, and mental and/or physical illness. Saturn rules Capricorn and Aquarius and is exalted in Libra. It is in detriment in Cancer and Leo and is in fall in Aries.

Uranus ♅ represents discovery, innovation, revolutionary thought, genius, unexpected or shocking events, surprises, originality, rebellious behaviour, invention, eccentricity, change, and future trends. Uranus rules Aquarius.

Neptune ♆ represents inspiration, poetry, art, dreams, music, illusions, delusions, intuition, confusion, spirituality, compassion, fantasies, mysticism, reclusiveness, film, visions, metaphysics, photography, imagination, and escapism. Neptune rules Pisces.

Pluto ♇ represents transformation, death and rebirth, power, healing, occult, resourcefulness, stamina, domination, control, manipulation, subconscious mind, obsessions, determination, and passion. Pluto rules Scorpio.

POSITIONS OF STRENGTH AND WEAKNESS FOR THE PLANETS

Planets usually have one or two signs that they rule, one or two signs they are in detriment in, one sign they are exalted in and one sign they have a fall in. Uranus, Neptune and Pluto, the three planets that were last to be discovered, only have one planet they rule.

Rulership conveys that the qualities of the sign and planet fall in natural harmony with each other. The qualities of a planet are most naturally placed in the signs they rule so they have an easy time expressing themselves well. The Sun rules Leo. Sun sign Leo people usually love the spotlight, are dramatic, and are good self-promoters.

Exaltation conveys that the qualities of a planet find the highest expression; their energies express themselves to their best potential. The planet's sign of exaltation is where it is like a King or Queen, it performs majestically. Venus is exalted in Pisces, here the love nature is idealistic, compassionate and unconditional. Love can transcend physical limitations.

A planet's **detriment** is the sign opposite to their rulership. Detriment conveys that the planet has a hard time expressing itself, and the negative manifestations can more easily occur if the person does not consciously work on improving them. The planet functions with obstacles in its path. The Moon is in detriment in Capricorn, here the emotional nature can be reserved and cautious. Emotions and affection are not spontaneously expressed.

A planet is said to be in fall when it is in the sign opposite to its exaltation. A planet in **fall** feels uncomfortable expressing itself so its expression becomes muddled. The principles of the planet and the characteristics of the sign are at odds with one another. Mars is in fall in Cancer, here there is a tendency for passive aggression, and giving the silent treatment rather than expressing anger in a direct manner.

Planet	Ownership	Traditional ownership	Exaltation	Detriment	Fall
Sun	Leo		Aries	Aquarius	Libra
Moon	Cancer		Taurus	Capricorn	Scorpio
Mercury	Virgo/Gem		Virgo	Pisces/Sag	Pisces
Venus	Taurus/Lib		Pisces	Scorpio/Aries	Virgo
Mars	Aries	Scorpio	Capricorn	Libra	Cancer
Jupiter	Sagittarius	Pisces	Cancer	Gemini	Capricorn
Saturn	Capricorn	Aquarius	Libra	Cancer	Aries
Uranus	Aquarius			Leo	
Neptune	Pisces			Virgo	
Pluto	Scorpio			Taurus	

Mutual Exchange

Planets that are in each other's signs gain favourability and are able to function as if they were in their own sign. For example, if you have Mercury in Taurus and Venus in Gemini, this is a mutual exchange.

The mutual exchange is particularly helpful when one sign is debilitated or fallen. For instance, Venus in Virgo (sign of its fall) and Mercury in Libra (Venus' sign). Sophia Loren had this combination and is known for her ageless beauty. She entered a beauty pageant at age 14 and became first runner-up, the exposure helped her breakthrough into a career of starring in movies. Venus in Virgo can sometimes give a tendency towards lack of confidence in beauty and appearance. In contrast, Loren's self-confidence is shown through her statements, *"I think the quality of sexiness comes from within. It is something that is in you or it isn't and it really doesn't have much to do with breasts or thighs or the pout of your lips"* and *"Beauty is how you feel inside, and it reflects in your eyes. It is not something physical."* [4]

Planets in signs	Dispositor
Aries	Mars
Taurus/ Libra	Venus
Gemini/Virgo	Mercury
Cancer	Moon
Leo	Sun
Scorpio	Pluto
Sagittarius	Jupiter
Capricorn	Saturn
Aquarius	Uranus
Pisces	Neptune

---

4 http://www.brainyquote.com/quotes/authors/s/sophia_loren.
html#TZ9yjxTcX2PdSRPC.99

DISPOSITORS

A planet's dispositor is found by finding which sign a planet is in and looking at its ruler. For example, Venus in Gemini's dispositor is Mercury, we know this because Mercury rules Gemini. Mars in Cancer's dispositor is the Moon, we know this because the Moon rules Cancer. The dispositor of a planet is the deeper essence of that planet and reveals another layer to its functioning. For example, the person with Mars in Cancer has ambition (Mars) directed toward enhancing their sense of security (Moon).

When going through your natal chart, you may find one or more final dispositors, these are planets in their own sign and they gain increased power from the number of planets that feed into it. The more planets that feed into it, the more powerful it becomes. For example Mars is in Taurus, Venus is its dispositor. Then you have Venus in Leo, Sun is its dispositor. Then you have Sun in Sagittarius, Jupiter is its dispositor. Then you have Jupiter in Sagittarius. Because Jupiter is in the sign it rules, it would be the final dispositor for Mars, Venus, and Sun. Final dispositors have increased prominence in personality.

PLANET BEHAVIOUR IN DIFFERENT SIGNS

Each planet behaves differently in different signs. For example, a person with Mercury in Gemini will be logical, a fast learner, quick-witted, and able to express ideas clearly. Meryl Streep and Audrey Hepburn have Mercury in Gemini. A person with Mercury in Taurus will take longer to process information but will be very through in whatever they study. They may have a pleasant speaking or singing voice and are likely to take more time to respond to you. Clint Eastwood and Barbra Streisand have their Mercury in Taurus.

An in-depth celebrity case study is helpful in illustrating these concepts. Don't worry if you are not understanding all the astrological language just yet, you can always return to it later.

Bruce Lee had his Sun in Sagittarius but had his Moon, Venus, Mars and Mercury in Scorpio. He was born on November 27th, number 9 vibrates to Pluto (the modern ruler of Scorpio) and Mars (the traditional ruler of Scorpio). From this pattern, we can see the incredibly strong passion, focus, and discipline that allowed him to be a pioneer among martial artists. He had tremendous personal magnetism and a very strong will. Mars represents the warrior archetype. In his chart, Mars is in Scorpio. Mars is the traditional ruler of Scorpio and is able to give optimal results.

Looking at his chart holistically, we see that he is the epitome of possessing positive warrior energy. Yet because the Sun is at the core, his Sagittarius traits are apparent in several ways as well. He majored in philosophy in University; in papers he would focus on the philosophies behind martial arts techniques. Sagittarius is the sign of the teacher, he made martial arts his career and founded multiple schools to teach gung fu and his own Jeet Kune Do techniques to students. Sagittarius represents publishing, and Bruce was a prolific philosophical author, sharing his thoughts about the nature of combat, his method of physical training and fighting, self-actualization, spirituality, and filmmaking.

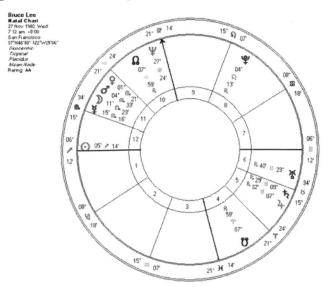

ASTROLOGICAL HOUSES

The next part of analysis is the 12 astrological houses, as each house governs a different area of life. The houses move counter clockwise starting from the 9:00 position (the first house). The first house represents our body and first impressions, the second our finances and personal values, the fourth family and home, the tenth career and public status, and so forth.

Each house--depending on what planets and signs are influencing it--will provide a different dimension to interpretation.

The ascendant (the cusp of our first house), is so unique that it changes every four minutes. This means that two people born only minutes apart in the same place can have very different life experiences. The astrological houses are covered in detail in *The Wisdom of Astronumerology Volume 2.*

PLANETS IN THE HOUSES

Planets placed in houses give energy-- the more planets in a house, the more attention the house receives. Three or more planets in a house are termed a stellium. The planets also influence the mode of operation of the house. For example, if Mercury is in Gemini in the tenth house, the person's career will probably have a large communications component where their speaking or written ability is relied on. Their intelligence or thinking style will be publicly spotlighted. Marilyn Monroe had this placement, and in contrast to her dumb blond persona for the movie screen, it is reputed that she had an IQ score of 168!

Returning to the case study, Bruce Lee's Sun in Sagittarius is tightly conjunct his Sagittarius ascendant (cusp of the first house). This means that the first impressions he gives to people will be Sagittarian. The Sun on the ascendant gives him an interest in being center stage and having people recognize his talents and accomplishments. We know that he had a huge interest in acting and filmmaking, having starred in and produced several popular movies (i.e. *Enter the Dragon, Fist of Fury, The Big Boss*). He was a film icon who broke box office records. The Sun's placement by sign and house is where we shine, the fact that his Sun was on the ascendant gave a big boost in gaining fame in his field of expertise. The first house also represents the physical body and he was respected for his dedication in maintaining a well-chiseled physique. If the Sun was not on the ascendant, it is likely that his Scorpio stellium of planets would have overshadowed the Sagittarian influence in the public eye.

The **tenth house** represents career and we see that Bruce has Virgo on the MC (cusp of the 10th house) with Mercury ruling it. This means that a prominent part of his career would deal with communication and media, indeed he authored multiple best-selling books and appeared on television. Mercury can represent teaching; he founded schools based on his Jeet Kune Do. Mercury is conjunct the 12th house cusp, coloring his writing towards philosophy, wisdom, and spirituality. Mercury is in Scorpio, and its modern dispositor is Pluto or traditional dispositor is Mars, this is clearly reflective of his career as a martial artist and his public reputation of being interested in fighting and combat.

Neptune is in the tenth house and is in Virgo, another indication of his communication being colored by philosophy and spirituality. Neptune represents acting and filmmaking so its placement in the tenth house helped him attain success in those pursuits. The North Node's position by house represents the area of life we should concentrate on for our personal growth. If the North Node is in the 10th, a person benefits from concentrating on their career and public reputation, positive recognition is easier to attain. Bruce's North Node in the 10th house enhanced fame in his career.

The 11th house is the most prominent in Bruce's chart. This is because of the stellium of planets in Scorpio placed there. The

11th house represents dreams, desires, large groups, humanitarian efforts, charities, friendships, and social movements. This shows that many of his heartfelt dreams came true in his life and his wishes were fulfilled. He would no doubt be pleased with The Bruce Lee Foundation, a charitable organization that "preserves, perpetuates and disseminates" Bruce Lee's philosophies and art of Jeet Kune Do through education, martial arts instruction, and the Bruce Lee Museum.[5]

ASTROLOGICAL ASPECTS

Astrological aspects add yet another layer to one's personality. The circle of the zodiac is comprised of 360 degrees, and every planet was located a certain number of degrees away from every other planet at the exact time you were born. The relationship dynamic between two planets--and whether they will express their energy harmoniously or not--is determined by the number of degrees (or angle) between them.

You need a good balance of easy and hard aspects to be successful in life. In other words, trines and sextiles give gifts but you need squares and oppositions to give the inner drive to do something with these gifts.

MAJOR ASPECTS:

Trine △ This is a 120 degree or approximately four signs apart aspect. An orb of seven degrees between planets and nine degrees for Sun and Moon is permitted. The trine is considered easy in that there are natural gifts and talents between the two planets involved. The planets are well integrated in a person's psyche. In predictive work, a trine brings harmonious conditions but some effort must still be made by a person to reap the full benefits.

Conjunction ♂ This aspect occurs when two planets are in the same sign and no greater than eight degrees apart between

---

5 http://www.bruceleefoundation.org/index.cfm/page/Mission/pid/10245

planets or 10 degrees for the Sun and Moon. The conjunction can be either easy or hard depending on the planets involved. Conjunctions have a lot of energy and that is why a larger orb is permitted. The conjunction is the blending of two planets energies into one combined energy. If the planets' characteristics work well together the conjunction is easy. However, if the planets clash, the conjunction is hard. In predictive work, conjunctions can produce either positive or challenging circumstances depending on the planets involved.

Sextile ✱ This is a 60 degree or approximately two signs apart aspect. An orb of seven degrees between planets and nine degrees for Sun and Moon are permitted. It is considered easy because there are natural gifts between the two planets involved. They are well integrated in a person's psyche but require more effort than a trine to make use of. In predictive work, sextiles bring harmonious conditions but as compared to the trine, a greater degree of effort must be made by a person to reap the full benefits.

Opposition ☍ This is a 180 degree or approximately six signs apart aspect. An orb of eight degrees between planets or 10 degrees for the Sun and Moon are permitted. The opposition is considered hard because the characteristics of the signs are on opposite polarities. There is an inherent dual nature and the planets involved will have a more challenging time integrating their energies. In predictive work, the opposition can signify a confrontation or challenge, this will usually arise from an external person or situation.

Square ☐ This is a 90 degree or approximately three signs apart aspect. An orb of eight degrees between planets or 10 degrees for the Sun and Moon are permitted. It is considered hard because the characteristics of the signs clash, they have a harder time understanding each other. This aspect produces tension, stress and drive between the two planets involved to integrate their energies. In predictive work a square between planets can signify a problem, major frustration or sometimes even crisis. In contrast to the opposition, the obstacles created by a square will have their origins within the person rather than arising from any external source.

MINOR ASPECTS

Minor Hard Aspects:

The quincunx/inconjunct ⏀, semisquare ∠, sesquiquadrate ⊡ and semisextile ⋎ are all minor hard aspects. An orb of three degrees between planets and luminaries is usually used. Psychologically, this means it is more difficult to integrate the two planet's qualities in a person's psyche. However, the person who has this minor aspect will not feel it as sharply as they would with a square, opposition, or conjunction. In prediction, these aspects will signify challenging circumstances but to a lesser degree than a square, opposition, or conjunction.

Minor Easy Aspects:

Quintiles Q (72 degrees) and Biquintiles bQ (144 degrees) are minor easy aspects. An orb of two degrees between planets or luminaries is permitted. Technically, these aspects are called minor but personally I have observed them having considerably more power than the other easy minor aspects. These aspects between planets signify creativity, imagination and the potential to make a truly novel contribution in those planets' domains.

Returning to our analysis of Bruce Lee's chart, recall that Mars and Pluto rule Scorpio and he has a stellium of Scorpio planets. To add to this theme we see that Bruce has an exact Mars-Pluto square: Mars is at 4 degrees Scorpio and Pluto is at 4 degrees Leo meaning that they are 90 degrees apart. Squares between planets cause obstacles to be overcome but give a very strong inner push of energy to overcome them, a big cosmic kick in the butt you could say! In particular this square gives tremendous reserves of concentration, strength, stamina, endurance, and focus. People with this square are unstoppable once they set their mind and heart to a goal. There could be anger, aggression and power/control issues but once channeled in a healthy physical outlet such as competitive sports or high intensity exercise, these influences can be worked off.

Uranus in the 6th house makes a trine (120 degree aspect) to the MC (cusp of the 10th house of career). This means that his reputation could be that of a visionary or a pioneer, someone who breaks out of the traditional mold. Uranus is in Taurus in the 6th house. The sixth house represents exercise, diet and nutrition. Taurus represents the cultivation of aesthetic value to the body (proportion, shape, symmetry). Since the trines represent gifts, he was able to make a name for himself with his revolutionary training techniques that allowed him to have a razor sharp physique and unconventional fighting style. For example, he would train different moves on different days, like the jab and hook on Mondays and the side and hook kick on Thursdays. His diet and nutrition routines were way ahead of the times with four or five smaller meals throughout the day, protein shakes to develop strength without bulk, avoidance of empty calories, and vitamin supplements. He was meticulous with his diet and extremely disciplined with regards to what he would eat and in what portions.

Another consideration with the planets is to see how well connected they are in the chart. **A planet that makes many aspects with other planets is going to be prominent in the psychological wiring of the person.** Usually a planet will make two to four aspects with other planets so if a planet makes five or more aspects, its energy is going to be powerful in the personality. In Bruce's chart, Mars aspects six planets (Moon, Jupiter, Pluto, Sun, Venus and Saturn) and Pluto aspects eight planets (Moon, Mars, Neptune, Sun, Jupiter, Saturn, Venus and Uranus) reinforcing that their energy is very powerful. Mars is the warrior; strong positive Martian energy manifests as ambition, drive, determination, bravery and independence. Pluto is the transformer; strong positive Plutonic energy gives one the ability to be transformed from the inside out. It makes a person powerful, strong-willed, and in control of their desires.

NUMEROLOGY

Numerology, similar to astrology, can be used to help people gain enhanced self-understanding and to predict future energies and trends in their lives. An ancient study dating back thousands of years, numerology was used by a wide variety of cultures such as the ancient Chinese, Japanese, Egyptians, Babylonians, Greeks, Hindus, and Tibetans to assist in a variety of endeavours.

Pythagoras, a key figure in the development of modern day numerology, was a Greek mathematician and philosopher who believed that there existed a certain number pattern in all of creation. He observed that these numbers all possessed a unique energy that would help us appreciate the nature of the universe on a much deeper level.[6]

Contemporary numerologists use numerology to help individuals gain a better understanding of their own personality, karma, strengths, weaknesses, motivation, and overall life purpose. Those who understand themselves on a deeper level are better able to fulfill their soul's true calling. In addition, they possess the courage to follow the goals that bring them joy, rather than allow others to dictate to them what they should do with their lives.

The numbers in your birth date and the letters in your name are used to calculate several important numbers that influence you psychologically, and are important in predicting the energies and trends influencing your life for any given period of time. The five core numbers in numerology include: birthday, life path, expression, soul urge, and personality.

---

6 http://www.tokenrock.com/numerology/

These numbers reveal important information about your dreams, desires, skills, inclinations, and motivation. When you make important life decisions that match these numbers-- you will experience greater fulfillment.

The **life path number** tells us about a person's natural gifts and skills and what course of action they need to take in this life to be happy. This number is reflective of our purpose in life, by acting in accordance with it life flows a lot more easily and with a lot less stress.

The **birthday number** tells us about a person's personality traits, what they value as important in life, and their motivation.

The **soul urge number** is a very personal number and its energy is not always obvious to anyone other than the person himself. It is a person's secret wishes and desires; we need to fulfill the needs of this number in order to feel comfortable and secure. If the needs of the soul urge number are not met, there is a sense of dissatisfaction, even if on the surface everything in our life seems to be going well.

The **personality number** describes the impression we make on people when we first meet them. It influences our personal style and dress, our mannerisms, and our outward demeanour. These are our most public characteristics. These characteristics are not necessarily what we wish to convey to others because they manifest without our conscious knowledge.

The **expression number** reveals conspicuous characteristics of a person. This is a number whose energies we are consciously aware of, and when informed of these characteristics by others, we immediately identify with them. The expression number is similar to the life path number in that it is important in showing us our purpose, the goals and activities we should prioritize in order to evolve the most in this life.

NUMBER KEYWORDS:

Number 1

Positive traits- Independent, self-starter, ambitious, assertive, competitive, original, high energy, entrepreneurial, willful, confident

Negative traits- Selfish, insensitive, arrogant, inconsiderate, aggressive, egotistical, self-centered, domineering, impatient

Number 1 people like to blaze new trails and be the first to make original discoveries. They are not afraid to travel where no one else has ventured before. They like to create their own path rather than following established traditions.

Number 2

Positive traits- Loyal, sensitive, sociable, helpful, sincere, diplomatic, sense of balance, peace loving, co-operative, nurturing, flexible

Negative traits- Clingy, sappy, moody, dependent, indecisive, trying too hard to please others, petty

Number 2 people enjoy spending their time with other people; in fact they do not really like to be by themselves for extended periods of time. They like to maintain harmony among people in their lives and they do their best to not deliberately create conflict.

Number 3

Positive traits- Optimistic, philosophical, creative, entertainer, joyful, humorous, articulate, versatile, flexible, generous, charming

Negative traits- Taking on too many activities at once, overdoing things, laziness, procrastination, sarcastic, blunt, melodramatic

Number 3 people have a fun-loving nature and like to entertain other people. Sports and the outdoors may be an interest. Artistic expression may be a skill. Philosophical, they like to discuss important matters with others of like mind.

Number 4

Positive traits- Dependable, responsible, loyal, realistic, sensible, hardworking, practical, self- reliant, stable, disciplined, methodical, original, futuristic, creative, unconventional, friendly

Negative traits- Pessimism, possessiveness, lack of imagination, resistance to change, perfectionist, argumentative

Number 4 people want to know what is expected of them so that they can fulfill their end of the bargain. They are excellent on following through with the practical work that needs to be done for innovative ideas. Another side to their nature is their unconventionality—they like to be unique and stand out from the crowd. Visions for how things could be done in the future and coming up with innovative ideas could be their forte. This dual nature to the number 4 is related to its dual correspondence with Saturn and Uranus.

Number 5

Positive traits- Curious, logical, quick-witted, versatile, fun-loving, freedom loving, good communication skills, bright, adventurous, open-mind

Negative traits- Enjoys gossip, tendency towards escapism, hedonistic, restless, fickle, nervous, scattered, irresponsible

Number 5 people are spontaneous and cherish their freedom. Skilled communicators, they desire to share their perspective, experiences, and stories. World travel is a major interest, meeting foreign people and learning about foreign cultures is something they greatly enjoy.

Number 6

Positive traits- Magnetic, nurturer, compassionate, appreciation of finer things, entrepreneurial, excellent aesthetic sense, fair, good team player, hospitable

Negative traits- trouble receiving criticism, unrealistic expectations, taking on too much responsibility, selfish, giving unwelcome advice

Number 6 people love beautiful things and they generally have excellent taste. Gracious hosts; they enjoy inviting others to their stylish homes. Being service-oriented, they enjoy helping other people. They must feel that they are doing meaningful work for their community or the world, otherwise they often aren't satisfied. They do best when they are self-employed.

Number 7

Positive traits- Spiritually connected, intellectual, insightful, observant, intuitive, imaginative, introspective, philosophical, sophisticated

Negative traits- Perfectionist, verbose, fussy, anxious, aloof, judgemental, pedantic, snobbish, critical, analysis paralysis

Number 7 people are thinkers, they like to read, write, analyze issues, philosophies, mysteries; anything that is mysterious or puzzling fascinates them. They enjoy their solitude more than any other number and come up with their best ideas when alone. If they are spiritually or religiously inclined, they devote a lot of time to thinking about these matters, and may even be reclusive.

Number 8

Positive traits- Good business sense, good provider, confident, competitive, organized, ambitious, high stamina, entrepreneurial

Negative traits- Workaholic, materialistic, blunt, arrogant, aggressive, stubborn, too status conscious, self-important, insensitive, careless

Number 8 people are business and power minded. They enjoy high status, the benefits of having money, and a luxurious lifestyle. Advancement and recognition in their career and/or public standing is very important to them, and they may become workaholics. Their discipline usually means that they are good providers for their family.

Number 9

Positive traits- Humanitarian, compassionate, intuitive, fair, ethical, insightful, authoritative, natural leader or teacher, powerful, creative, astute, strong-willed, tolerant

Negative traits- Holding on to past resentments, critical, intolerant, self-righteousness, stubborn, judgmental, impersonal, suspicious

Number 9 people are interested in global affairs and often have an interest in humanitarian and charity work. They are interested in religious and spiritual matters, and are quite tolerant of other people's beliefs. Artistic, they do well in the performing and visual arts. Number 9 people are natural born leaders and do very well when in charge of people. Teaching comes naturally to them.

Number 11

Positive traits- Inspirational, charismatic, spiritual vision, intuitive, mystical, imaginative, illuminating, strong leader, very bright, benevolent

Negative traits- Escapist, impractical, deceptive, nervous, self centered, confrontational, self-important

Number 11 people are interested in personal growth, spirituality, mysticism, and connecting with a higher power in the Universe. They can be inspirational catalysts for other people's growth as they get them to see new possibilities that were not apparent before. Because they are imaginative and their inner world is rich and fulfilling; they may not always be that interested in the outer world.

Number 22

Positive traits- Inventive, revolutionary thinking, visionary, master builder, trailblazer, genius, charismatic, original, wise

Negative traits- rebel without a cause, instability, extreme thinking, delusion, fanaticism, exhaustion

Number 22 people are visionaries; they are future oriented and detect trends/ ideas ahead of their time. They are good at designing or coming up with ideas for innovative and technological products. Original and creative, fitting into the crowd is not a goal. Blazing their own trail rather than following a set hierarchy comes naturally.

Master numbers 11 and 22 have a higher vibration than the first nine numbers and contain elevated energy. They are special because people who are able to tune into these extraordinary inspirational and illuminating energies have a significant advantage in becoming successful at their pursuits, which are usually unconventional and more complex than the other numbers. At the same time, keep in mind that 11 and 22 break down into the numbers 2 and 4 respectively, and people having characteristics of the master numbers also are influenced by the energy of the base number to some extent. In some cases, if a person does not identify with the characteristics of 11 or 22, they may be exclusively having the characteristics of the 2 or 4. Significant effort and dedication on the part of a person to use the benefits of a master number is critical to maximizing its vast potential.

CALCULATION OF NUMBERS

The birthday number is the day you were born. Bruce Lee's birthday number is 9 because he was born on the 27th. His life path number is 7, to get this we add 11 for November + 27 + 1+9+4+0 that is 11+27+ 14 = 52 =7.

Pythagorean Number-Letter Conversion:

1= A, S, J	2= B, K, T	3= C, L, U	4= D, M, V
5= E, N, W	6= F, O, X	7= G, P, Y	8= H, Q, Z
9= I, R			

The expression number is the total value of the full name, the soul urge number is the total value of the vowels and the personality number is the total value of the consonants. The soul urge and personality numbers must add to the expression number, if they don't you have made a mistake in the calculation.

There are 143 possible combinations of personality, soul urge and expression numbers when taking into account the master numbers.[7]

The chances of you having the same four or five core numbers as someone else that you would meet in person are very small. They would need to have one of the 143 combinations that contained at least two of the same numbers and have the same birthday and life path; or they would need to have exactly the same combination as you and either the life path or birthday number also the same. There are 11 possible options for both the birthday and life path numbers (1-9, 11 and 22). It is understandable then that you will only meet a handful of these people in your lifetime. He or she would have a highly similar temperament, and the relationship would have a special karmic purpose. You may consider both a person's birth name and current name when comparing your numbers to them.

Returning to the case study, the name Bruce Lee gives an expression number 8, personality number 8, and soul urge 9.

BRUCE LEE

29335   355

Adding the entire name we get, 2+9+3+3+5+3+5+5= 35 = 8
Adding the consonants we get, 2+9+3+3= 17 = 8
Adding the vowels we get, 3+5+5+5 =18= 9

His birth name Lee Jun-Fan gives an expression number 7, personality number 2 and soul urge number 5.

LEE JUN-FAN

355 135- 615

7 Since the soul urge plus the personality number must equal the expression number, each number from 1-9 in addition to master numbers 11 and 22 have 13 possible combinations. For example for number 1, they are 1+1=2; 1+1=11; 1+2=3; 1+11=3; 1+3=4; 1+3=22; 1+4=5; 1+22=5; 1+5=6; 1+6=7; 1+7=8; 1+8=9; 1+9=1. 13x11=143.

Adding the entire name we get, 3+5+5+1+3+5+6+1+5=34=7

Adding the consonants we get, 3+1+5+6+5= 20 =2

Adding the vowels we get, 5+5+3+1= 14 = 5

Your name at birth will continue to influence you all throughout life, even if you change it. Upon changing your name, you come to be influenced by a different set of numbers **in addition** to your birth name numbers. In other words, you cannot erase the effects of your birth name numbers, but some people do notice that they become less prominent.

To summarize, for his public name Bruce Lee, his numbers were 9, 7, 8, 8, 9. His birth name gives 9, 7, 7, 2, 5. People born with 9 influencing them can have strong leadership qualities, and he was the founder of his own method of martial arts. Innovation is the hallmark of 9 and through his movies, he changed the way Asians were portrayed in the media by portraying a charismatic action hero. Number 9 has a humanitarian streak and he received the Ethnic Multicultural Academy Legend Award in 2004.

Number 8 corresponds to Saturn and gives the persistence, work ethic, and ambition to constantly be striving towards his personal best. The number 8 desires power, wealth and status and will put in long hours to achieve them. After overcoming setbacks in his youth, he become more resilient to move ahead in life.

Number 7 corresponds with Neptune and gives the interest in philosophy, spirituality, writing, publishing and filmmaking. It can be very creative, imaginative and reflective. Having two number 7's in his youth also caused him to spend a lot of time by himself reading and perfecting his craft. Even into adulthood he needed a good amount of solitude to read and write his many books. He enjoyed presenting his thoughts in a way that would give others food for thought.

The number 5 corresponding to Mercury also gives him a skill for oral and written communication, a compelling style of writing that engages the reader to learn more. The 5 gave him interest in foreign travel and higher education, he was endlessly curious. His ability to learn quickly, be charismatic, possess good humour, and be quick-witted can also be attributed to 5.

The **intensity number** is the number that repeats most often in your name, it is a minor number that adds a layer of analysis in addition to the core numbers. This number pushes its expression into the outer world with power, it is a part of a person that they naturally express without thinking about it. Lee-Jun-Fan has an intensity number of 5 (5 is the number that repeats most often in that name). The name Bruce Lee has three 5's and three 3's. Both 3 and 5 are associated with writing and publishing. Five extends to media and broadcasting, hence the acting and film production. Number 3 corresponds to Jupiter which strengthens the Sagittarius Sun and ascendant.

CELEBRITY CASE STUDY: DR. MAYA ANGELOU

To further illustrate the power of numerology, let us examine the life of Dr. Maya Angelou. She was born Marguerite Annie Johnson on April 4th 1928. Her birthday number is 4. People born on the 4th are responsible, dedicated and hardworking but at the same time have a side to their nature that is visionary, offbeat, and creative. The first letter of her first name is M, which if you recall converts to 4 according to the Pythagorean system. **This first letter of the first name's corresponding number energy** is an additional insight into the natural way of being for a person, which is usually observable after getting to know him or her for a while. Maya participated in the 1963 *March on Washington for Jobs and Freedom* and was involved with fundraising efforts for the *Southern Christian Leadership Conference* that would help challenge the Jim Crow laws. She wrote about the struggle for civil rights in her poetry and books and helped to raise public awareness about social justice.

There are three **life cycle numbers** that affect us at different stages in our life. The number of a life cycle will present opportunities to you characteristic of that number, and you have a chance to develop these traits in your personality to a greater extent in that time period. Maya's 1st and 2nd life cycle numbers until age 53, were both 4, further enhancing her legacy as a cultural pioneer. She said, "It is time for parents to teach young people early on that in diversity there is beauty and there is strength." [8] The first life cycle is your month of birth, the second life cycle is your day of birth, and your third life cycle is your year of birth.

Maya's life path number is 1, this gives her a need for independence and autonomy, and a desire to blaze her own trail in life. In fact she wrote the script for *Georgia Georgia* in 1972 and it was the first by an African American woman to be made into a movie. It was also nominated for a Pulitzer Prize. She is self-confident and has the ability to inspire, lead and direct. Creating her own opportunities; she was self-employed for the majority of her life.

The name Maya Angelou gives an expression number 7, soul urge number 8 and personality number 8.

MAYA ANGELOU

4171   1575363

Adding the entire name we get,
4+1+7+1+1+5+7+5+3+6+3=43 = 7

Adding the consonants we get, 4+7+5+7+3=26 = 8

Adding the vowels we get, 1+1+1+5+6+3=17 = 8

The name Marguerite Annie Johnson gives an expression number 3, personality number 7 and soul urge number 5.

---

8 http://www.africanamericanquotes.org/maya-angelou.html

MARGUERITE ANNIE JOHNSON

4197359925   15595   1685165

Adding the entire name we get, 4+1+9+7+3+5+9+9+2+5+1+5 +5+9+5+1+6+8+5+1+6+5 = 111 =3

Adding the consonants we get, 4+9+7+9+2+5+5+1+8+5+1+5 = 61 = 7

Adding the vowels we get, 1+3+5+9+5+1+9+5+6+6 = 50 = 5

All of the numbers from both names have their influence on her. The numbers 5 and 7 make her a writer, with a compelling message that she wants to get out into the world. She writes "There is no greater agony than bearing an untold story inside of you." Bringing to the reader's mind vivid memories of the painful racial discrimination she faced growing up, as I read her books, I am irresistibly pulled into her world.

Number 7 could have skill as a poet; for writing beautiful, descriptive pieces to evoke deeply held emotion. *Phenomenal Woman* and *Still I Rise* are my two favourites but many of her poems have an inspirational tone to them. She certainly used her sassy words to empower people! Number 5 helps her to gather her thoughts in a clear, eloquent style that makes the reader curious to find out more. She published several best-selling and critically acclaimed autobiographies, essays and books of poetry. A skill for languages can be prominent with number 5, and Maya fluently spoke English, Spanish, French, Arabic, Fanti, and Italian.

The 8 influence gives her the motivation to work hard on her various pursuits as well as a desire to achieve recognition for her work. It also inclines people to be more willing to bestow her with honours. She received numerous honorary degrees, three Grammys, Pulitzer Prize and Tony Award nominations, the National Medal of Arts in 2000, and the Presidential Medal of Freedom in 2011.

The 3 influence gives her talent in the arts. At the age of 14 she won a scholarship to study dance and drama, however dropped out to take care of her son. She resumed her formal study of dance later on, and even danced with Alvin Ailey on variety shows. Maya also recorded an album and danced professionally to Calypso music. She performed in the opera Porgy and Bess in Europe, and took an active role in creating, directing and performing in different productions within the United States. When she was in Ghana, she taught at a University's music and dance program.[9]

PRACTICAL APPLICATIONS IN NUMEROLOGY

THE POWER OF A NAME

The idea that every name has embedded within it a unique destiny based on its numerological vibration is a fascinating one with many practical implications. Since each number corresponds to a particular set of characteristics, any name or concept that adds up to it will carry the essence of that number.

When a baby is born, his or her parents choose a name based on a variety of factors such as ancestry, culture, and personal taste. What many parents don't realize is that they are helping shape their child's character and destiny by having them come under the influence of a certain combination of numbers.

When a woman marries, she often changes her name. However, what she may not realize is that she is also changing her personality and destiny by choosing to be influenced by an additional set of numbers.

When you start a business, the company name can have a direct impact on popularity, prosperity, and profit. The numbers

9 http://voiceseducation.org/content/maya-angelou-0

will shape the "personality" of the company. Choosing a name in harmony with your vision for the company maximizes your likelihood of success.

People often intuit that certain houses, cities, or countries are luckier for them to live in without knowing why. The very real reason has to do with the location's numerical vibration. One may be naturally more blessed and successful in some locations, while living in other areas may restrict this individual's potential.

Obviously, there exist huge potential personal ramifications when deciding what house to purchase in which city. The number of practical numerology applications is endless.

CHOOSING A DATE FOR A SIGNIFICANT OCCASION

When you set a date for an important occasion such as a business launch, fundraiser, or wedding, the numbers derived from that date have a direct influence on the event and the outcome. By consciously choosing a harmonious date, you are giving it the best chance to prosper. While its overall outcome is dependent on a number of other factors, choosing a favourable date can give it that extra favour it needs to thrive. For example, choosing to hold a fundraiser on a given day may increase the probability that the guests are satisfied with the catering, program, and banquet hall. In addition, they may feel compelled to donate more money. Factors for success that are variable include the organizers involved, effort and resources expended in planning, and the nature of the charitable cause.

We have all noticed that some brands seem to gain long-lasting popularity and have endured for a long time. When I examine the founding date of some of these iconic companies such as Walt Disney World or McDonalds, it becomes evident that they had a number of advantages to help them start off on the right foot. The date they founded their business has given them a number of unbeatable competitive advantages. On the other hand, other brands that may have had excellent quality products and/or services go out of business too soon. Again in examining the founding date, there are some major drawbacks that held them back from the start.

The day you get married shapes the themes, trends and energy influencing the marriage. By choosing an auspicious date, you are giving the marriage a desirable type of energy that makes it easier to sustain a happy union. At the same time, the overall success will depend on the relationship karma of each individual, the karma of the couple as a unit, the life events they face together, and the effort they each exert in making the marriage work.

Through this chapter we have seen how there are many components of analysis within astrology and numerology separately. This forms the basis for understanding how they will be blended together in astronumerology to form a more comprehensive analysis. In the next chapter let us take a look at how astronumerology can help us live our best lives in the world today.

CHAPTER 2

THE VALUE OF ASTRONUMEROLOGY IN THE WORLD TODAY

"I have always believed, and I still believe, that whatever good or bad fortune may come our way, we can always give it meaning and transform it into something of value."
- Hermann Hesse, *Siddhartha*

LIVING LIFE CONSCIOUSLY

Astronumerology holds practical information about our personality, relationships, career, finances, and health; it sheds light on our karma and life purpose in each of these areas. When we understand the deeper reason for every event that occurs in our lives, we gain a sense of inner peace. Instead of judging events as good or bad, we view them as learning opportunities in our school of life.

Every event--even those worthy of our worst nightmares-- plant a seed within. From this seed, the pathway to finding the hidden gifts we all possess can grow. Having read *Man's Search for Meaning* by Victor Frankl, and *Left to Tell* by Immaculee Ilibagiza, among countless other amazing stories of forgiveness and transformation, I know that this is true. We attract into our lives events and relationships not meant to make us perfect, but to give us opportunities to find our own inner greatness.

Instead of giving up because of life's battles, we can see the life lessons inherent in them, waiting to be mastered. The astronumerology chart sheds light on where our obstacles reside. When we consciously channel effort into these areas and behave in the best possible way, we find we can deal with them.

Right now, at this very moment, we are creating our karma for better or for worse! **Events may happen in our lives, but we can change the way we react to them.** This makes all the difference in our personal evolution.

Every life decision contains within it a conscious decision of whether to gain strength or become bitter. We are using our freedom of thought to process the experiences that we are faced with either in a creative or destructive way. We can either work with the planets and numbers in an effort to learn their life lessons, or we can resist their influences and create more complicated karma for the next time around. As the saying goes, when life hands you a lemon, don't complain. You can make lemonade!

To a certain extent we are faced with the results of our past actions, and this is our *fixed karma*, which may be seen in a chart through numerous factors pointing to the same tendency.[10] [11] Although this **fixed karma** must happen at a designated point in our lifetime, with knowledge of *why* it is happening we can consciously seek to learn from these situations as we develop through life. When, for example, someone doesn't have any idea why he or she experiences "bad luck with the opposite sex," there is nothing they can do to change it. It will never resolve on its own unless and until they sincerely commit to changing from within.

STAYING TRUE TO YOURSELF

Being true to who you are in a world constantly trying to change you is indeed one of the most difficult challenges life has

10 Rao, K. N. (2003). Karma & Rebirth in Hindu Astrology. New Delhi, India: Vani Publications
11 Kelleher, J. (2006). Path of Light, Volume 1. Ahimsa Press.

to offer. I believe that in today's world, possessing a firm sense of self is more important than ever. From the time you were born, the people around you were already planning the type of person you should be, and what you should do when you grow up. As you mature, friends, the media, and society in general tell you how to act, who to spend time with, and what you should do. During your teenage and adult years, your romantic/marriage partner, employer, and institutions with which you are affiliated also try to influence your life. It might be said that everyone is trying to write your life story for you--according to the vision they have for you in their mind!

Opposition can be fierce when we don't listen to others' "friendly advice," and those close to us can proceed to act in a way that is not conducive to our success. They might make us believe that our dreams are impractical, our talent not "good enough," or comment "you can't make a living doing that!" And on they go...

While these folks may have the best of intentions, no one except God knows the real you--your true passion and purpose for living. [12] In my view, the astronumerology chart is God's way of communicating to us on earth a person's purpose in life. A gift from the Universe, it's a map of information revealing our skills, aptitudes, and karma that assists us to navigate through life with a flashlight in an otherwise dark room. By having the confidence to become what God intended us to be, we are a first-rate version of ourselves and not a second-rate version of someone else.

Society and the media tell us that wealth, status, possessions, nice cars, fancy houses, exotic trips, number of friends and fans, and sexy partners are markers of success. Young, ambitious people may have dreams to climb the corporate ladder, wishing that someday it will be them in the corner office with all the outer trappings of success. They may pursue careers that they are not

12 Throughout this book I use the term God to refer to a higher power and intelligence, not in a specific religious sense. I believe that there is a Universal divine intelligence far greater than what we could imagine that guides our lives. Astronumerology is not a religion and you do not have to be religious or spiritual to benefit from its symbolic wisdom. However, you do have to be receptive to the idea that there is more to the world than we experience with our senses.

really interested in or suited for. Instead of being what nature intended them to be and what would have given them inner satisfaction, they choose a job for the glory, wealth, and power.

As many people have realized, and often too late, is that the soul is not satisfied with "being somebody." We are born with a mission that is uniquely ours, we must do it regardless of opinions to the contrary. Moreover, when you do something that you have a passion for and that you have figured out a way as to how your knowledge and skills can uplift people, you owe it to yourself and the world to express your gifts.

I believe that the key to our happiness and fulfilment lies in finding what it is that puts that light in our eye, that kick in our step and that we find our natural groove in. There is no sense in working against our natural tendencies and feeling frustrated with the lack of success. Yet so many of us today do precisely that. Imagine if we could find out and clearly express our soul's true purpose! We want to feel like we are intelligent, talented beings who make a positive contribution to this world. Once we find our purpose and we declare to the universe that we intend to proceed with it, regardless of our present circumstances, the universe will make a way for us to live out our destiny.

There are many inspirational people I could highlight here who are using their skills and abilities to express their soul's true purpose, but one who stands out in my heart is Amma, the hugging saint. This July I had the opportunity to meet her and receive her darshan. I felt wonderful upon hugging her as she said a prayer out loud for me. Even after hugging thousands of people, I felt it was incredible that when I got onto the stage to hug her she still smelled of the beautiful fragrance of lavender.

Amma had the courage to write her own life story from a young age. Her family punished her for giving away food and clothing to the poor but she persisted in doing this to help alleviate their suffering.[13] She was scolded for going into her

---

13 http://www.amritapuri.org/amma/life

ecstatic meditative states but her faith was so strong she would not stop. Her family tried to get her married several times but she refused because she knew her purpose was much greater than that.

In honour of her courage and incredible contribution to humanity, I am including a chart analysis so that you can see the transformation that can happen on a world scale when you are living your life in alignment with your karmic purpose. If you are new to astrology and numerology and not familiar with all the terms used, you can skip the case study and return to it later in your studies.

CELEBRITY CASE STUDY: AMMA

From a young age, Sudhamani Idamannel, better known as Amma, knew her purpose was to comfort the poor and aid in bettering their quality of life in practical ways. As a young girl she felt compelled to embrace people in an effort to reduce their suffering. She is now known as the hugging saint, having hugged millions of people worldwide. It is reported that she has been known to hug people continuously for up to 22 hours.[14]

Through her charitable organizations, she has donated millions of dollars to humanitarian efforts such as disaster relief, education, and vocational training for people desperately in need.

---

14 http://www.amritapuri.org/amma/who

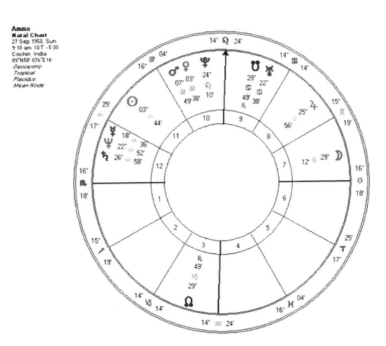

The ascendant is Scorpio showing a person who is intuitive, persistent, sensitive, and empathetic. Her birthday and life path numbers are 9. Number 9 can have a very strong charitable side to their nature, particularly with people they feel have been oppressed, marginalized and abused. The sight of suffering can be deeply painful, and compassion springs forward as a natural response. Their transformational leadership style can be seen in Amma as she is the head of several organizations; her values and mission are used as a guide in providing resources for those in need. Number 9 has the potential to have a deep capacity for selfless service; it being more universal, it can sacrifice personal interests for the interests of others.

Ascendant ruler Pluto is in the 10th house. The 1st house ruler being in the 10th house is helpful for fame and capturing the interest of the public. Pluto in Leo allows her to embrace her authority and power. The ruler of the 10th house, the Sun, is in the 11th house representing dreams, desires, wishes, humanitarian movements, social causes, and helping the underprivileged. In both her birth name Sudhamani Idamannel and her public name Amma, the expression number is 1, which corresponds to the Sun and its sign Leo. Through her various charities, Amma has fulfilled the dreams of many people who faced horrendous circumstances. Through her, they were given a second chance to thrive and be productive in their communities. The 1 influence gives her very strong leadership qualities and she does a great job inspiring people as she leads not just by words but by example.

The 9th house contains Uranus in Cancer. The 9th house represents higher education and foreign relations. Uranus is revolutionary change and ground-breaking ideas. The University she founded (Amrita University) is highly ranked for research and teaching, and is involved with many international research projects and exchanges. The Uranus in Cancer also is linked with the mother archetype-- Cancer symbolizes the mother and Uranus is new approaches. She is the first hugging saint in history and her hugs are a symbol of motherly love. Incidentally, her Jupiter in Gemini can also be symbolic of her blessing; Jupiter represents how we show our good will and generosity and Gemini rules the shoulders, arms, and hands. When we embrace someone we love, we throw our arms around them. Jupiter is in her 8th house showing that her hug can have a healing and transformative effect on people.

The Moon is exalted in Taurus and can provide its most productive function there, that of nurturing, comfort, affection, and security. The soul urge of the name Amma is 2, which corresponds to the Moon, indicating that a deeply felt desire of hers is to be a compassionate source of selfless love. She is most at peace when she is able to personally alleviate suffering and donate her resources to implement practical programs to provide comfort to the poor. Interestingly, 29 degrees Taurus is conjunct Alcyone, a traditionally malefic fixed star said to bring something to cry about. The Moon is in the 7th house which represents one-on-one relations. I think that this is symbolic of her encounters with people worldwide who are in desperate living conditions, who have lost hope and are in need of help and comfort. Her global charities are named *Embracing the World* and her beautiful hug provides that sense of caring and protection that people are seeking. The Moon is out of bounds showing that she is able to exceed the boundaries of the traditional mother role (nurturing one's own children) and nurture children and adults from all over the world. The chart shape is a bowl with lead planet Moon so this is the central focus of her chart.

There is Mercury, Neptune and Saturn in the 12th house and her birth name personality number of 7 showing her interest in spirituality, transcendence, meditation, enlightenment, and intimate relationship to the Divine. Number 7 corresponds to Neptune and Neptune's natural house is the 12th. Number 7 can be the most spiritual among the numbers, with a tendency towards mysticism. With a personality number 7, these characteristics are prominent to others on first impression. The IAM Integration Meditation Technique is a form of meditation that Amma developed to bring an integration of body, mind, intellect, and heart. It is taught by trained volunteers to interested students free of cost.[15]

Critical degrees are points of added strength and emphasis in the chart, they are located at different degrees in the cardinal (13 and 26), fixed (8-9 and 21-22), and mutable (4 and 17) signs. Saturn is at critical degree 26 Libra, emphasizing her responsible and service-oriented nature. The 12th house planets make Amma come in contact with extreme suffering but also give her the compassion and empathy to strive to change their quality of life. This is especially true as the ruler of the 11th house (Mercury) is in the 12th house. Libra is represented by the scales of justice: with this stellium she is trying to correct inequalities, alleviate isolation, and restore wholeness to people's lives by implementing various social initiatives. Her ashram Amritapuri is the center of spiritual life for many devotees who have dedicated their life to

15   http://amma.org/groups/north-america/projects/iam-meditation-classes

serving God. Countless people come here to receive Amma's darshan.

The ruler of the 12th house Venus is in the 10th house, showing that her career is focused on 12th house matters. Venus in Virgo shows the humble and dedicated way in which she serves God. Venus in close conjunction with Mars is indicative of her immense vitality and energy, she hugs thousands of people in a single day and she travels all around the world, never seeming to tire of this service.

Quadrants are the four subsections of the natal chart. If a person has a dominance of planets in any given quadrant that will give us an idea of what they are focused on. The first quadrant is the first three houses, relating to a focus on the self and development of personal identity. The second quadrant is the fourth, fifth and sixth houses; it focuses on how a person relates to people in their immediate environment. The third quadrant is the seventh, eighth and ninth houses; it focuses on relation to society and culture on a broader level. In Amma's chart, there are 7/10 planets in the fourth quadrant (10th, 11th and 12th houses) of the chart. People with this pattern have a focus on universal matters, humanitarian efforts and serving people on a global scale. They are able to see the interconnectedness of people and are able to unite them. This may be seen in her quote *"Amma sees everything as part of the whole, as an extension of Her own Self."* [16]

Amma's chart is a completely Southern hemisphere emphasis, all 10 planets are on the top half of the chart, this is extremely rare to find. This indicates her complete involvement with the world outside her and the collective consciousness. Some of her initiatives include cleaning India, nature composting, puja revolution, and empowering villages. She has little interest in herself-- rather she spends all of her energy in service to other people and increasing quality of life worldwide. She derives fulfillment in life from being able to serve. There is a good deal of objectivity in that she is able to understand other people's

16 http://www.amritapuri.org/

experiences even when she hasn't lived through them. Her vision is embodied in her quote:

Everyone in the world should be able to sleep without fear, at least for one night. Everyone should be able to eat to his fill, at least for one day. There should be at least one day when hospitals see no one admitted due to violence. By doing selfless service for at least one day, everyone should help the poor and needy. It is Amma's prayer that at least this small dream be realised.[17]

The personality number of the name Amma is 8, which gives her a lot of discipline and ability to endure difficult circumstances in order to better serve the needs of those she wants to help. The number 8 is associated with structure and global enterprises, and her charities run amazingly well based primarily on volunteers. Number 8 attracts other people to recognize her for her service. She was chosen by the *Huffington Post* as one of the 50 most powerful women religious leaders in 2014, she was awarded the Golden Goody Award (Oscar for social good) in 2015, and the Saint Jnaneshwar World Peace Prize in 2006 among many others.[18]

Overall it may be said that Amma is a self-realized being, she was born with a strong sense of purpose as to what her life's work would be. She had the confidence to boldly pursue her vision and in the process she changed countless lives.

HEALING OUR MINDS

In contrast to Amma, most of us were not born self-realized and we don't always have a clear vision of our life purpose. We may have some idea as to what it may be, but there is a lack of conscious clarity. This is where anxiety, uncertainty, and doubt creep in and prevent us from living the life we want to live.

An understanding of our astronumerology chart is helpful

---

17 http://www.ammanewengland.org/blog/about
18 A full list of Amma's honours and awards can be found at http://amma.org/about/awards-honors

to gain conscious clarity by helping us see our true nature more accurately, but this is only the **first step** in achieving our potential. An awareness of the chart will not magically give us a sense of fulfillment in our lives. In the real world, knowledge without action is useless! For example, a client looking into a career change can get their chart read by multiple qualified practitioners who all say essentially the same thing about the types of career paths that they are best suited for. Nevertheless, they chose to ignore the advice given and instead continue in their current career that they have admitted is making them feel bored, excessively stressed, ill, uncomfortable, or incompetent in some way. Perhaps they believe that they won't really be able to succeed in this new career, that they lack the intelligence to complete the necessary schooling, or that they lack the connections to get a job in the field. The common denominator is that these are **erroneous beliefs** that exist within the person. There is no practitioner or system of knowledge that can help someone if they don't take constructive action towards important goals in their lives.

The most important thing is your mind, you must affirm to the universe with great feeling what you would like to be and how you want your life to manifest. Your thoughts are what create your reality. If you say something but really you believe in your heart you won't get it, that the odds are stacked against you, or that you are not good enough for it, the universe will respond to that.

Every day we must be willing to consciously change the negative thought patterns in our mind and get rid of thoughts that don't serve us. The vast majority of our thoughts are repetitive and automatic. While it is normal to have these fleeting thoughts, the trouble occurs when we linger on them. The narrative around the thoughts can consume our mind with feelings of regret, worry, guilt, or anticipation of how things will be in the future.

There is a compelling discussion of "the roommate in one's mind" in Michael Singer's book, *The Untethered Soul*. Prior to this, I was aware of the endless stream of thoughts in my own mind, and while I felt it was irritating, I did not see it as destructive. Thus, I did not really make significant efforts to stop it. It was only later that I realized how harmful this endless stream of thoughts was to living my best life. Not only did unkind thoughts keep replaying about myself and why I couldn't do something, other people's perceptions, opinions, and expectations of me took up much more space than they should. At times, one thought of worry or regret was quickly fueled by another, and then another, until it became a vicious cycle and ruined the tone of my day.

Each time we think about a prior conversation or experience, we add an additional layer of meaning. This could be our own reflection of what we did or said, and how someone else interpreted it, or could be a reflection of what another person said or did, and how we responded. Instead of clearing up ambiguities directly, our natural tendency is to try to analyze it, and try to infer what their true intention was. Subsequent words and actions by that person are analyzed in the context of earlier conversations. The story of the original conversation or incident keeps building in our mind until what we believed happened, has very little resemblance to what the other person believes happened. This can contribute to misunderstandings and wounds that take years to heal.

In other situations, the passing of time can reveal the true intentions of people, because we all know that actions speak louder than words. In this case, retrospective analysis of what occurred can be priceless in learning from the situation, as long as we keep it simple. For instance, I'm sure many people can relate to the experience of making the same mistake in judgement with different people. When I look back on things, I realize that I tended to believe people who repeated the same promise on different occasions. As long as I observed in an objective sense, that they had the resources, or were in a position to fulfill the promise, I assured myself that they would keep their word. After some major disappointments, I learned that this wasn't necessarily the case. But all mistakes are learning opportunities, and as a result, I adjusted my expectations. I accounted for the fact that in order for a promise to be kept, other variables needed to be considered. Two of the most important being that the person must be ethical enough to keep their word, and/or and they must care enough about me to take the time to fulfill it.

The roommate in our mind can also become active when thinking about a future goal or outcome. There are many steps involved with reaching most of our dreams, and within each step is a possibility for something to go wrong. Think about the common occurrence of deciding to go back to school mid-career: first you must first decide what to study--there is a possibility that you could make a choice you don't end up enjoying. The next step would be obtaining entrance to that particular program-- there is a *possibility* that you aren't able to get in. After you get in, you must do well enough in that program in order to graduate-- there are many external factors that could get in the way of this despite your best effort. Finally, when you do graduate, you are faced with the task of obtaining a job that utilizes your new knowledge and skills-- some job seekers are unable to find work in their field.

The truth is that anything worth doing in life has risks associated with it, some of which are not apparent at the time we start. In pursuing goals, there are other people whose actions directly impact our success, and it is not always possible to anticipate or control their actions. Then there are life's curveballs that we could never have imagined happening but they do! Intellectually, we know that there is no possible way to have total control over the outcome, and a lack of success is not always our fault. Yet, we can get so anxious trying to avoid life's inherent uncertainty by repetitively thinking about all the details and possible outcomes. The ego can cause us to get so caught up in these negative possibilities, and feel frozen with fear, unable to take risks that could add joy to our life. This endless stream of "what if" scenarios stops us from implementing change and instead we stay stuck in a situation that is slowly draining our happiness.

Although I have not yet mastered the art of present moment awareness, I do make a significant effort to be aware that these unconscious repetitive thoughts are not really my own, but are the ego's way of stopping me from reaching my highest potential. The best way I have found to counteract the tendency to linger on thoughts is to fill my mind with affirmations, mantras, and words of wisdom from inspirational people and texts. It is like getting rid of a bad habit--you need to consciously replace it with a good habit. Gradually, the good habit becomes a natural response. I also meditate on this powerful quote from *The Initiate* by Cyril Scott:

> Why forestall things which, who knows, may never materialize, and so allow the mind to embrace all manner of apprehensions totally futile in themselves? Nay, to fear a thing is the most likely way of giving it birth, seeing that the mind is creative, and what a man thinks, that does he create sooner or later; while conversely, that on which a man refuses to think at all he starves, so that the very germ of it dies for want of sustenance.[19]

ACCURATELY INFORMED EXPECTATIONS

The reason I mention "the roommate in one's mind" is because I believe it is the single biggest obstacle in reaching the full potential shown in the Astronumerology chart. When you were born, the planets were at a specific position in time and space, this snapshot is your natal chart. However, the planets are dynamic and will never stop moving. When the planets in the sky make astrological aspects to your natal chart, they bring the promise of your natal chart to fruition. You will experience feelings and events reflective of the type of transit.

19 Scott, C. (1991). The Initiate. Weiser

Sometimes I hear people lamenting that they just went through what was supposed to be a very favourable period but they didn't feel they got what they wanted out of it. Perhaps they had been unemployed a long time and were hoping that this particular transit would bring them a job. Or maybe they had been single for the past X amount of years and they believed that this transit was supposed to bring a romantic relationship. In other words, their desired outcome was not a match with their reality, and as a result they felt disappointed.

There are a couple of reasons why people could feel disappointed when what they were expecting from a transit did not align with reality. One reason is that the practitioner they consulted with didn't consider all of the possible meanings of that particular transit, or did not ask enough questions about the circumstances of the client's life at the present time. For example, the 7th house represents marriage and romantic relationships, but it also represents clients, business relationships, contracts, legal matters, divorces, and open enemies. Although people hope that 7th house transits will bring a new romance, the truth is that when transiting planets activate your 7th house, any of these domains can get highlighted. The domain(s) that come to fruition depends on the themes that are prominent in your life at that time. If your marriage has been on the rocks for a long time, a 7th house transit could bring a divorce. Alternately, if you are currently in a loving relationship, a 7th house transit could bring marriage, or a deeper level of commitment to each other. Therefore, an understanding of context—time, place, and circumstance is critical to giving accurate readings. The more the practitioner knows about you, and what you would like to get out of the reading, the better they can interpret the transits of the stars and numbers in your life.

Another reason for the disappointment is that the person shifted the responsibility of a desired goal onto an external force, instead of examining what type of inner dialogue may be preventing them from achieving it. In many cases it is thoughts in the subconscious that prevent people from getting what they want. The Universe always delivers to us the same energetic vibration that we are putting out, so if we are expecting something but don't believe it can happen at a heart level, it will not manifest for us. There has to be the power and clarity of intention behind the words and actions.[20]

It is important to keep in mind that the natal chart is comprised of several potentials of what could be. The transits bring the chart to life but we have to cultivate the right attitude and action to maximize the energy at a particular time. Knowledge of astronumerology is only useful in conjunction with a strong positive intention, a resolution to get rid of all sabotaging thoughts that don't serve us, and a firm commitment to taking action in making our dreams come true.

We are at a point in history when the study of astronumerology is needed more than ever before. We live in the age of information where there are endless choices to make and so many paths we could take. With the "roommate in one's mind" and so many conflicting messages in society as to how we should live, it is easy to feel confused and lacking a sense of direction. I believe that unlocking the secrets of the astronumerology chart can greatly aid in this critical process of self-discovery. We can achieve so much more when we engage in activities that highlight our natural talents, and that allow us to follow an authentic direction in our life journey.

---

20 Wayne Dyer has written an eye-opening analysis of the power of intention and the effects our individual intentions and vibrations have on the consciousness of humanity. See Dyer, W. (2005). *The Power of Intention*. Carlsbad, California: Hay House.

CHAPTER 3

KARMA, FATE, AND FREE WILL

A child is born on that day and at that hour when the celestial rays are in mathematical harmony with one's individual karma. The horoscope is a challenging portrait revealing one's unalterable past, and probable future results.

The message boldly blazoned across the heavens at the moment of birth isn't meant to emphasize fate—the result of past good and evil—but to arouse our will to escape from this universal thralldom. What we have done, we can undo. None other than oneself was the instigator of the causes of whatever effects are now prevalent in this life. We can overcome any limitation, because we created it by our own actions in the first place, and because we have spiritual resources which are not subject to planetary pressure.
- Swami Sri Yukteswar in *Autobiography of a Yogi* by Paramahansa Yogananda

One of the biggest questions around astronumerology is the curiosity pertaining to how much of our life outcomes are predestined, and how much is due to our own actions. Everyone practicing astrology and/or numerology has their own opinion based on their experience, and there is no definitive answer.

I think of someone's astronumerology chart as a genetic inheritance. For example, the trait of intelligence has been found to be about 50% heritable. The other 50% is due to circumstances such as family background, upbringing, culture, society, motivation to learn, and personal dedication to acquiring knowledge and experience. Similarly, a person is born with an astronumerology chart reflecting potentials and tendencies, but it will be modified by his or her external circumstances and personal effort.

Astronumerology works within parameters. The chart will reflect a certain range of experiences. Our experience will depend on our personal desire and specific direction in which we expend our effort. By way of illustration, with regards to career, there are many personality traits and skills that we possess that could enable us to succeed in different careers. A person can have strong abilities to heal, to teach, to work with clients, and to write. In today's world with so many career choices, there are many paths that would allow someone to make use of a combination of those skills. In light of this information, the Astronumerologist will not tell you which specific career to pursue, because ultimately it is best you make that decision based on your own heart's desire. Rather, he or she can help you identify your skills and aptitude so you are spending your tuition, and focusing your job search, in areas that are more likely to lead to fulfillment and personal growth.

As we progress through life, we make choices, which affect our actions, which in turn affects our future experiences, much like a domino effect. Our interests change as we grow up, which influences the experiences we seek out, and people we bond with. For these reasons, I believe the chart is not 100% fate. We do have a good degree of control over what happens to us.

Charts represent potential, of which we can choose to work on the higher end or the lower end. A person's soul cannot be seen in a chart; we cannot tell a sinner from a saint, because it's up to free will as to how a person works with the energy in their chart. In other words, there are no specific birthdays for bad fate versus good fate. Every planet, sign, and number has both positive and negative characteristics and proclivities: how a person expresses themselves is due to their level of consciousness. Someone with a higher level of consciousness is more likely to express the highest positive potential, whereas someone who is low in consciousness will tend to magnify the worst tendencies of the same birthday.

We observe that saints and criminals were born on the same day, but expressed their energy in different ways. Saint Rose of Lima, the first canonized saint of the Americas, and Adolph Hitler, leader of the Nazi party, both born on April 20th are a good distinction. Both of them are Taurus number 2 people. On the positive side, such people can be very nurturing, compassionate, and empathetic, able to provide people with a sense of comfort and security. Saint Rose of Lima consciously lived a life of self-inflicted suffering and denial, praying to God to increase her trials so she could develop more love in her heart for others. Despite being a natural beauty, she chose not to get married and instead most of her life was spent in seclusion studying scripture and praying. She practiced extreme dedication to helping those in the poorest and most desperate living conditions.

On the other hand, Taurus number 2 can use their skill for psychology and understanding of public tastes, to influence large crowds of people into believing their propaganda. If their motive is pure then this can be a great contribution to humanity, but if their motive is malicious, it can leave far-reaching and long-lasting damage. In an attempt to purify the Aryan race, Hitler used propaganda to convince the German people that "inferiors" such as Jews, Gypsies, Africans, disabled people, retarded people, and homosexuals needed to be eliminated in mass extermination. In particular, he understood that many German people were hurting financially, while Jews seemed to be running thriving businesses. He distorted the facts to make Germans believe that Jews were responsible for taking away their financial prosperity, effectively portraying them as the enemy. He made the highly attractive promise that once these "subhumans" were gone, Germans would be comfortable and secure again.

Sometimes we want to make the most out of certain tendencies, so we consciously engage in behaviours reflective of it. This can be productive in many areas of our lives. Perhaps if you have Mercury prominently connected to your astrological career house (tenth house), you can consciously choose a communications-based career, so that your skill for expressing yourself can help you get ahead. Or if your life path is 1, you choose a career where you are self-employed or have a great deal of autonomy, to account for your need for independence.

It is wise to use our natural gifts and inclinations in our favour, rather than working in a job that emphasizes our weaknesses or is focused on areas that we are just average in. Even so, natural gifts that we are born with must be consciously practiced to make the most of. A child may have a lot of musical talent reflected in their chart, but without many hours of practice, she will not achieve greatness in that area. When you find out what your natural proclivities and skills are, and then commit those subjects to practice, you have the best chances of being successful.

This naturally brings up the controversial question; can a person do *anything* they set their mind to? I have no doubt in the power of positive thinking and affirmations; both of these have served me and many people I know very well. We literally do become what we think about all day long. For this reason, it is critically important to be aware of what is entering our stream of consciousness from the various sources around us. There are so many stories from around the world of people doing the impossible and far surpassing what was previously thought possible. Rarely does anyone have the heartfelt desire to work so hard for something that is totally against the grain of their personality. What happened in these outstanding stories of success, is that the person chose to exert their effort in an area that *complemented* their natural proclivities. Their deeply held dream was supported by their chart.

Sheer determination without natural interest will only go so far. I don't believe you can set your mind to do things that you have no natural interest for in the long-term. This is because it is not an internally motivated desire but rather an externally based one, which, eventually the motivation will exhaust for. I feel that every experience in life teaches us something, and that no experience is ever wasted. At the same time, it is much better for a person to follow their heart's desire as soon as they are in a position to do so. The free will component is always available to us should we choose to take it.

For almost everyone living today, the planets and numbers do reveal their karma. By sincere devotion, good works, and the grace of God, certain negative events may be alleviated, or in rare cases, avoided. However, if a person is ignorant of the nature of the planetary forces at play, there is no possible way for them to try to reduce the deleterious effects. Astronumerology is not a religion, and does not require a belief for it to have its effects on us. Rather it is like gravity, regardless of our belief in its existence, its force is too great for us not to succumb to it.

Sri Yukteswar succinctly explains this to his disciple Paramahansa Yogananda in in chapter 16 of *Autobiography of a Yogi:*

Mukunda, why don't you get an astrological armlet?

Should I, Master? I don't believe in astrology.

It's not a question of belief; the scientific attitude one should take on any subject is whether it is true. The law of gravitation worked as efficiently before Newton as after him. The cosmos would be fairly chaotic if its laws could not operate without the sanction of human belief.

Charlatans have brought the ancient stellar science to its present disrepute. Astrology is too vast, both mathematically and philosophically, to be rightly grasped except by men of profound understanding. If ignoramuses misread the heavens, and see there a scrawl instead of a script, that is to be expected in this imperfect world. One should not dismiss the wisdom with the 'wise'.

Man is a soul, and has a body. When he properly places his sense of identity, he leaves behind all compulsive patterns. So long as he remains confused in his ordinary state of spiritual amnesia, he will know the subtle fetters of environmental law.

There are a few self-realized souls on the planet today who have obtained enlightenment and have reincarnated to help us out of our state of maya (illusion). For example, Yogananda, while acknowledging the effects of the planets, also managed to supersede them as he had risen above the human limitations that all of us are still subject to. His sole purpose for living was to teach people methods of gaining inner peace and deepening their connection with God. He wrote, "The starry inscription at birth doesn't mean that we are puppets of the past. The message is rather "a prod to pride;" the very heavens seek to arouse our determination to be free from every limitation." Astrology gives a means of understanding karma so that we can use our inner spiritual resources and other external resources to overcome it. Sri Yukteswar states:

By a number of means—by prayer, by will power, by yoga, meditation, by consultation with saints, by use of astrological bangles—the adverse effects of past wrongs can be minimized or nullified.

It is only when a traveler has reached his goal that the traveler is justified in discarding the maps. During the journey, one takes advantage of any convenient short cut. The ancient rishis discovered many ways to curtail the period of man's exile in delusion. There are certain mechanical features in the law of karma which can be skillfully adjusted by the fingers of wisdom.

I believe that in a sense it is part of one's karma as to whether he ever finds out how the planets and numbers are affecting him in different ways at different times. If he does find this out, the issue then becomes whether he is willing to consciously learn the lessons presented to him. The best way to keep a man in prison is for him to believe he is not in a prison. If one is not aware of the root of the problem, there will be no permanent way to fix it; temporary fixes will only result in the same problem in different guises. At the same time, everyone does their best from their level of consciousness, and we only come to understand advanced teachings when we are ready.

Everyone has a unique life journey, we have different experiences which have shaped our beliefs and perspective on life. Perhaps you can change a person's theories, but once they have lived through something, it is real to them and not a vague notion in their mind.

I have lived through the transits of Pluto, where an old part of me died to make room for powerful healing and transformation. I have experienced the feeling of the rug being pulled out from under me due to shocking Uranus transits that ultimately were a stepping stone to greater success. I have been subject to the influence of Neptune, in seeing only what I wanted to see in people and situations, and then being blindsided. At the same time, Neptune transits were times when my creativity and imagination were at an amazing high and allowed me to do some of my best writing. The return of Saturn to its natal position and concurrently going through the heart of Sade Sati (my Moon is conjunct Saturn by one degree) has brought me face to face with very tough situations in line with the karmic lessons of Saturn. In facing them head on, I am able to tap an inner well of wisdom within me and discover strength I never knew I had. Jupiter's transits have brought me luck, fortune and foreign travel, especially as Jupiter is placed in my 9th house. By making it a point to travel abroad during the transit of Jupiter through my first and ninth houses, I had unforgettable trips filled with wonderful people and excellent learning experiences. Jupiter also represents writing and publishing. The bulk of Volume 1 and Volume 2 of *The Wisdom of Astronumerology* was written while Jupiter transited my first house. Concurrently being in a Venus-Jupiter dasha really allowed Jupiter's energy to positively manifest in my life.

The planets have unfolded their various karmas in my life and that has always been my lived reality. Just as no one can convince me that the planets and numbers do not have a discernible influence on human affairs, I would never try to force people to believe in astronumerology. If people find they can benefit from its wisdom and express an interest in learning more, I think that is wonderful. Likewise, if they don't find it helpful at this point in their life journey, I understand that too. It's important to stay true to yourself and follow the teachings that resonate with you on a heart level.

Everyone is at a different stage in their evolution. Some people are old souls relatively close to liberation, some are new souls trying to learn the ropes, and many others are somewhere in between. Everyone has to progress at a pace that they can cope with. There is no "right way" to freedom from the never-ending cycle of death and rebirth (moksha). In fact, the majority of people on this planet do not have an ultimate goal of moksha. This is perfectly fine for them at this point in their journey. Everyone has their unique karma in life that they are trying to navigate, and when you know better, you do better. Making the most of the process of learning leads to wisdom and discernment.

What everyone has in common is the fact that there are imbalances created from life to life. Sometimes we make good decisions resulting in gifts that are brought forward. This is where we reap the results of our previous actions, our past life credit. Other times we fail to learn a lesson or we make a poor choice resulting in a more difficult set of circumstances. But these difficult experiences are not solely meant to punish people. As the level of consciousness rises, the soul chooses to work out its more difficult karma in order to purify it from memory. At this level, difficult experiences and people are more accurately seen as teachers meant to take you to your next evolutionary stage. St. John of the Cross states this idea eloquently in his book *Dark Night of the Soul,*

> For, if the soul be not tempted, exercised and proved with trials and temptations, it cannot quicken its sense of wisdom. For this reason it is said in Ecclesiasticus: He that has not been tempted, what does he know? And he that has not been proved, what are the things that he recognizes?.... For how long a time the soul will be held in this fasting and penance of sense, cannot be said with any certainty; for all do not experience it after one manner, neither do all encounter the same temptations. For this is meted out by the will of God, in conformity with the greater or smaller degree of imperfection which each soul has to purge away. In conformity, likewise, with the degree of love of union to which God is pleased to raise it, He will humble it with greater or less intensity or in greater or less time. Those who have the disposition and greater strength to suffer, He purges with greater intensity and more quickly. But those who are very weak are kept for a long time in this night, and these He purges very gently and with slight temptations.[21]

Our souls undergo experiences to purify any karmas and move to the next level. I agree with the spiritual teachings that say the key to progress is in trying to face all experiences with an attitude of equanimity, a calm acceptance of everything that happens without letting emotions disturb us. In the real world, as we all have experienced, living in community with others makes this much easier said than done! Nevertheless, it is not impossible. It is really the decisions we make on a daily basis that shape the direction of our lives in the long-term.

---

21 St. John of the Cross (2003). *Dark Night of the Soul*. Dover Publications

Some years ago, I saw Bishop T. D. Jakes do a demonstration by asking several audience members to keep walking in a circle around him. Initially he started turning his body in an attempt to keep pace with them but found that continuing to do this resulted in dizziness. He subsequently explained to the audience the purpose of his demonstration: the people walking around the circle represented various external components of life, including career, finances, family, relationships, and health. If he let his internal state be dependent on changes in external circumstances, he was working himself into dizziness as he didn't have full control of what other people did. This is why he stopped in the center of the circle and let people continue to walk around him. By doing so he maintained his peace and composure. Regardless of the chaos that was going around outside him, he found his serenity within. The externals represent karma, and his conscious choice to maintain inner peace represents our free will. As spiritual teacher Wayne Dyer frequently taught, what other people do to you is their karma but what you choose to do in return becomes yours.

One of the most dreaded periods for people familiar with astrology is Saturn's return around age 28-30 and 58-60. Similar to this, Vedic astrology has a period called Sade Sati, the seven and a half years that Saturn passes over your Moon and the two houses adjacent to it. These periods do not necessarily overlap, unless your Moon is in the same sign as Saturn or in an adjacent sign to Saturn. Many people experience some form of crisis at these times that puts them in touch with their deepest fears and anxieties. Emotionally, it is very difficult as pressures from every source seem to be mounting with no easy solutions. In Vedic astrology, the Moon represents the mind and happiness: Saturn transiting over it can make the mind pessimistic, and make it harder for a person to feel satisfied with their circumstances. It takes a lot of conscious effort to stay upbeat and motivated to succeed at this time. Saturn is the disciplinarian and task-master who is often feared because of malefic influences that it brings about. These time periods are filled with many challenges and can be a time of serious testing. Things will not just naturally go our way. If one does not understand the nature and timing of Saturn's tests, it is very easy to fall into a state of despair as a result of things not going the way we planned. Unfortunately the feelings of despair often cause a lack of motivation to try in the first place which of course does not create positive results. However, this is not to say that this period must necessarily be completely disastrous. Some people do very well during these periods and use Saturn's influence to work the hardest they have ever worked in their life towards accomplishment. They are able to use the positive characteristics of Saturn to overcome the difficulties:

1. After many years of hard work and dedication, Alexander Graham Bell (born March 3rd 1847), received the patent for the telephone on March 7th 1876,[22] right in the heart of his first Saturn return.

2. On April 17th 1961, with transiting Saturn making an exact conjunction to her natal Saturn, Elizabeth Taylor (born Feb 27th 1932), won her first Academy Award for lead actress in BUtterfield.

3. During her first Saturn return in 1919, best-selling novelist of all time, Agatha Christie (born September 15th 1890), had her first detective novel, *The Mysterious Affair at Styles*, accepted for publication. In her Vedic chart, Agatha has her Moon in Virgo and her Saturn in Leo, so she was concurrently going through Sade Sati.

4. During her second Saturn return in 1984, Louise Hay (born October 8th 1926), started Hay House publishing as a way to self-publish her international best-selling books, *Heal your Body* and *You Can Heal your Life*. Hay House has gone on to sell millions of products worldwide. In the Vedic chart, Louise has her Moon in Libra and her Saturn in Scorpio, so she was concurrently going through Sade Sati.

---

22 Document for March 7th: Alexander Graham Bell's Telephone Patent Drawing, 03/07/1876 http://www.archives.gov/historical-docs/todays-doc/?dod-date=307

5. During Clara Burton's (born Dec 25th 1821) second Saturn return, she set the groundwork for the founding of humanitarian organization, the American Red Cross in 1881. The American Red Cross has provided disaster relief, health and safety services, blood services, and education within the United States to millions of people in need of assistance. In her Vedic chart, Clara has her Moon in Aquarius and her Saturn in Pisces, so she was concurrently going through Sade Sati.

6. During her second Saturn return in 1978, Susan B. Anthony (born Feb 15th 1820) introduced the Susan B. Anthony Amendment requesting women to have the equal right to vote in the U.S. Congress. The 19th amendment giving women the right to vote was finally approved in 1919, after her death. Her portrait was placed on dollar coins, the first woman to receive this honour in 1979.[23]

7. During her first Sade Sati, Angelina Jolie (born June 4th 1975), won several major awards from 1998-2000 (Academy, SAG, Golden Globes) for her work in *George Wallace*, *Gia* and *Girl Interrupted*. In her Vedic chart, her Moon is in Pisces and transiting Saturn was moving through Pisces and Aries at that time. During her first Saturn return in 2004-2005, she met her future husband Brad Pitt while filming *Mr. & Mrs. Smith*. This film was her highest grossing up until that time.

8. During his first Saturn return in 1925, F. Scott Fitzgerald (born September 24th 1896) had his novel *The Great Gatsby* published. The novel received mixed reviews and did poorly in terms of sales during his lifetime. However, it became popular during World War 2 and is now widely considered a literary classic. It has also been made into many stage and film adaptations.

9. During the peak of his Sade Sati in 1987, Stephen King (born September 21st 1947) released his book *Misery*. According to a 2014 poll by Rolling Stone Magazine, *Misery* was the 5th out of the top 10 Stephen King books as rated

---

23 https://www.brooklynmuseum.org/eascfa/dinner_party/place_settings/susan_b_anthony

by fans.[24] On the official release date of June 8th 1987, transiting Saturn was conjunct his Moon by 1 degree! *IT*, the #2 ranked book released in September 1986, was also during Sade Sati. *The Shining* ranked #3 was published during his first Saturn return in January 1977 and the #1 ranked novel *The Stand* was published just as he was coming out of that Saturn return in September 1978.

These celebrity examples are used to illustrate the positive potential of Saturn, but definitely not to make light of the real feelings of pain, sadness, guilt, and hopelessness that can just as easily occur instead of, or even concurrently with, great accomplishments. Saturn can lower your self-confidence and cause you to be really hard on yourself, wondering if you are really worthy. You can start to think you are not good enough, and allow other people's criticism to affect your perception of yourself. There is nothing wrong with you if you are in this period now and are feeling this way, or you haven't accomplished what you had hoped to by this time. It is important to feel your emotions and not repress or deny them, otherwise they just start to affect you subconsciously by influencing your beliefs, decisions and actions. The honest acceptance and expression of emotion can be very cathartic.

These periods of Saturn's testing are fate but we have free will in how we choose to deal with Saturn's energy. Saturn does bring about difficulties but the ultimate purpose of it is to strengthen ourselves and purify karma. Beautiful people do not just happen, they are created by withstanding significant trials and emerging on the other side victorious with their newfound wisdom. By being aware of times of trial, we can have the peace of knowing that our failures are not necessarily due to some internal defect, rather it is a natural life cycle that everyone goes through at some point. It is much better to keep trying and fail a few times before getting it right, than not to try at all.

---

24 http://www.rollingstone.com/culture/lists/readers-poll-the-10-best-stephen-king-books-20141105/misery-20141105

Transiting Saturn is not the only planet that can cause challenges. The outer planets Pluto, Neptune and Uranus all will bring some form of upheaval reflective of their nature.

Pluto's transits primarily focus on power, control, transformation, healing, death and rebirth. This could be a time when you get involved in external power struggles, but are also most challenged to step into your personal power by staying true to yourself.

Neptune's transits can bring a huge surge of creative, idealistic and compassionate energy. However they can also cloud your vision, and bring confusion and uncertainty. You are encouraged to consciously look at certain parts of your life more realistically, especially with regards to the house Neptune is travelling through.

Uranus' transits bring revolution, sudden changes, surprises, innovative ideas, and an urge to express your unique style. They are focused on getting you out of old ruts and embracing necessary change in your life.

These slow moving planetary transits last a long time and during their period of exactness really put the pressure on to learn their lessons. Easier aspects like the sextile and trine do this in a more gentle way. If we are awake enough to absorb the lesson and take the necessary action, it saves us a lot of grief later on. If we don't take the necessary actions at the sextiles and trines, the hard aspects like the conjunction, square and opposition will force us to take action, it can feel like being hit over the head with a hammer.

CELEBRITY CASE STUDY: CAITLYN JENNER

To illustrate transits, let us use a celebrity profile. On June 1st 2015, by making a debut on the cover of *Vanity Fair*, Bruce Jenner, a former U.S. Olympic Gold Medalist, revealed that she had changed her name to Caitlyn, and revealed her status as an openly transgender woman.

Uranus the planet of revolution, shocks, surprises and upsets was making several aspects to her natal planets. Concurrently, Pluto the planet of transformation, healing and rebirth was also making several aspects to her natal planets. On June 1st 2015, Uranus at 19 degrees Aries was making an opposition to her Mercury-Neptune conjunction in Libra in the 12th house of secrets, and Pluto at 15 degrees Capricorn was making a square to this conjunction, suggesting something kept hidden coming to light. She struggled with these feelings for a long time but previously didn't feel ready to share them with the world.

Libra a sign ruled by Venus is representative of the female essence. Venus also represents beauty, and poses the thought-provoking question, who defines what is beautiful? Her natal Venus being in the 2nd house speaks to her values and sense of self-worth. Transiting Uranus made a conjunction with his North Node in Aries, and completed a grand trine with her Venus in Sagittarius in the 2nd house and her Pluto in Leo in the 10th house. This transit is suggesting that she felt confident in her decision to come out, she wanted to define her own sense of what is beautiful in the public eye and she was eager for the world to get to know her as she truly is.

Transiting Pluto's trine to Saturn in the 11th house indicated that she made the decision to value her own authenticity over any possible societal judgements and that one of her heartfelt wishes was coming true in being able to express her sexuality openly. Transiting Pluto made an exact square to his North Node in Aries in the 6th house. This aspect indicates that by transforming her body, she was taking a step in the right direction and advancing her personal growth. The North Node's position represents where we are trying to evolve and Aries is a sign of blazing new trails. By her courageous example, she has made it easier for other transgender people to come out publicly. The 6th house traditionally is associated with health and taking care of the physical body through exercise and proper nutrition. Pluto's square to the North Node in the 6th house can indicate the new health issues she may have to deal with by having breasts and female reproductive organs.

Transiting Uranus made a trine to Pluto in Leo in her 10th house. The 10th house is your public reputation. Leo represents being center stage and doing things in a flamboyant manner. The 3rd-9th house axis represents communications, broadcasting and publishing; sharing your message with the world. Transiting Uranus made a square to Jupiter in Capricorn in the 3rd house. At the same time the transiting North and South Nodes at 6 degrees Libra and 6 degrees Aries respectively squared her natal Uranus at 4 degrees Cancer which is conjunct her natal 9th house cusp by 1 degree. Thus she felt the need to come out as transgender in a flamboyant way by capturing the world's attention on the cover of the magazine in a corset. The clear message was that she embraced her sexuality and hoped that others would too.

Transiting Pluto's exact sesquiquadrate to Mars and quincunx to natal Pluto in the 10th house indicates the public transformation and rebirth. This shows the urgency with which she felt a need to come out in order to experience healing. Feeling trapped in the wrong gender's body reached a point that it was too painful and she needed to close the gap between her inner feelings and her physical appearance. She literally transformed her physical body into the opposite gender. It was a psychological death of Bruce Jenner and a rebirth of Caitlyn Jenner.

Keep in mind that transits only serve to time the natal promise. Natal promises are your karma in specific areas of life and work in ranges, not absolutes. For instance with regards to finances, a general range of prosperity is shown. If you have very lucky money karma, the destined transit can bring you your first million. If you have a more typical money karma, you may win or inherit some money, receive a raise at work, or start a new job at a higher salary. In other words transits are proportionate to the natal promise. Caitlyn Jenner must have an extreme natal promise to first become an Olympic Gold Medalist, and then come out as a transgender woman.

Looking at her chart shape, it is a locomotive with lead planet Uranus. We know that when Uranus gains a central focus, the person may be a revolutionary, pioneer, or trendsetter in some way. Uranus in the 9th house adds an international/ foreign flavour. The Moon in Aquarius participates in a mutual exchange with Uranus in Cancer strengthening the expression of both and enabling them to perform to their strongest potential. As she was formerly known, Bruce Jenner set a 1976 world record in winning the Gold Medal in the Olympic decathlon held in Montreal, Canada. Uranus makes a trine to the Sun which is closely conjunct the ascendant, this helped him have his talents applauded by other people, and he became a celebrity. After this he launched a career in television and film. Cancer is a patriotic, home-loving sign and with his win, he became an American hero. He won the James E. Sullivan Award as the top amateur athlete in the United States.

In 2015, the time came again for another major natal promise to be fulfilled. This natal promise also reflected the essence of Uranus, but with the added influence of Pluto. Uranus is semisquare Pluto in his chart. Natally, Pluto makes a trine to his Venus, and by transit Uranus at 19 degrees Aries made a tight trine to his Venus at 20 degrees Sagittarius. Venus is a female planet that represents beauty and appearance. A planet is termed out of bounds (OOB) if it is greater than declination 23 degrees 27 minutes. **Note that declination degrees are different from the degrees shown on the chart.** In the chart displayed here, you can see that Venus is at 20 degrees Sagittarius but you can't see it is out of bounds at declination 25 degrees 59 minutes. Declinations can be displayed by astrological software programs.[25]

Venus OOB indicates that Venusian energy is extremely strong in him so I can understand that psychologically he felt he was a woman trapped in a man's body. Venus OOB can express itself in embodying unconventional expressions of the feminine principle, and being a transgender woman certainly fits the bill.

25 You may go to http://www.astro.com/cgi/genchart.cgi, and when the chart is displayed click view additional tables (PDF) in the top left hand corner to view the declination of the planets.

Planets that are out of bounds can express themselves in ways that are outside the normal structures that society creates. In fact in his chart, the Moon (also reflective of the female principle), Venus and Uranus are all out of bounds (OOB). In a study I did, I found that only about 3% of the population has three out of bounds planets.[26] People with this many OOB planets can feel a strong urge to break the traditions and limitations held by society, and usher in new thought and action. They do not try to mold themselves into society's ways and need to be able to creatively express themselves. Recall that Jenner's natal Pluto is in Leo in the 10th house, his transformations would be done publicly in a flamboyant way. Pluto in trine to Venus could indicate a transformation in appearance and because Venus is the female planet, one literal expression is a physical transformation into a woman.

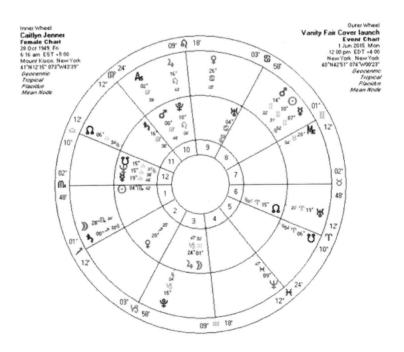

---

26 The full study is at http://www.astronumerologywisdom.com/out-of-bounds-planets.html

Numerical energy is similar to planetary energy. We are born under a certain set of numerical combinations which shape our personality and life trends. The numbers that are affecting us at any given time period need to be properly understood, so that we can work with the natural trends rather than against them. Each number has a set of characteristics as well as activities that it favours. Making a conscious choice to engage in these activities and cultivate the positive traits of a number during its transit over your life makes it much easier to maximize your potential.

Personal year numbers are calculated by adding your month and day of birth to the current year. For instance, if you were born on March 20th, you add 3 (March) +2 + 8 (2015) = 13 = 4. Therefore you would be in personal year 4 in 2015. The personal year number changes every calendar year, and you will always go through the sequence in order from 1-9.

The personal month is similar in effect to the personal year, but lasts for just one month. It is calculated by adding the personal year to the current calendar month, for example if you are in personal year 4 and we are in November, you would add 4 + 11= 15= 6. You would receive the energy of the number 6 for November. The personal month number changes every calendar month, and you will always go through the sequence in order from 1-9.

The personal day is similar in effect as the personal year and month, but lasts only for the day. Taking the previous example of being in a personal month 6 for November, you would add this to the calendar date. For instance, if you wanted to know what your personal day number is on November 3rd, you add 6 + 3, which would mean your personal day number for November 3rd is 9. The personal day number changes every calendar day, and you will always go through the sequence in order from 1-9.

To conclude the example, if you were born March 20th, on November 3rd 2015 you would experience the energy of numbers 4, 6, and 9. You can combine the meaning of those numbers to get an insight as to the type of activities you many engage in that day for enhanced productivity.

Returning to the case study, Caitlyn Jenner was in a personal year 1 in 2015. October =10, +28 (birthday) + 2+0+1+5= 10+ 28+ 8= 46 =1. Certainly coming out as a transgender woman in public on a global scale would count as taking a new direction in life! She could not stand to hide her true feelings any longer, and she became a leader in the transgender movement. The date of the Vanity Fair cover was June 1st. To get the personal month, we add personal year 1 to the month of June (6). Her personal month 7 indicated the emphasis on the written word and publishing; the top secret cover story reportedly took the author Buzz Bissinger hundreds of hours shadowing Caitlyn during the final stages of her physical transition.[27] To get the personal day, we add 7 to the calendar day 1st. Her personal day 8 was reflective of increased power; with revealing of her identity in a hugely public way, she was stepping into her personal power. Her confidence was within her, rather than relying on any external source for validation.

If you are in a personal year number 1, you are at the start of a new nine year cycle in your life. This is the year of new beginnings, of embarking on goals that you have previously spent time preparing for. This is a year of having your firsts, being independent, and taking action. You can handle more leadership and responsibility, and you will feel most fulfilled if you find roles that allow for this. Making an effort to include more innovation and risk-taking in a number 1 year will result in creative self-discovery.

Current U.S. President Barack Obama (born August 4th 1961) was in a personal year number 1 when he began his United States Senate career on January 4th 2005. In 1987, another of his number 1 years, he visited Nairobi, Kenya, his father's homeland for the first time. He had a chance to connect with his African

---

27 http://www.vanityfair.com/hollywood/2015/06/caitlyn-jenner-photos-interview-buzz-bissinger

roots, meeting with his brothers, sisters and grandmother. For Barack, any year that adds to 7 (1969, 1978, 1987, 1996, 2005, 2014) is a personal year 1, since his birth month and day add to 3 (8 for August + 4).

As another example, Oprah Winfrey (born January 29th 1954) got her first morning talk show co-host position at WJZ-TVs *People are Talking* which premiered on August 14th 1978. This is where her talents as a T.V talk show host were noticed, and it set the stage for *The Oprah Winfrey Show*. At this time she was in a personal month 9; often when you have a combination of 9 and 1 for your personal year and month or vice versa, it indicates finishing one chapter of your life and beginning a new one. The personal day of 5 was auspicious for any activity relating to communications. On September 17th 1996, another year where her personal year was 1, she launched her world famous Oprah's Book Club. For Oprah, any year that adds to 7 (1960, 1969, 1978, 1987, 1996, 2005, 2014) is a personal year 1, since her month and day add to 3 (1 for January + 2).

The **four pinnacle numbers** typically last between 9-40 years, with their exact length differing based on your life path number. The first pinnacle cycle number is your month and date. The second pinnacle cycle number is your date and year. The third pinnacle cycle number is calculated by adding pinnacle cycle number 1 and pinnacle cycle number 2. The fourth Pinnacle cycle number is your month and year.

Let us use Caitlyn's birthday of October 28th 1949 to illustrate the calculations:

First pinnacle is 10 (October) + 28 = 38 = 11 or 2

Second pinnacle is 28+ 1949= 28+ 23= 51 or 6

Third pinnacle is 2 + 6 = 8

Fourth pinnacle is 10 + 23 = 33 = 6

These numbers reflect a developmental lesson that needs to be integrated into the personality at certain periods. To find out the length of each pinnacle, start with subtracting your life path number from 36. Adding the month, day and year of birth, 10+ 28 +1949 = 61 =7, we get 7 for Caitlyn's life path.

Since her life path is 7, 36 – 7 = 29. Therefore Caitlyn's first pinnacle was from birth to age 29. The second pinnacle is the next 9 years (30-38) and the third pinnacle is the 9 years after that (39-47). The fourth pinnacle is from age 48 and continues for the remainder of the life span.

At the time of coming out, Caitlyn was in pinnacle 6. Number 6 vibrates to Venus. Both symbolically and literally, we see his powerful embrace of the female principle as well as his physical transformation into a woman.

The **four challenge numbers**, each lasting 25-30 years represent the nature of challenges that will be dominant at a given time in your life. The third challenge, also known as the main challenge, will affect you all throughout life.

The first challenge number is arrived at by subtracting the month from the day, in Caitlyn's example, it is 28 (1) – 10 (1) = 1 – 1= 0. Don't forget to break down the numbers before adding, otherwise you would get 28 -10 = 18, which is incorrect. In the event you get a negative number, convert it to a positive, i.e. -6 is the same as 6.

The second challenge number is subtracting the day from the year, 23 (5) – 28 (1) = 5 – 1 = 4.

The third challenge number is arrived at by subtracting challenge 1 from challenge 2, 4 – 0 = 4.

The fourth challenge number is arrived at by subtracting the month from the year, 23 (5) – 10 (1) = 5 – 1 = 4.

Caitlyn's second, third, and fourth challenge numbers are all 4, meaning that she struggled with the feeling of being different from others, and may have worried that people wouldn't accept her because she didn't fit into society's traditional gender roles. Her challenge was to rise above the fear of other people's judgements.

The **maturity number,** arrived at by adding your expression number to your life path number, reveals characteristics that you embody more consciously around the age of 35. This is when you have developed more self-awareness, and have a clearer idea as to what is most important for you to achieve. For instance, the expression of Caitlyn Jenner adds to 6, and adding 6 to her life path 7, gives 13=4. Since 4 vibrates to Uranus, we observe in the latter half of life, Caitlyn gradually developing the confidence to be unique, and setting the stage that will enable more transgender people to feel comfortable coming out in public.

As we can see, there are many planetary and numerical themes affecting us at different points in life. Returning to the wise quote by Sri Yukteswar, the stars and numbers don't completely control our fate. In contrast, they are there as indicators of our life purpose, and signal the timing of important events. By making an effort to work cooperatively with their energy, we have the power to create success we never dreamed possible. Don't let anyone else or external circumstances convince you that your actions cannot change what will happen to you. Indeed, you are the only one who ever was, and who ever will be the co-creator of your destiny. You are shaping your future one day at a time.

CHAPTER 4

KNOW THYSELF

"Your own Self-Realization is the greatest service you can render the world."
- *Ramana Maharshi*

The question "Who am I?" is probably one of the most difficult to answer, yet one that if answered honestly could transform our lives. Many philosophers have spent their lifetimes trying to answer this question, and there is no book of answers to check if you got it right! My intention is not to get too deeply entrenched in the philosophical basis behind this question but to approach it in a way that benefits everyday men and women trying their best to live their lives to their highest potential. People sometimes think of astronumerology as an esoteric study that is too difficult or abstract to be of use in the real world. Nothing could be further from the truth! The reason I am so passionate about this subject is because it helps to understand the many layers of a person, it's a completely unique karmic blueprint.

Understanding astronumerology charts isn't intended to make judgements or to try to fit people into a box, but rather to understand a person's inner blueprint, which leads a greater compassion towards oneself and others. There is already enough judgement on us from the media, from society, from people at work, family, friends, and even strangers, but-- we are often our biggest critic.

Our thoughts zero in on what went wrong instead of focusing on what we did right. The truth is that most of us fixate on our shortcomings and compare ourselves to other people. We may wonder why we couldn't be just a little more _____ or a little less_____. Or you may think "I wish I could be more like _____ , he always seems to be so good at _____" or-- "It seems to be so easy for_____ I'm trying so hard, why can't I do this?" This sort of thinking leads to comparisons that are not productive and can be very destructive to self-esteem. There is a reason why you are the way you are and why _____ is the way he or she is. There is nothing wrong with you because you aren't performing like someone else.

It is important to remember that we all have our own trials and tribulations in private, and what we show publicly is usually a highlight of our highest points in life. Nowadays many people create various social media profiles of themselves, but these are public images. They are carefully chosen to project a certain image to the world. The photos shown are not of sorrow, and lack, but of fond memories. Similarly, most of the people we come into contact with online or in person are not people we would share our deepest vulnerabilities with. On the contrary, the conversation usually remains at a relatively pleasant level with the normal response to "How are you?" being "Good, thank you." Even if things are not going our way, we are hesitant to get into the true details, possibly fearing what others may think of us. Thus, comparing our private life to the public lives of others based on everyday conversations and social media is a surefire way to create disappointment and a sense of lack.

Judgements are often black and white, with very little grey. Something is right or its wrong, good or its bad. Judgements emphasize opposites instead of a spectrum. While this type of decision-making has certain productive uses, personality traits are not one of them. Personality traits are neither good nor bad, they simply are a part of who we are as an individual. I should make the distinction that personality traits are not the same as personal choices. Choices can be thought of as good or bad, however these are not who we are. For instance, there is no positive way to frame constantly being late. But should a person with this bad habit be committed to improving themselves by being more considerate of other people's time, they can make the conscious choice to be punctual from that moment forward.

In contrast, two people looking at the same personality trait can frame it differently, one way can be used to empower and heal, the other way can be used to punish and blame. Understanding your astronumerology chart helps you understand your personality traits more deeply and to frame them to their best advantage. You don't need to fix what other people don't understand about you. **Your unique blueprint allows you to think of your traits to your best advantage rather than letting them be labelled by others as something to be fixed.** A good case in point is when a man and a woman display the same trait, it can often lead to social advantage for one of them and a disadvantage for the other. The judgement is determined by society's expectations for how each gender should behave. While being assertive usually pays off for men, the same behaviour in a woman can be framed by others as mean or angry. In truth, assertiveness is a good quality regardless of which gender displays it.

Positive terms lead to positive self-concept which leads to increased happiness and productivity. Having this information readily available can lessen any guilt or harsh self-judgement that could easily be created by the negative tone of those around you. Having knowledge of your blueprint gives you the confidence to stay true to yourself rather than allowing others to frame your characteristics from their perspective. You should never have to apologize for being who you are.

CHAPTER 5

STEPPING INTO YOUR PERSONAL POWER

"Don't be satisfied with stories, how things have gone for others.
Unfold your own myth."
- *Rumi*

Labels are all around us! Everywhere we look, it seems
that society has a name, definition and set of expectations for
everyone, everything and every place. It is seemingly quicker and
more convenient to fit people, places, and things into set boxes
in our mind, so we don't really have to think much about it. In an
age when there are many demands on our time, we are tempted
to use these shortcuts to make quick decisions.

In cultures all around the world, we have developed unique
languages to create mental representations of our surroundings
and the people in it. When we think of that name, preconceived
notions that originate from the culture we live in immediately
come to mind. For example, the words *love* and *beauty* calls to
mind certain images, expectations and feelings that are generally
positive. These are very different from the negative images and
feelings associated with the words *hate* and *ugly*. Yet in reality,
these words are nothing more than unique combinations of
letters we have constructed in the English language to represent
night and day concepts.

Sometimes labels can be useful in our everyday lives. If I'm at a restaurant and I order my favourite meal of flame grilled chicken with spicy fries, I expect to receive exactly that. I would be very disappointed if I ordered this meal, but instead received a cheeseburger with salad. For the waitress and cook to fulfill my expectation accurately, the three of us must share a similar idea of what chicken with fries looks like. We do have to have some degree of labelling for us to work together in creating an efficient world.

The trouble enters the picture when we place labels on people when we should be keeping an open-mind. Labels prevent the process of looking deeper into an individual to discover the essence of who they are. In the most negative sense, labels turn into unflattering stereotypes of a person based on a group they belong to. While stereotyping is a natural human process, it is still wrong. Sadly because it is a default reaction, it is not only strangers that stereotype us. Teachers, classmates, colleagues, bosses, teammates and acquaintances stereotype us based on their subjective perceptions of our ability. Sometimes positive stereotypes lead to higher expectations and higher achievement. More often though, it is negative stereotypes which lead to lower expectations and lower achievement.

As a child we look to the people around us for clues to what our strengths and weaknesses are, what are acceptable pursuits, and what are not acceptable. Based on this feedback, we choose to engage in certain activities and ignore others, even though the activities we are ignoring may actually be something we are really interested in. Some teachers who are supposed to take the role of encouraging and inspiring their students to their highest potential-- do exactly the opposite. At school, some children are fortunate enough to get the label of being "smart" while others are labelled "slow" or "challenged." These premature judgements towards a child or adolescent are a negative stigma that can cause discriminatory and/or differential treatment at school which may lead to long-term problems such as lower self-esteem, lower academic achievement, and lower levels of job attainment. Regardless of age, imposing labels on a person could result in self-fulfilling prophecy, a process whereby fallacious beliefs are communicated to someone about their ability, and they believe them, thereby causing the beliefs to come alive. This could manifest in a direct or indirect way.[28]

As we grow up, the people we work with take the place of teachers, but the patterns can be very alike. Some employees get more promotions, raises and responsibilities, even though another employee may be more qualified. Employers can consciously or unconsciously signal to the employee how much they value them. For some, this helps them achieve more, and for others, it is upsetting to realize that their efforts are not being rewarded.

Worldly power imbalances still exist. Although individual exceptions are becoming more common, and a growing number of glass ceilings are being broken, the general pattern is still that men have more power than women, and Caucasians have more power than visible minorities. In some countries, within the same race, caste systems allow those at the top of the hierarchy, to manipulate the lives of those at the bottom. There is no meaningful or urgent incentive for those in power to stop, as they enjoy a better quality of life at the expense of exploiting others to do menial and degrading work. Societal stereotypes further exacerbate the power imbalances. For example, in India, the Hindu belief that Dalit people (formerly called the untouchables) committed sins in a past life and now are born into the lowest rung of the social ladder to atone for them, causes Dalits to be forced into a life of modern day bonded slavery. On top of being forced to do the dirtiest jobs, they are humiliated, tortured, and socially ostracized by the higher castes.[29]

In several articles, it has been documented that the greatest gap both in status and in wealth, is between White men and visible

28 Brophy, J.E (1982). *Research on the Self-Fulfilling Prophecy and Teacher Expectations*. Retrieved from http://files.eric.ed.gov/fulltext/ED221530.pdf
29 I highly recommend reading the best-selling book *Dalit Freedom* by Joseph D'souza to find out more about the Dalits and their ongoing struggle for emancipation.

minority women. Yet in my own experience as a visible minority woman trying to raise awareness of this systemic problem, I have found it very disturbing that people who are closer to the top of the hierarchy tend to minimize the seriousness or completely deny there is a problem on a societal level. Even worse is that some of them try to deny or make light of the individual experiences of oppression faced by those closer to the bottom. They attack them by attributing their experiences to a personality deficiency.

Sometimes even within the same traditionally oppressed group, some people who have done very well for themselves negatively judge others experiences of oppression in an effort to psychologically distance themselves. They don't want to believe that what happened to the victim could possibly happen to them, so they assign the blame to the victim rather than uncontrollable external forces. Some of these people want to believe the victim is lying or blowing things out of proportion, while others openly state that since they accomplished a goal, everybody else who couldn't is somehow inferior, or is otherwise exploiting their situation for their own gain.

Regardless of who is making the judgements towards them, it can be especially painful, as people who have already been pushed down are now being kicked. Each person within a group has had different life experiences. The fact is that unless you have walked a mile in another's shoes, their experience is just theoretical. You don't really know what it feels like despite how many external similarities you share with them.

I vividly recall my last year of undergraduate studies when I was finishing up my last few credits and desired to gain entrance into a psychology graduate program upon graduation. I had worked very hard and managed to obtain all As and A+s in my last two years. Additionally I had competitive GRE scores, excellent references, research experience, and volunteer experience. Even so, to gain entrance to the graduate program I learned that I had to locate a potential supervisor for my thesis who was willing to admit me into their lab. One can have the best objective record but unless you find a professor who thinks you are the correct "fit" for them, you will not be able to get in.

In light of this, a family friend referred me to the institution where she worked so that I could participate in a research project that would mirror the type done in graduate school. She told me the man who was in charge of it was a professor affiliated with a psychology program, and one of his graduate students was also currently working on it. I agreed to volunteer because on the surface, it seemed like a fruitful opportunity. Thus I volunteered on the project under the supervision of one of his colleagues.

Several months later, I met the professor in person and expressed my keen interest in entering the graduate program. He directly expressed to me in what seemed like a sincere manner that he was satisfied with my work up to this point and that if I continued to do a good job that he would likely be able to accept me as a graduate student (in other words recommend to the admissions committee that I was a good candidate for the program). I thought to myself, if he believed I wasn't a good fit for his lab, he probably wouldn't have said anything at all, or at least he wouldn't have said as much as he did, especially in such a nice tone of voice. If he reacted this way, I would have quit working on the project shortly after, as I didn't sign any contract, and I had already volunteered there for a significant amount of time. In looking at his website in greater detail at that point, I noticed that he did not have any visible minority graduate students in his lab. In any case, due to our meeting I believed that I could be the first, and I increased my volunteer commitment from one day per week to two days per week, even though it was a 1½ hour commute each way that costed $14 in bus fare. Each day I was there I spent four to six hours. I also spent a considerable amount of additional time doing a literature review for the research report at home. I volunteered for about 10 months in total.

In all his communication with me via email, he never expressed any problems with my work. In fact on the second in person meeting, he told me my work was great. Later that year when I checked in with him, he told me was accepting a graduate student for next year, and that I should apply. A few months later, I paid the mandatory fees of over $150, but never even got to the interview stage. I received a form rejection letter from the school, and never heard a word from him since.

It became crystal clear to me that he believed I was good enough to be a source of free labour for his project, but that I was not worthy of being a student in his lab within the graduate program. I know that millions of young people doing free internships or volunteer work are exploited this way, and it is usually not related to race. Although this practice is despicable, the benefit for not hiring is clear-- employers want to save money on hiring employees. However, in my case, there was no economic benefit to not accepting me: there is an allotted stipend for students to be there. On top of that, the school is dependent upon students to enrol in their graduate programs and work as teaching assistants for undergraduate courses.

When I expressed my disappointment to the school, and pointed out the conspicuous lack of diversity within his lab, it came back to me via other people at the institution that his colleague had been spreading rumours that my performance was poor, and that I was using my race as an excuse. Considering that she had written me a reference letter prior to this, in which she rated, and commented, on my performance highly, it was upsetting that she began slandering me to cover up what had taken place. While it was disappointing not to get in on a personal level, more harrowing was that fact that everyone was not given an equal chance to succeed. I strongly feel that if enough people speak up, change will occur.

Regrettably, while the professor's actions were not ethical, I was unable to take it up legally. I did not have anything in writing stating he would accept me into the program, and he had formally denied it. This was despite the fact that it made absolutely no sense for me to continue, let alone increase my time commitment after our first in person meeting if he was truthful about his intentions. He could not give a suitable explanation for the discrepancy. It has been five years since then, and a recent look at his website shows that there are still no visible minority graduate students in his lab…

HAVE THE COURAGE TO SPEAK YOUR TRUTH

The reason I relate this personal experience is because it resonates so deeply. I've spoken to countless people who have had similar experiences in different contexts. Although it happens more often to people from certain groups (women and visible minorities), it can happen to anyone. The common theme I hear is that what is more upsetting than the original discriminatory experience, is the shame, guilt, and condemnation projected onto the courageous souls who dare to let their voice be heard.

Some people silently internalize those projections, believing there is something wrong with them. Or perhaps they don't speak out because they are afraid of future consequences, and what other people will think of them. Sometimes, they are worried that even if they do speak up, people won't believe them, which adds insult to injury. This is particularly true with high-status and powerful perpetrators, they are counting on the fact that their victims don't ruin their reputation. It doesn't help matters that the public is slower to accept that a high-status person would engage in this type of behaviour.

This scenario happens in the workplace all the time—everyone knows that a certain person mistreats people, but because that person is near the top of the hierarchy, he or she consistently gets away with their bad behaviour. Or perhaps a person's direct supervisor instructs them to knowingly do something wrong— such as grocery store employees tampering with expired food to make it look fresh, or changing the best before labels. Even though it is a risk to public safety, most employees are too afraid of losing their jobs to complain or refuse to do it. Employees may notice that other employees who speak up, are put on the chopping block or are otherwise criticized or ostracized—which discourages them from taking action. Even if employees do take legal action, companies have access to corporate lawyers, who are paid very high salaries to defend their actions, even if they know they are on the wrong side of the law.

Most of the time, applicants feel pressured into a settlement. Settlements typically give some monetary and non-monetary benefits but there is no public admission of wrongdoing. If applicants go through with the case to the end, there is satisfaction of winning, and forcing a public admission of wrongdoing. But the stress of being involved in a legal battle takes its toll, and in almost all cases, the monetary award is not even close to being proportionate to the suffering and tangible losses they faced. Deciding to go through with the case also introduces the risk that the applicant could lose; especially if they are lacking skilled legal assistance and/or their case is assigned a judge that usually sides with corporations. Even in cases where it would be clear to the public that a particular judge would have reasonable bias or a conflict of interest (due to their background and/ or results of previous decisions), it is solely up to the judge's discretion to recuse themselves from the case in the event they are formally requested to do so. This is unfortunate as numerous studies have documented that even well-meaning people can have trouble recognizing their own biases and conflicts of interest.

Going back to the same workplace after taking legal action can be detrimental to one's peace of mind, and gossip among people in the industry may cause lengthy delays in obtaining a comparable job elsewhere. It is understandable given the relatively grim outlook, that people feel that their actions won't really payoff in the end, so they don't try in the first place. But at the same time, the forced silence can impose an even heavier burden on a person's mind, body and spirit, even resulting in physical illness and disease. Our biggest regrets in life are always what we didn't do, rather than what we did. This is true even if we failed to get the desired outcome. When employees do take a company to court for a legitimate concern, it sends a message that treating people with a lack of dignity and respect has consequences. It takes someone with a lot of strength of conviction, tenacity, and faith to pursue these types of cases to try to hold powerful wrongdoers accountable, even if there is significant personal risk and sacrifice involved.

While workplace silence can be psychologically deadly, there are other domains where silence can be physically deadly. For instance, rape and sexual abuse victims must first come to terms with their own feelings of what occurred. Then they would have to participate in a court proceeding to get justice and re-live the traumatizing events by telling their story in court. Sometimes when they are on the stand, victims get torn to shreds by callous attorneys who aggressively question their sexual history, trying to distort the facts to portray them as someone who they are not. Both in and out of court, the process of "slut-shaming" causes millions of women to experience degradation, isolation and serious mental health issues. Another common occurrence is if the attacker is famous/ wealthy, the victim may be portrayed as a liar and opportunist. In these cases, it seems that it takes several victims to come out for it to be taken seriously. It is painful to witness that one woman's life-changing experience is not worthy of being heard.

If the attacker is affiliated with a powerful organization, the victim might even receive direct threats that prevent her from taking action so that their reputation is not tarnished. For instance, I read the story of Dana Liesegang[30], a woman who at the age of 19 enlisted in the U.S Navy. One day, she left the ship to mail a letter to her boyfriend back at home. On the way back she was offered a ride with a male sailor. Things took a turn for the worse when he took her to a 75 foot cliff, raped

---

[30] Her inspiring and courageous story is detailed in her recently released book *Falling Up*

her, and then threw her off. She survived but was paralyzed from the neck down and became confined to a wheelchair. She reported the incident to the Navy but they threatened that to remain 100% service connected on disability (financially taken care of), she could not take them to court. Further they told her that she would not win, she would not get any money, and that she could assert her right to remain silent. She did suffer in silence for over 20 years. With the legal system having so many flaws, and the Navy being so powerful, the truth does not always prevail, and it was too big a risk to take at that time. But with the encouragement of her social worker, Dr. Wayne Dyer, and his daughter Serena Dyer, she realized that she didn't have to be silent anymore, and finally wrote a book about how she regained her sense of peace through forgiving her attacker. Her inner process of being able to forgive was more challenging than the outer physical training she took part in to be able to walk with crutches. But she would not let one man's selfish and cruel actions define her life! Inspiring others to go from being a silent victim to an empowered victor through speaking their truth became her mission.

Whatever the circumstances surrounding sexual assault, the social stigma, and other potentially negative outcomes, often discourage victims from speaking their truth immediately after the traumatizing event. The may wait years, or perhaps they never find the courage to come out. If the crime is made light of-- and perpetrators don't face severe enough consequences, statistics show that they reoffend. Researchers tracking 404 368 prisoners from 30 states after their release from prison in 2005 found that 76.6% of them were rearrested within five years. Of those prisoners, 56.7% were rearrested within the first year.[31] The next crime might be even more brutal, and silence could result in critical injury and/or death for the next victim.

Fortunately, an increasing amount of people have realized that silence is what keeps the cycle of abuse going, and they don't want to see other people in their position mistreated in the future.

31 http://www.nij.gov/topics/corrections/recidivism/pages/welcome.aspx

In seeking to be the change they wish to see in the world, they are labelled troublemakers, complainers, and difficult personalities. They are ostracized, penalized, expelled, and fired. Depending on the part of the world they live in, some of them are even tortured and killed for daring to speak up.

Instead of acknowledging that there is a problem, those in power seek to bury it, finding fault with the victims in an attempt to evade their own wrongdoing. They hope that victims will stay silent, feel ashamed, and quietly move on with their lives. This way the perpetrators can continue doing what they are doing, without feeling public pressure to change their policies and actions.

There are countless examples of large scale man-made oppression, and throughout history, we have seen that these injustices were never discontinued by the perpetrators by their own free will. To the contrary, when the powerless initially began to stand up for themselves, they were met with extremely violent attacks by those in power. We would still have Black slaves if it weren't for the first defiant acts of courage displayed in the Civil Rights movement, and the persistence of those acts of courage by countless brave souls despite savage murder, aggression, and jailing. In a very similar human rights issue, it is other religions such as Christianity and Buddhism, which the Dalits are converting to, as a means of hope out of their bonded slavery. They know that by remaining a Hindu, they will always be regarded as sub-human, regardless of any education or wealth they may attain. When the Dalit people dare to take action against the gross injustice inflicted on them on a daily basis, either legally, or in their communities, they are brutally attacked, raped, humiliated, and tortured by the higher castes. Yet, they persist in taking back their rights! An increasing amount of people globally are taking a collective stand on this issue, and change is slowly occurring.

CELEBRITY CASE STUDY: MALALA YOUSAFZAI

Part of the inspiration for this chapter comes from the story of Malala Yousafzai, a young girl from Pakistan who dared to publicly speak up about the importance of education for girls, despite death threats from the Taliban. She had witnessed numerous young girls marrying in their early teens in her community, and she did not want her life to turn out like that. She realized the only way out was to get an education. But since the Taliban took over, they burned down the girls' schools, slaughtered the students, and burned female teachers alive. As a result, Malala felt compelled to publicly speak about girls having the right to an education. Agonizingly, her courage had a price-- on the bus from school one day, a gunman shot her and she was left in critical condition, needing multiple surgeries to survive.

Even though the Taliban continued to consider her a target, during her recovery, she continued to speak out, and released her autobiography, *I am Malala: The Girl Who Stood Up for Education and Was Shot by the Taliban.* For her outstanding display of courage, she was awarded several prestigious awards worldwide. At age 17, she became the youngest Nobel Peace Prize recipient. Today, she continues the fight in raising public awareness to get world leaders to spend more money on education. Because of her bravery and determination, real change is happening in the world. It is so inspiring to realize that it all started with one young girl...

Malala was born on July 12th 1997 in Mingaora, Pakistan.[32] She is a Cancer number 3: since Jupiter is exalted in Cancer, and Jupiter vibrates to the number 3, this is a very harmonious combination. Cancer is concerned with protecting and nurturing children, giving them a sense of safety and security. Number 3 is associated with optimism, inspiration, education, and foreign travel. It makes sense that she is happy to travel all over the world raising awareness for millions of young girls to be able to receive

---

[32] http://www.astro.com/astro-databank/Yousafzai,_Malala. Her chart is not shown here because her birth time is not accurate. However, you may view the positions of the planets

an education. The Malala Fund has experienced exponential growth since she introduced it.

Her mutual reception of Mars in Libra and Saturn in Aries, allow these two planets to work as if they were in their own sign. Along with her life path of 9 (Mars' number), it is natural for her to display toughness, determination, and a courageous warrior spirit. It doesn't matter how outwardly powerful or intimidating her enemies are, she has more power within her.

Her leadership skills and ability to take center stage are shown by her Mercury and Venus in Leo and her life path of 1 (Sun's number). Since the number 1 repeats six times in her name, number 1 is her intensity number as well, which gives her that extra boost of courage and confidence.

Her eloquence and persuasive communication style are in part due to her personality and soul urge numbers both being 5 (Mercury's number). Her North Node in Virgo, a Mercury ruled sign, shows that her soul's purpose has a service-orientation, and also involves communicating a specific message to the world. Since Mercury also represents how we learn, it is fitting that her message deals with education. This work allows her to grow spiritually.

Malala's significant interest in social justice, fairness, and equality is shown by her life path 9, her Moon-Mars conjunction in Libra as well as her Jupiter and Uranus in humanitarian Aquarius. Uranus is expressing the fullest extent of its power in its own sign Aquarius. Thus, we see she is a revolutionary thinker passionate about a large scale social justice movement. In fact, the generation born with Uranus in Aquarius will bring forth technology, innovation, and social justice issues on a whole different level from what we have seen before.

Malala is a special example of a girl having the courage to reject her attacker's vision for her life, and turn her test into a testimony.

The Taliban didn't want her to live to see her 16th birthday, but with God's grace, she survived and is thriving. She made the conscious choice to not allow the erroneous belief system that girls are less worthy than boys poison her life, and the lives of millions of other girls.

On the other hand, many people do struggle with everyday experiences of discrimination, stereotyping, oppression, marginalization, and power abuse. Throughout life, as experiences such as these accumulate, we find that other people's projections can subtly seep into our beliefs without us even realizing. We may act upon this erroneous belief system, potentially limiting ourselves and future accomplishments in significant ways. For this reason, it is important to do a regular inventory of our beliefs with the refrain, "is it *really* true?"

Exercise:

Take a sheet of paper and divide it into two columns. In column A, write down all of the negative comments or actions toward you from other people and how it made you feel. This could be from anyone you have ever met as long as it had a memorable impact. On column B, write down all the negative beliefs you have about yourself at the present time. Below the columns, write down what comes to mind about how the harsh criticisms made about you have been carrying into your self-image today.

When I first did an exercise similar to this one, I found it incredibly cathartic and healing. Don't save this one for later! Words that were long "forgotten" came flooding back to mind from the subconscious. After you are finished your writing, you may choose to repeat the affirmation: **I am beautiful and worthy of being loved just as I am.** You may wish to tear up the piece of paper to solidify the process of letting these old, false beliefs out of your heart and mind.

Doing this exercise is like pushing a reset button on your mental programming. Erroneous beliefs only change **when we question where they come from** and realize that they are not based in truth. A rose retains its essence regardless of how many times it is crushed. People can say and do whatever they want but they can't diminish who you are unless you let them, only you hold the power. Just because someone makes a judgement about you, it doesn't make it true. It says more about their own dissatisfaction with themselves than anything else.

Stereotypes and prejudices are viruses that infiltrate societal belief systems both consciously (explicit) and unconsciously (implicit). They cause practical disadvantages to certain groups of people in different situations. Potentially more harmful than the practical disadvantages are the mental and emotional wounding that can occur as people internalize these judgements, even though they are only based on a *subjective* appraisal.

For instance, women in traditionally male-dominated professions such as engineering, science, technology, math, firefighting, law enforcement, politics, construction, the skilled trades, and surgery, face stereotypes about their ability to do the job. People have preconceived notions about what people in these professions should look like. This translates into practical disadvantages for women in these fields.

Research on gender bias in STEM (science, technology, engineering and maths) faculty, revealed that when employers saw two identical resumes, one with the applicant's name "John" and the other "Jennifer", Jennifer faced several disadvantages. The faculty perceived Jennifer as less competent, thus they were less likely to hire or mentor her. They also suggested paying Jennifer a salary that was significantly lower than John. Interestingly, even the female faculty exhibited the same biases. Results suggested that the faculty in the study were likely unaware they were discriminating against Jennifer, in other words it was an implicit bias.[33]

33 http://gender.stanford.edu/news/2014/why-does-john-get-stem-job-rather-jennifer

In the same vein, several studies have documented that identical resumes with stereotypically ethnic sounding names are less likely to get calls for interviews. In other words, employers consciously or unconsciously discriminate against ethnic sounding names. [33]

While we are fortunate in many countries to have equal opportunities to attend elementary and high school, millions of girls don't have that privilege. In many countries stricken with poverty, there is a widespread belief that only boys are worth educating. This explicit stereotype about females' lack of intelligence further exacerbates the cycle of poverty for a woman and her children.

A relatively recent trend is the stay-at-home dad, which the 2015 film *The Intern* put a spotlight on. In this movie, Jules Ostin is the successful founder of an e-commerce fashion company. Her husband Matt stays at home to take care of their daughter while Jules continues to run the business. Earlier in their relationship, Matt was earning more money than her, at a job he found fulfilling, but now the roles are reversed. He made a sacrifice to let her capitalize on the success of the rapidly growing business. There is judgement from the other stay-at-home moms at the daycare that Jules doesn't have enough time to cook, or do other tasks she "should" do as a mom. As the plot goes on, we learn that Matt has been having an affair with one of the stay-at-home moms from his daughter's daycare. Jules is unsure what to do about this, but is considering hiring someone to become CEO of her company to give her more time to spend with her family and hopefully restore the marriage. It becomes clear that Jules does not want to sacrifice control of her company, but feels it may be the best option to give her more time to spend with her husband. Fortunately, after the confrontation about his affair took place, Matt encourages Jules to retain control over her company.

The reason this scenario is interesting, is because in real life, the roles are reversed most of the time. When the man is the CEO, there isn't a stigma, and there are better family dynamics. With an increasing number of wives earning more than their husbands, the stay-at-home dad is becoming more common. Unfortunately, societal stereotypes about masculinity may cause negative judgements towards these families. This may also contribute to strained family dynamics within the home, as men feel less masculine, and women feel guilty pursuing successful careers, and/or being the sole income earner.

Stereotypes are a topic that I am especially passionate about for several reasons, but perhaps the most salient is that I have personally been the recipient of derogatory stereotypes about my ability. Several studies have documented that visible minorities are disproportionately labelled as learning disabled as compared to White students, leading to overrepresentation of certain races in special education classes. I was also quite surprised as I did the research, to find that there are stereotypes of South Asian students as memorizers who lack critical thinking abilities.[34] I gained entrance to a graduate program that only accepted the top 6% of its applicants: entrance statistics showed that every student accepted had an A average. Despite this, I was told by a professor, Kristin,[35] on my very first meeting with her that I was "a memorizer who was unable to critically think and apply information." Kristin prematurely predicted based on one meeting that I wouldn't do well in her courses (I had to take three of her mandatory courses over two semesters) because I memorized information. I was surprised because all I did was ask for a few clarifications to course content—it would have been simple for her to just answer my questions. In all my academic life, I had never experienced something like this, and was very confused as to why she made these assumptions so quickly. The first midterm was in a week's time, and despite my best efforts, her words kept replaying in my mind, distracting me during my study periods. This made me anxious, and caused me to lack

---

34 See for example, http://tribune.com.pk/story/387854/why-indians-win-the-spelling-bee/ or http://www.uni5.co/index.php/en/uni5-education-system-ues-2/pisa-reveals-indian-education-status.html
35 Not her real name

confidence that I could pass her exams. In the end, I failed one of her course's written and practical exams by 1-2%.

As time went on, Kristin would repeat these comments whenever she saw me, drilling it into my mind that I needed to be formally tested for a learning disability, otherwise she didn't know how to help me, and I would fail at finals. I told her the first time she said this that I refused to be tested. But she didn't take no for an answer—she told the chair of the department, Dawn[36] about her belief. In a mandatory meeting soon after that, Dawn was echoing the same comments about memorizing and not thinking, even though I had done well in all the courses last semester and was doing well in every other course this semester (including hers) which obviously required critical thinking and application. There was a huge power imbalance between us, and she was adamant that I at least get disability screening since it was free. Dawn told me that she was also the acting director of the department, and that if I failed a course my appeal would get sent to her to decide. It was clear that the result of her decision would directly impact my ability to stay in the program. The conversation was excruciatingly painful and I felt the only way not to upset her was to give in to her demand.

About three weeks later, I visited the Services for Students with Disabilities center and met with the learning strategist, Michelle.[37] She did not request access to my developmental, academic, or medical history. During the meeting, I told her that I did not believe I had a learning disability, but that Dawn requested that I attend this screening, and I needed her to send an email that I actually attended. During our meeting I did not see her taking notes, but it is possible she did when I left her office. In the ensuing legal proceeding when the school released these notes, I noticed there were also some unflattering things written that I never told her (but that were the same things Kristin or Dawn wrote on their witness statements).

---

36 Not her real name
37 Not her real name

It is important to note that Michelle assured me that the meeting would remain confidential, as would any other paper work that I filled out. SSD encourages you to reveal details as they want to portray the image that they are making efforts to help you. But I chose not to reveal anything too personal, as I knew nothing students fill out really remains confidential in the case of a dispute. If there is something the school thinks they can use against you, they won't hesitate. My intuition turned out to be correct, as during the ensuing legal battle, opposing counsel requested that I give her permission to access my "confidential" file, otherwise she would file a formal request for it. The court can order the documents to be released against your will. So if you are a student being required to visit disability services, please do keep in mind that nothing you ever tell them or write down is truly confidential. Be cautious with what you reveal.

In her witness statement, Michelle correctly noted that I told her that I didn't participate in sports (except swimming), that I did not drive due to some trouble with parking, and that I had problems navigating a map. In her view, this constituted visual-spatial processing deficits. But she also admitted that I told her I was good at math, that I did not have attention problems, and that I did not have trouble interpreting others nonverbal language—that is three major criteria of nonverbal learning disorder (NVLD) that I did not possess. Nevertheless, Michelle stated on her witness statement that based on what I told her, she felt it was appropriate to refer me for a psychological educational assessment because I endorsed some symptoms consistent with NVLD. To sum it up, because I did not play sports, I had trouble with parking, and I had difficulty with maps-- like millions of others worldwide-- she thought it was appropriate for me to spend nearly $2000 to test out the possibility that I may have a learning disorder.

Incidentally, NVLD is characterized by over-reliance on rote memorization as a survival skill.[38] In addition, this disability has

38 http://www.ldonline.org/article/6114/

a negative impact on conceptual skills and abstract thinking.[39] I certainly did not tell her that I memorized things, nor did she ask me. Not surprisingly, NVLD fit with the South Asian student stereotypes and the two subjective assessments given to me by Kristin and Dawn. Keep in mind Michelle was not even qualified to administer the testing, she had to refer me to a psychologist to get it done. She ended the meeting by informing me about the cost and procedure of the disability testing, and said she would be emailing me literature describing nonverbal learning disability in detail.

In the time span of one month, three White female authority figures were telling me I might have a learning disability. I was dumbfounded that it had never crossed their minds to think about how I had gotten this far in my studies if I all I did was memorize stuff. Prior work included an honours thesis, essays, assignments, projects, and presentations! They had no hard evidence, only their irrational beliefs about my ability. It was hurtful and infuriating.

Each time I would meet with her, Kristin continued to make several derogatory comments about what she *perceived* to be my tendency to memorize only what would appear on exams, rather than critically think about different scenarios that could happen in real life. Despite her lack of formal training on learning disabilities, she opined that she had an extensive background in teaching students using a variety of techniques, and since I didn't seem to understand the concepts in the way she explained them, it is appropriate that I be formally tested. The insinuation was clear: because my learning style did not match with her teaching style, it was due to some fault I, and definitely not her, must have. And it was my duty to be tested to correct this fault.

Perhaps this dilemma could have been solved if I was able to gain clarification from a teaching assistant, as their teaching style may have been a better match for me. Unfortunately, both of

39 https://www.understood.org/en/learning-attention-issues/child-learning-disabilities/ nonverbal-learning-disabilities/understanding-nonverbal-learning-disabilities

them refused to meet with me when requested, or answer my emailed questions (despite the course outline stating that they were available by appointment and held virtual office hours). I found out later that the reason for their differential treatment towards me was that Kristin had been having multiple discussions about me with them. She discouraged them from meeting with me, or answering my emails. She wrote to Holly,[40] "you might be wasting your time...we are trying to get her tested for a learning disability." Kristin even went so far as to tell Holly that I told her that I had hired tutors throughout my academic career to get me through! Besides this being an outright lie, she never even asked me how I got through my undergraduate studies because she had already told me in our second meeting that psychology just involved memorizing things. When the other teaching assistant, Andrew[41] asked her if he should answer my email, she responded that he should forward it, as well as any subsequent emails I send to her. She told him that she would explain why when they met. Andrew responded by agreeing to her request and adding that he had assumed as much from their previous conversations.

Owing to Kristin's gossip, no one else would meet with me for help when I needed it. She was creating a hostile learning environment for me, one in which even infrequent questions posed to Andrew or Holly during lab classes were met with vague answers and a clear disinterest. Regardless of their personal feelings, they did not make an effort to behave professionally, and it was crystal clear to me that they *believed* I wasn't good enough to be in the program. This also translated into a lab participation score of 2/5 and 2.7/5 from Holly and Andrew respectively, even though I attended over 95% of the lab classes, never being late and being prepared with the required pre-readings almost all the time. On my peer feedback sheet (each classmate wrote something they admired about the others), numerous people commented that I was hardworking, persistent, and determined. They witnessed the sheer amount of time that I would be practicing in the labs, even outside of classes, and studying the

40 Not her real name
41 Not his real name

material on the break times. Ironically, it was Kristin's idea to compile the peer feedback sheet, and she also wrote that I was a hard worker and determined to succeed, yet she gave me 2/5 on the lab participation score. When I formally requested the objective criteria on which this score was based, and any notes from the teachers in coming to these abnormally low scores, the school could not provide me anything in writing. As a result they omitted this score from my final mark.

Every time Kristin and I met, she spent the majority of time insulting me for asking questions, rather than just answering them, and kept reinforcing that I needed to get disability testing. My firm refusal to get testing only exacerbated her behaviour. Even in grading my performance on practical exams, Kristin always marked me two full grade levels below the grades given to me by the other examiners at the other stations. Looking at the class grades overall, the difference between her and the other examiners was only half a grade level. This difference caused me to fail at finals. If she had marked me to the same differential she marked the class, I would have passed.

I had used up one of the two remedial examinations permitted to re-write one of Kristin's written exams that I had failed in her course the previous semester. According to the student handbook, I had one more remedial exam left that I could use to stay in the program, and I requested to use it for the practical exam in the current course. But the school administration refused to give it to me, and I was required to withdraw from the program immediately. They justified it by stating that since I refused to get disability testing, formal accommodations could not be identified or implemented to allow me to succeed in the program.

The school did not see it this way, but what they were actually doing was discriminating against me on the basis of a perceived disability. For them, my testing was a necessary prerequisite in order to graduate, and without it they *believed* I wouldn't be able to. To the best of my knowledge the second remedial exam was not refused to any other student in the department's history. They had a graduation rate of nearly 100% each year, so there were only a handful of cases of withdrawal. Of those withdrawals, the school refused to release whether they were denied their second remedial exam them under the guise that it was an invasion of privacy and they would have to manually search through all student files from the last five years. This was clearly untrue as I was not requesting specific names. Moreover, they would only need to look at the enrollment versus graduation lists for any given year that graduation was slightly below 100%, and any discrepancy would quickly become apparent. They simply did not want to release any information that would help me prove discrimination and differential treatment.

My formal written appeals to the progressively higher levels of school administration were denied. Kristin had many years of experience, several publications, and had won teaching awards, so she had a lot of credibility. Without taking into account my excellent academic record, or interviewing her about the cause of the grading differential, and log of derogatory comments I had recorded her making since we first met, they concluded that she was correct in recommending me to be tested for a learning disability and providing *continual reminders* to be tested throughout the semesters. Specifically, they wrote that she was acting "conscientiously" and fulfilling a "positive duty" by giving me an opportunity to achieve my academic potential through formal accommodations; as a student who may have a learning disability.

Although Kristin was wrong regarding the first time she suggested that I may have a learning disability, I may have been angry but I would have been able to shake it off—if only she had stopped there and respected that I was an adult capable of making my own decisions. But the school did not take into account the potentially far-reaching and long-lasting effects of her *continual reminders*. Her constant harsh comments about my abilities had a negative impact on my self-confidence, and her gossip to the teaching assistants about my abilities had a negative impact on my ability to receive constructive assistance with material. Both of these factors had a cumulative effect in me doing worse in a general sense in her three courses—which were my lowest grades of any professor's courses in the program. Additionally, in her mind, was a strong *belief* that I could have an undiagnosed learning disability, and that I could not graduate without formal disability related accommodations. Regardless of how well I actually performed, she had *lowered expectations* for me. My overall performance was just hovering around the pass mark of low sixties on the practical portion of the course, and the other examiners had marked me at a level that would allow me to pass. It was the huge grading differential between Kristin and the others that made me fail. Whether it was conscious or not, the grading differential was a direct result of her beliefs. In my view, the events that went on for about two years after this point was really due to her decision to continually remind me, and the teaching staff, about the disability she thought I may have.

Dawn stated that since Kristin had met with me many times, she could not be biased against me, and went 'above and beyond' to help me. But she didn't take into account that I was forced into meetings with Kristin because the teaching assistants refused to help me. Dawn never interviewed Kristin about the log of interactions-- what good is it if I met with her if I was not getting questions answered and instead being insulted the whole time? It was a conflict of interest for Dawn, who had been colleagues with Kristin for the past 20 years to be deciding my first appeal, the one that was relied on a lot in the higher levels. On top of it she believed I had the disability and that I was wrong for refusing to be tested. When the emails on my student file were released, I found out she was breaking privacy rules by talking about the suspected disability with another professor in the program, telling her she doesn't think I'll make it through the program. I have no idea how many other people in the department she may have discussed me with.

The Vice Provost didn't interview Kristin about the log of interactions either, stating that since she decided to allow me my first remedial exam for her written test, she could not be biased. Conveniently, she had forgotten that two remedial exams are granted to all students in the program, with no formally stated rules for exception. Kristin had no right to deny me my first remedial exam. In response to my complaint that the teaching assistants refused to help me, she responded that she did not find evidence of this. Apparently she interviewed them and they both said I was a student who relied too heavily on memorization and had trouble applying my knowledge. She didn't consider that since I barely spoke to Holly or Andrew, they were not in a position to make these extreme comments first-hand. They had to be influenced by someone else, but at that point they had denied talking about me with Kristin. The assistants continued that I would be confused if given slightly different answers to the same question, so they forwarded the questions to Kristin to answer—this was fine in the Vice Provost's opinion. The fact is I never once asked Holly and Andrew the same question—what would be the purpose? But Kristin liked to tell people that I asked her the same questions repetitively to justify her learning disability hypothesis.

It was only during the legal proceeding, more than a year later, that they conceded that several students failed Kristin's exams, and she had not attributed their failures to an undiagnosed learning disability. They admitted that students could have failed for a variety of other reasons that didn't include disability—but still refused to acknowledge the possibility that I could be one of them. There was a huge significance to this, as these other students weren't required to pay for disability testing in order to receive help, or to graduate from the program. Comments recorded in the log such as:

"Why is it so hard for you to think?"

"You just memorized, didn't you, why don't you just think for once and maybe you can come up with a good answer."

"You don't seem to be showing any interest in developing critical thinking skills, memorizing isn't going to get you to pass this course or get through the program."

"You have to stop acting like a robot, you don't have enough time in the day to memorize all this information, what are you going to cut out next? - Sleep?"

"Your C.I. is going to come right back to me and complain that you are an incompetent student and wonder why I am training incompetent students, it looks bad for me and the School, it's embarrassing."

"You are not a good reflection of the quality of training in this program" and

" ...You are really scaring me, I mean it, you are *scaring* me,"

were not denied by Kristin when she was legally confronted. Sadly, these comments were just a snippet of all the things she said, and the school decided to defend her anyway.

I was deeply dispirited that the administration could behave like this. Many of the decision-makers deciding the outcome of my appeals had children of their own. How would they feel if their child was demeaned in this way? Would they still see nothing wrong? I guess they never gave it much thought because the tenure system guaranteed that they would still have their jobs, even if they made wrong decisions. Thousands of students come and go, but professors still had to interact with their colleagues on a daily basis, so why make life difficult? After all, faculty lives are more precious than the dreams of the students who worked hard and made sacrifices to get into their desired programs.

I knew that this deeply engrained pattern of behaviour would not correct itself on its own, and for the sake of future students, I felt compelled to take action. I was determined to incentivise these people to use their critical thinking ability before making unfair judgements that went against the objective evidence the next time around.

THE POWER IS WITHIN YOU

Like most external events, this is one in which I had no control over other people's actions. At the same time with the wisdom of my astronumerology chart, I was in a much better position to stand firm against these judgements and step into my personal power. The school pointed a finger at me, but my actions signaled that there were three pointing back at them. It was a decisive moment in my life journey--I could either let a few wretched opinions throw me off track or I could stand up for myself. I explained in no uncertain terms that there was no evidentiary basis to suggest I may be learning disabled and I refused to pay thousands of dollars to test out their baseless hypothesis. Once again, I displayed the quiet confidence that I have always had that conveys to people that I know who I am, and what my abilities are. Their behaviour angered me but there was no way I was going to let this poison seep into my mind and influence my self-perception. I decided that instead of internalizing these projections into my self-image, I would make sure that they were returned to the sender where they rightly belonged.

With the psychology professor discussed earlier in the chapter, my actions did not cause him to change his behaviour: there was no meaningful avenue to hold him accountable, and he had no external pressure to change his actions. But his behaviour lit a fire and brought out my inner warrior goddess! It set the stage for this incident years later, when I was finally given the chance to get some form of justice.

By sharing my story through the proper legal avenue, I was ultimately able to ensure that Kristin and the school were forced to be held accountable for their actions. Although at first, things didn't appear to be going my way; the legal proceedings were a huge test of faith. The school retained a ruthless corporate lawyer, Lisa, who was an alumna of their law school. She had been successful in getting another student disability case against the school dismissed (the applicant was self-represented in that case). Lisa had experience representing schools against students, as well as corporations against employees, in disability cases. She started playing hard ball right from the beginning.

When I was self-represented, and emailed her for arguably relevant documents prior to formally filing a request for it, she denied that the school had basic information like graduation or employment figures, even though this information was actually available online, as I later discovered. When I requested my student file, Lisa also denied the school had a student file for me. In other written documentation months later, she conceded its existence when trying to advance another of her arguments. When she was confronted about the inconsistency by the lawyer I later retained, she tried to use the technicality in wording that there was no *single*-copy student file but that there were *multiple* hard copy files for me in a variety of places in the university. For other requests she admitted the school had the documents, but refused to give them to me, often with no explanation. At that point they had refused mediation, meaning that I would have to examine my own witnesses, and cross-examine their witnesses. The task before me was daunting, and I knew I couldn't do it on my own—not because the facts weren't on my side, but because I didn't have specialized legal knowledge.

It was clear at this point that if I wanted to be taken seriously, I needed to get a lawyer. Finding a skilled and affordable lawyer is very difficult. It took me numerous phone calls to find Wade, who I felt understood my perspective of the case and was genuinely interested in helping me win. Given the four planet-nodal connections between our charts within an orb of one to three degrees each (his South Node conjunct my Saturn-Moon conjunction, my South Node conjunct his Mercury, and his North Node conjunct my Sun), it was a destined meeting. The South Node dominance meant that there was a disparity in giving and taking in past lifetimes and now the balance had to be restored. Wade knew nothing about astrology, but because the planets exert their influence regardless of belief, without even meeting me in person, he unconsciously gave me a contract in which the firm ended up running a significant loss. He later admitted he didn't think about the possibility that it could happen. But this was the only way I could afford to retain him, and at certain times fate takes over. Thankfully, God works through the right people to show you His favour at just the right time. It was a relief to know that the playing field was now more evenly matched.

With Wade's help, I was able to present a stronger case but we still had no control of external factors. Out of all the judges available, the one assigned to my case, Jennifer, was an alumna of this school's law program. Worse still, Wade told me that the vast majority of her previous decisions (with a few notable exceptions) had gone in favour of the defendants. It was especially distressing to learn that in one of her previous decisions, she concluded that a professor was not being discriminatory towards a visible minority student by suggesting she may have a learning disability upon failure of an exam—even though there were no other known difficulties in her academic history. Jennifer's sole reasoning was that because she performed differently on the multiple-choice versus short-answer sections of the exam, the professor's suggestion had been valid. Needless to say, students usually have variations in the way they perform on different sections of the exam-- for a multitude of different reasons, which most of the time don't include having a disability. She failed to consider that learning disabilities don't just pop up like the common cold! They *must* have a developmental pattern. Through my research I learned from the Diagnostic and Statistical Manual of Mental Disorders (DSM-5) learning disability diagnostic criteria that,

> Specific learning disorders can be diagnosed any time after formal education starts, but can be diagnosed afterwards in children, adolescents, and adults, provided there is evidence

during the years of formal schooling (i.e. the developmental period).[42]

In other words, difficulty with just one course at the university level with no other documented difficulties in one's academic history, does not justify adequate cause for suspecting an LD.

Prior to retaining Wade, I filed the application citing discrimination on the grounds of a perceived learning disability. Although it is a myth, people with learning disabilities are still stereotypically perceived to be less intelligent and less competent.[43] Besides ill-informed beliefs about my ability, there was no other rational explanation for the significant grading differential exhibited on multiple exams. Common sense dictates that the two or three other examiners at the other stations on each of her three practical exams wouldn't give me bonus marks equivalent to two full grade levels! I had a strong feeling that race was an additional factor for Kristin's beliefs, however I was unsure as to how to get evidence to prove it, and thus omitted this ground. However, when Wade strongly urged me to investigate potential racial causes, I discovered the South Asian student stereotypes, and it was eye-opening that they were the specific comments being made to me. We compiled several references to show the similarity between her comments and the stereotypes referenced in the media.

Regardless of the abundance of stereotype research to the contrary, Jennifer's first decision went in the school's favour: she refused to let my visible minority status be an additional ground on which I could argue the case. She gave the explanation that adding race as a ground would necessarily result in an adjournment of hearing dates, change the type of discrimination alleged, and prejudice the respondents by having to call evidence in response. She was incorrect on all these points as:

---

42 American Psychiatric Association. (2013). Diagnostic and statistical manual of mental disorders: (5th ed.): Washington, D.C
43 http://www.pbs.org/newshour/rundown/five-misconceptions-about-learning-disabilities/

1. The school had already set out their position with respect to race in their witness statements: even though they acknowledged that there were those stereotypes in society, and that Kristin echoed those exact sentiments, they maintained that there was no credible evidence that she specifically held those views.

2. Racial beliefs do not have to be explicitly stated or even intentional.[44] Such beliefs are exhibited in an unconscious, deeply systematic embedded way. For example, the *OHRC Policy and Guidelines on Racism and Racial Discrimination* state "Practical experience and psychology both confirm that anyone can stereotype, even those who are well meaning and not overtly biased. While it may be somewhat natural for humans to engage in racial stereotyping it is nevertheless unacceptable."[45]

While the school may have called evidence to justify the comments and actions taken by Kristin, there was no additional evidence to be called to "prove" that her comments and actions were not influenced by racial stereotyping. This would be determined by her answers on cross-examination. Her intention not to stereotype was irrelevant, and additional evidence was not required to address the same. Moreover, neither party had alleged that further witnesses would have to be called if the amendment was granted. Therefore it wouldn't prejudice the school by having to call evidence in response.

3. The allegations regarding race were directly related to the factual claims that Kristin harassed and discriminated against me after forming the early and unsupported view that I was not capable of critical thinking. While a further ground of discrimination was being added to at least partially explain the reasons for her conclusion in this regard, the facts such

44 See for example http://www.ohrc.on.ca/en/racial-discrimination-race-and-racism-fat-sheet
45 http://www.ohrc.on.ca/sites/default/files/attachments/Policy_and_guidelines_on_racism_and_racial_discrimination.pdf at page 18-19

claims had been based on had already been plead. Therefore there would be no adjournment of hearing dates, nor would this ground have changed the type of discrimination alleged.

These points were all made on a formal request for reconsideration. Jennifer quickly dismissed it on the basis that it wasn't a final decision in spite of the Divisional Court previously weighing in on the matter:

> Even though other issues may remain to be resolved, if the decision disposes of a substantive right of a party, it will be considered final. Courts have also held that there may be more than one final judgment in a matter, such as when a substantive issue is disposed of while other matters are reserved for subsequent determination.[46]

> It was clear that she did in fact finally dispose of the racial issue: she prevented me from arguing a racial ground of discrimination at the trial.

On the same decision, she refused to order relevant documents pertaining to the treatment of other students in the class (names redacted) that I requested from the school in order to prove differential treatment. By definition, I couldn't prove differential treatment without the use of a comparator group to measure against. As all lawyers know, framing of the issues to be determined is important in the final outcome of the case because it determines what each side can argue and the type of evidence that can be presented. The way in which Wade framed the issues were much broader than the way Lisa did for the obvious reason that the school did not want to argue issues like differential treatment that they knew were weak. Unfortunately, Jennifer decided to ignore the issues from my perspective and use the same framing of the issues Lisa used-- which were limited to two narrow points focused solely on me. Jennifer knew that establishing differential treatment was one of the three requirements set out by the OHRC that was necessary to prove

46 [1994] O.J. No. 1585

a case of prima facie case of discrimination due to disability[47] —yet in trying to gloss over this fact she labelled my request for class information as a "fishing expedition," the exact term used by Lisa. By very specific and selective framing of issues, they prevented me from presenting critical arguments that would damage the school's position in this regard.

I received Jennifer's preliminary decision about a month before the trial was set to begin. It was easy to feel discouraged given all the time and money I spent thus far. At the same time, I knew that there was a purpose, plan, and right time for everything. The seeds have to be planted before the flower can grow. Lucky for me, over 130 pages of documents the school had no choice but to release were finally sent to Wade the afternoon before the proceeding. These were the documents in the multiple hard copy student files that they had to submit because they had inadvertently admitted its existence in writing. The documents contained information I needed to help me prove that some of their witnesses had not been truthful about some of the most crucial claims made in their statements.

Many of the things that I had suspected but didn't have evidence for, were now in my hands. For example, Holly denied the following facts on her witness statement: 1. that she had any conversations about me with Kristin regarding a learning disability, 2. that Kristin told her to forward my questions and 3. that it was her obligation to answer student emails or to meet with students. In other words she was trying to portray the appearance that she was not treating me in a differential manner as compared to the class. All her points turned out to be false. I found out that there was significant email correspondence between them about the learning disability, and that Holly admitted she would answer questions for other students in the class but "given the recent history and personality we are dealing with," she felt it was best to forward my questions to Kristin "to be correctly dealt with." I was disappointed she had prematurely

---

47 http://www.ohrc.on.ca/en/policy-and-guidelines-disability-and-duty-accommodate/3-prima-facie-discrimination-because-disability

formulated negative ideas about my personality given that: I had gotten a B in her class the previous semester, I had never met with her for an appointment, and I had minimal interaction with her in labs (either in her course or in Kristin's). Holly had no first-hand experience of me to form any conclusions. Regardless, she had written on her witness statement that when I was in her class, she was "concerned" that I was using rote memorization as a learning strategy for the material. If she had hardly ever spoken to me, there is no way she could know what learning strategy I was using.

Holly had been lucky in a legal sense that I didn't have this evidence in the beginning, for I would have singled her out as an individual defendant just like Kristin. But in a personal sense, she had two daughters of her own, and I wonder how she would feel if one of their teachers treated them this way—and then proceeded to lie about it when confronted.

Just like Holly's statement, there were other important inconsistencies concerning various key players that were very helpful to me. Regardless of the way in which the judge appeared to be leaning, there were only so many times when the facts can be overlooked or denied...

God is good! Regardless of how it looks at one moment, everything could turn around —but you have to keep the faith. Having knowledge of the planetary and numerical influences helped me to understand why all of this was happening at this time. I received insight into the cosmic dance symbolizing the interplay of surrender and action, uniquely applicable to my situation.

With regards to my natal promise, there are multiple factors in my chart for my decision to pursue the case: there is the Uranian side of my number 4 soul urge and first challenge number 4 which is my heart for social activism and equality; my life path and first cycle number 6's desire for fairness and justice; my exact Pluto opposition to the MC, compelling me to publicly challenge existing power and hierarchy structures; my birthday on June 11th and my four out of bounds planets, both of which cause me to push society's boundaries; in the Western chart, my North Node in Aries (soul growth through assertion of one's rights) in the 9th house of higher education; my chart ruler Sun, as well as Mars conjunct Mercury in the 11th house, and four planets in the 5th house aspecting the 11th house giving the 11th house of social justice a lot of emphasis; and in the Vedic chart, there is the dominance of planets (including my Moon and ascendant) in rakshasa nakshatras, making me a free-thinker who is not afraid to confront authority in an effort to bring about change. In all domains, when I see people being treated unfairly and not given the same opportunities, I feel compelled to take action.

In my Vedic chart, Jupiter conjunct Rahu in the 9th house is a promise of extreme, fateful experiences with respect to a 9th house matter—in my case of higher education. The 9th house also governs legal matters and justice. As Jupiter also rules my 6th house of enemies, and is found in the 9th house, there could be challenging circumstances in higher education. Fortunately, my Jupiter is vargottama in Pisces, and receives 18/20 points on the vimsopaka bala calculation, indicating it is very auspiciously placed. This means that regardless of who acts against me, they would not be able to defeat me in the long-term-- because Jupiter is strongly placed in so many of my divisional charts. In the Western chart, Jupiter is placed in my 9th house in Aries. Even though Mars, the ruler of my 9th house is fallen in Cancer, it participates in a mutual exchange with Jupiter in Aries, greatly strengthening both planets, and in the final analysis, allowing me to have a good deal of blessings.

In terms of transits, Pluto making a close opposition to my Mercury-Mars was highlighting my voice in challenging traditional power structures. The school was a formidable opponent; they fought hard, with their considerable resources, to prevent me from succeeding at every step of the way. My essence number at that time was 5, the number corresponding to Mercury. This speaks to a period where my ability to persuasively communicate my position, and adapt to quickly changing circumstances would be of critical importance. In the Western chart, with Pluto transiting through my 5th house, casting its opposition to Mercury-Mars in the 11th house, it was clear that the battle dealt with issues of human rights and social justice. At the same time, transiting Uranus in both the Vedic and Western charts was going through my 9th house triggering the natal promise of revolutionary events in higher education. Uranus brings surprises-- one minute things look one way, but the next they are completely different. The heavens were smiling at me on the day I was finished with the case: I was in a Venus-Jupiter dasha, Jupiter was transiting through my first house (in the Vedic system), and transiting Neptune made an exact conjunction to my 8th house cusp (in the Western system). In addition, I was in personal year 7, which corresponds to Neptune. Being in a personal day 9 and a personal month 1 indicated that a long battle in my life was finally over, and I was free to make a fresh new start (number 9 represents endings and 1 is new beginnings).

At the resolution, when all was said and done, things were okay. The Canadian legal system is far from perfect, but something tells me that the teaching staff won't be doing something like this to another student anytime soon, and the school administration will learn some valuable lessons about critical thinking and procedural fairness! Out of the very small number of withdrawals over the years, this was the second time within six years that this particular department faced a legal complaint with regards to visible minority, disability and being forced to withdraw. The more people who have the courage to take action, the more that decision-makers will be forced to change their policies and behaviour.

YOUR BREAKTHROUGHS ARE DIVINELY ORCHESTRATED

A repeating theme I want to emphasize is that while *we can't control stereotypical thought processes, and the actions of other people-- we can control our responses.* When people treat us unfairly, they are shaping their own karma and destiny. They can appear to get away with things in this lifetime, but ignoring universal laws has its consequences. People who are powerful and wealthy in one lifetime can be poor and powerless in another. The love-based definition of karma teaches that it is a learning opportunity for soul growth: the most memorable way to understand the pain you inflicted onto someone is to experience it yourself. The deepest feelings of compassion often arise out of first-hand experiences.

Of course even with this knowledge of karmic justice, it is still frustrating on a day-to-day level, because they may have the power to deny us something we worked hard for, such as an education, a degree, a job, a promotion, housing, citizenship, and so forth. *The most important thing is to realize that no person can stop us from achieving our destiny.* The wrong doors need to be shut before the right doors can be opened because there is a divinely orchestrated time for everything. A failure in one pursuit can be the catalyst you need to move into another direction in which you have unsurpassed success.

It is natural for us to have a life plan, we all have goals we are working towards, and dates for which we want to see them accomplished. When things don't go to plan, we may feel frustrated, anxious, or angry, in considering how much time, effort and money we spent working on it and the sacrifices made. Regardless of how hard we may try to do everything right, the cycles of life simply do not work on our desired timetable, nor should they for our most optimal growth. *Often, challenging detours along the way are actually fated events that are needed to prepare us for our future purpose.* It could be to help people who are currently struggling with the same issues that we struggled with in the past but were able to overcome. Our life story could be the inspiration that someone we don't even know needs to make an important turning point in their lives. Or perhaps these detours caused a necessary shift in our perspective, which resulted in a more enlightened awareness of our true purpose in life. We may have decided we wanted to take a certain direction, but one important person or event changes our lives and priorities forever...

CELEBRITY CASE STUDY: ECKHART TOLLE

One inspiring example of a divine breakthrough is Eckhart Tolle, born on Feb 16th 1948.[48] In interviews, Eckhart describes his childhood as unhappy and isolated; he felt as if he never fit in with the others, and that the 'pain body' of Germany was too heavy. Worth noting that in his Western astrological chart, he had three planets in detriment—Sun in Aquarius, Venus in Aries, and Mercury in Pisces. This could have exacerbated his feelings of pain and dissatisfaction when he was younger. To help him get through this challenging period, he read mystical books in his quest for knowledge. With his birthday 7, and his birth name Ulrich Leonard Tölle giving a personality number 7, this inclined towards sensitivity, solitude, and the seeking of spiritual knowledge. Blessed with a sharp intellect, he studied at the University of London, and then went to Cambridge University to do graduate work.

During his studies, he reported feeling long periods of suicidal depression. One night in 1977, around the time of his first Saturn return at age 29, the painful intensity of emotion culminated in his darkest night of the soul, followed by a life changing epiphany. This was an inner transformation that permanently changed his outlook from depressed to peaceful. People thought he was crazy because for the following two years, he wandered about in his peaceful state.

His Mercury-Mars opposition helped him achieve clarity and simplicity in his writing. *The Power of Now*, had a small first run and he personally distributed his first book in bookstores. Eventually, as his profound but simple teachings spread, the book became a #1 New York Times Best seller and was translated into over 30 languages worldwide. Eckhart's third book, *A New*

---

48 http://www.astrotheme.com/astrology/Eckhart_Tolle. His chart is not shown here because his birth time is not accurate. However, you may view the positions of the planets

Earth, also reached the #1 position on the NYT Best Seller list. In partnering with Oprah Winfrey, (who made it her book club selection in 2008), he was able to do webinars to reach millions of viewers worldwide. As of 2015, Eckhart is ranked as the third most spiritual person in the world by *Watkins Magazine.*[49]

Eckhart's life path is 4 and after he changed his name to Eckhart Tolle, his expression became 4 as well. Combined with his Sun in Aquarius, we see a revolutionary thinker who introduced us to an innovative way of looking at the importance of staying in the present moment. He has helped uplift consciousness levels on a broad scale through his meditations and exercises designed to develop present moment awareness. Characteristic of the hidden gift of multiple planets in detriment; his pain cut so deep that it plunged him into the dark depths of the soul, it was from here that he was reborn into his now peaceful state. As an example, although Mercury in Pisces is technically considered weak due to its lack of objectivity and nonlinear thinking process, it gives the mind an intuitive, creative, spiritual, and compassionate bent. Other dimensions of knowledge become available, particularly through intense meditation and spiritual practice.

The exalted Moon in Taurus helps him to sustain stability and calmness in emotion, and Jupiter in its own sign Sagittarius aids in his philosophical teaching ability. Mars making an exact semisquare to Neptune gives a spiritual tone to his ambition and goal-orientation. The name Eckhart Tolle gives a personality number 5, which enhances his ability to communicate his message to large audiences.

CELEBRITY CASE STUDY: ELLEN DEGENERES

Ellen DeGeneres is another brave lady who had the courage to publicly come out as a lesbian, back in 1997, when no other celebrities were doing so. Prior to 1997, Ellen (born January 26th 1958 in Metairie, Louisiana) had a booming career as

---

49 http://www.watkinsmagazine.com/1-20-on-the-spiritual-100-list-in-2015

a comedienne. She had a popular sitcom, *Ellen*. Despite her success, she felt uncomfortable because she could no longer hide her authentic self; she had to speak her truth. Therefore, on one episode, her character came out to the therapist, and she announced to her love interest that she was gay. Ellen herself also came out in a few interviews. This resulted in adverse outcomes such as ABC cancelling her sitcom, and backlash from the Christian community, who viewed it as a sin. She learned what it was like to not be loved and to be the butt of jokes on television and in magazines. Regardless, in viewing the double standards, discrimination, and statistics for gay teen suicides, she felt she had to stand up for what she believed was right. She is using her platform to convey the truth that it is okay to be who you are.

Even though she lost her career for three years, her income, and everything she had worked for, she realized she was strong and talented enough to start over, and make a comeback. She knew that lousy things had to happen for her to appreciate the good things, and sometimes the bad things are the biggest teachers.[50]

The Ellen DeGeneres Show has been running for 12 years, and gaining more awards as the years go by. Ellen has been happily married to her wife Portia De Rossi since 2008. She knows in her heart that she doesn't have to have everyone like or accept her, in order for her to feel fulfilled. Without a doubt, she changed countless people's lives. Because of her, they have the courage to be comfortable in their own skin, and let the world know who they really are.

Looking at Ellen's astronumerology chart,[51] it is clear that she is a humanitarian, social justice activist, and trailblazer. She has a Sun-Venus conjunction in socially conscious Aquarius, and the Sun participates in a mutual exchange with Uranus in Leo.

---

50 Ellen's life story is conveyed here as she told it in her own words on her television episode of Oprah's Master Class (first aired October 2015)
51 http://www.astro.com/astro-databank/Degeneres,_Ellen. Her chart is not shown here because her birth time is not accurate. However, you may view the positions of the planets

The Sun and Uranus are now able to express themselves most naturally—the Sun gives her the confidence to be in the limelight and to have a large, admiring audience; and Uranus gives her the interest in speaking up for a group who is discriminated against in society.

The Venus-Uranus opposition speaks to her unconventional (Uranus) approach to love (Venus). The opposition is also reflective of her efforts to create social equality (Uranus) in romantic relationships (Venus).

Her Moon in Aries makes her an independent leader, one who creates her own opportunities in life. She is assertive about issues that are important to her and she is not afraid to speak her mind.

The birth name Ellen Lee DeGeneres gives an expression 8, personality 4, and soul urge 4. Born on January 26th 1958, her birthday is 8 and life path is 5. Because there are so many E's and N's in her name, number 5 is also her intensity number. With Saturn having total influence over 8, and partial influence over 4, Ellen has an abundance of discipline, perseverance, and tenacity to succeed. Everything was taken from her, but she knew she had to get back up and keep trying to reach new goals. Saturn makes you work very hard, and puts a lot of obstacles in your path, but they are meant to make you stronger and wiser.

We can also see the Uranian side to the 4, which complements her Sun-Venus conjunction in Aquarius and makes her an inspiring leader for social change. With number 4 having a humanitarian side, she has been involved with several charitable projects such as Declare Yourself, the Humane Society, Music Rising, Red Cross, The Trevor Project, the It Gets Better Project, and the ONE Campaign. She also regularly surprises deserving guests on her show with generous gifts.

Her life path and intensity number 5 gives her the gift of comedic timing, she has the instinctive understanding of how to communicate her jokes to get the most laughs. Having the

5 influence also gives her the ability to create interesting and humorous interviews with guests on her show, in addition to giving her an articulate voice to raise awareness for the LGBT community.

THE HIDDEN GIFTS OF CRISIS

There are two choices in responding to periods of crisis in our lives, and ultimately we have control over which choice we make. One choice is to feel defeated, lose hope, and quit trying. The other choice is to keep the faith. God may be trying to give us opportunities, but if we are fixated on what we don't have, rather than being grateful for what we do have, we don't have the chance to take advantage of them. By focusing on the blessings in our lives in an overall sense, a sense of gratitude replaces the sense of disappointment over the perceived lack of success in just one or two areas of life.

When we respond with an attitude of faith in periods of crisis, the amazing thing is that the very people who treated us badly become footstools for us to achieve our personal bests. I know that for me, it was those people who tried their hardest to make me fail that really motivated me to succeed. I heard the saying, "your enemies are your greatest teachers" but only understood it in theory before. I really am thankful because without these "teachers" I wouldn't have had the chance to discover just how much strength, determination, and resilience I had within me. If everyone always likes you, treats you well, and gives you what you want, how can you ever know the full extent of your inner resources? Our enemies can be a catalyst for considerable personal growth. God takes what was meant for our harm and uses it for our good.

The astronumerology chart reveals our strengths, talents, and purpose. No matter who tells you that you are not good enough based on stereotypes and their own limited thinking, you know in your heart that is not true. In addition to your spiritual resources, you have another powerful tool for healing.

This is an unbeatable combination that will position you as well able to stand firm against false judgements, regardless of the prestige or "qualifications" of the person making these claims. Your full potential can only be released when you have the courage to believe in yourself. While other people are telling you all the reasons you won't succeed, you'll be too busy laying the groundwork for your personal breakthrough. After all, success is the sweetest revenge!

Chapter 6

Overview of the Planets, Signs, and Corresponding Numbers

Astronumerology is a complex field which involves the blending of 12 astrological signs with nine number archetypes, this comes out to 108 different combinations. The number 108 is of great significance religiously, spiritually, and in astronomy:

- The distance between the Earth and Sun is 108 times the diameter of the Sun. The diameter of the Sun is 108 times the diameter of the Earth. The distance between the Earth and Moon is 108 times the diameter of the Moon.
- The universe is made up of 108 elements according to ancient texts.
- There are 54 letters in the Sanskrit alphabet. Each has masculine and feminine, Shiva and Shakti, 54 x 2 = 108.
- There are 108 beads on a mala used for reciting mantras.
- The Vedanta recognizes 108 authentic doctrines
- 108 sacred books constitute the holy writings for Tibetans. In Tibetan Buddhism, it is believed that there are 108 delusions of the mind.

- In Kriya Yoga, the maximum number of repetitions allowed to be practiced in one sitting is 108.[52] [53]

The fact that there are 108 personality combinations is no coincidence. It is a sacred synchronicity revealing the magnificence of the awe-inspiring design of the Creator of the Universe. Our differences are wonderfully made to complement each other, and cause the profoundly rooted interdependence that allows us to engage in meaningful relationships, and in the process learn the karmic lessons we came to the school of life to learn.

The deeper reason for the existence of the 108 different personality temperaments is that each combination adds their own beauty and value to the world that no other will ever be able to replicate. Similar to the butterfly effect, the disappearance of even one combination would cause a large shift in the state of affairs in the world. *Without even one of these combinations represented, the world ceases to function as we now know it.* There is only one out of 108 combinations that is uniquely made to live out a certain destiny in life, and without this combination, humanity would be unable to make all the important breakthroughs that are necessary at the designated times. We need the unique personality, skills, and experience of each combination to constantly move forward.

The 108 combinations described in chapters 7-18 are primarily intended for your Sun Sign/birth date combination. At the same time, you can gain additional insights about personality by reading your Sun sign and life path combination, or Moon sign and birth date combination.

You may calculate your life path number by adding the month, day, and year of birth. The month is calculated as January=1, February =2, March=3 and so forth until December =12. You

---

break down the double digit number to a single digit at the end (except if it is a master number 11 or 22 and then it stays as is). For example if someone was born October 30th 1986, adding 10 (October) + 30 +1+9+8+6= 64=1. Therefore this person could also read Scorpio number 1.

You may find your Moon sign by entering your birth details at http://www.astro.com/cgi/genchart.cgi. The Moon changes signs every two and a half days; if you don't know your birth time, and you were born on a day when the Moon was changing signs, you will have to read both signs to see which one is a better fit with your emotional nature.

Be careful when reading your birthday combination if you were born on a cusp, that is at the beginning or end of a Sun sign. Typically, cusp dates fall from the 19th-23rd of a month. The Sun transitions into different signs at different times on each day. Therefore, people born on the same cusp day are not necessarily the same sign. For example, one person born on May 21st 1954 in the morning may be a Taurus, but someone born that same day in the evening would be a Gemini. This is because May 21st was the transitioning day from Taurus to Gemini in 1954.

People born on the same day in different years aren't necessarily the same sign. For example, some years the Sun transitions into Cancer on June 21st, but other years it remains in Gemini for the whole day on June 21st. For instance, on June 21st 1943, the Sun was in Gemini the entire day and only transitioned into Cancer on June 22nd. In contrast, on June 21st 1980, the Sun moved into Cancer. Keep in mind that you are either one Sun sign or the other, and not a mixture of two Sun signs. To confirm which Sun sign you are, you will need to enter your birth details into an astrological natal chart calculation software such as that found at http://www.astro.com/cgi/genchart.cgi.

Once you find out what sign you are, read your birthday number for that sign. For example, if you were born August 22nd, you may actually be a Virgo. In this book, August 22nd is listed as Leo, so you would read September 22nd for a more accurate description of your personality. You will always be reading your birth date number, but if you were born on a cusp date you may need to read the description of an astrological sign that is adjacent to yours.

The descriptions for the 108 combinations are based on my theoretical understanding of the unique blend between a sign and birth date, research on the lives of celebrities, and detailed observations of people I have interacted with over the years. Because people born under the same combination have certain life themes, and patterns of behaviour in common, my observations share similarities with previous literature.[54] It is a good sign that the previous literature displays consistency, meaning that different authors have written about the same personality traits for people born under the same combination. It would be very confusing, and inaccurate, if different books had a completely unique assessment on the same combination. At the same time, each author adds his or her frame of reference for a particular trait or tendency, and focuses on certain facets of personality over others.

My personal style is to inspire people to make the most out of their innate strengths and talents, thus I write mostly on the positive features of their nature, while keeping weaknesses to a minimum. Words can be interpreted very differently depending on the way in which they are said, and the person who is interpreting them. As a result, delivering sensitive personal information through the written form can cause a lack of clarity, and potential misunderstanding. Where drawbacks are mentioned, I offer constructive suggestions for improvement because I feel there is no point knowing about a weakness with no guidance as to how to overcome it.

54 The texts I used in comparison for the 108 combinations include *The Secret Language of Birthdays*, *The Element Encyclopedia of Birthdays*, *Your Stars are Numbered*, and Cheiro's *Astronumerology & Your Star*

The Sun and Number 1

The Sun is the brightest planet and has all the planets revolving around it, naturally it takes center stage. Making a complete trip around the zodiac's signs in one year, the Sun changes signs once per month. The Sun represents our life force, and the essence of who we are; our individuality, ego, and sense of self. This part of ourselves, which varies in its visibility to other people, is always a strong part of us. These are basic drives that form our motivation and natural way of being. Our vitality and where we focus our overall energy is governed by the Sun sign.

The Sun rules Leo, and is exalted in Aries, meaning that its nature is best exemplified in these signs. Leo is a sign that thrives on being the center of attention; they need to feel respected and admired. They are warm, creative, enthusiastic, and self-expressive, generally having high self-confidence and vitality. Aries is a sign that is me-first; their own priorities generally take priority over others. At the same time, they are strong leaders, self-confident, and willing to take risks. They have a strong sense of self, are independent, and competitive.

In numerology, the Sun is associated with the number one. Number one people are bold, courageous, and competitive. They are leaders, pioneers, and inventors. These are people who will venture into the unknown and come out with a visionary new idea. They are powerful and like to be top dog. They will state their needs, wants, and goals clearly; no beating around the bush for them. However, they can be short on diplomacy, and a challenge is to learn the art of compromise where needed.

Celebrity Case Study: Yves Saint Laurent

Yves Saint Laurent (born August 1st) comes under the influence of Sun/Leo/1 and is a perfect embodiment of using its abundant creativity and originality. He became a leader in his field, and influenced many designers after him. Saint Laurent had a very strong need to express himself artistically, and to have others admire his work. This world famous fashion designer's brand also includes world class perfumes, skincare, and makeup.

He started out by studying with his mentor, Christian Dior. In his own words, "Dior fascinated me, I couldn't speak in front of him. He taught me the basis of my art. Whatever was to happen next, I never forgot the years I spent at his side." In 1957, the House of Dior promoted him to Chief Designer. However, when he came back to Paris after a leave of absence, he found that he had lost his job. Being courageous from a young age; he sued the House of Dior for wrongful termination, and won a significant amount of money.[55] Although Christian Dior had died at this time, the company was a giant in the industry. It takes a person with a lot of guts to take that on.

After the incident with the House of Dior, Saint Laurent started his own fashion business, and introduced signature items like the reefer jacket (1962), and le smoking, the smoking tuxedo pantsuit (1966), and jump suit (1968).

He was the first designer to take men's clothing, and turn them into designs that looked good on women. This included pea coats, blazers, leather jackets, safari jackets, flying suits, the tuxedo, and the trouser suit.

Saint Laurent was the first designer who included women from a variety of ethnic backgrounds in his fashion shows. By doing this, he set a trend for diversity on the runway.

In the 1980s, he became the first designer to have a retrospective on his work at the Metropolitan Museum in New York City. There is a deep need to be honored with the Sun/Leo/1 influence, and Yves Saint Laurent was presented with many prestigious honours and awards throughout his lifetime.

---

55 http://www.biography.com/people/yves-saint-laurent-9469669

THE MOON AND NUMBER 2

The Moon shines bright in the sky at night, illuminating the darkness. Our emotions, subconscious reactions, instincts, moods, what we need to feel comfortable, our cravings, and our habits, are represented by the Moon. We will feel unhappy if we don't fulfill the needs of the Moon. For example if your Moon is in Gemini, you need to communicate with people, and be intellectually stimulated. If you don't have a chance to do this for long periods, you may feel frustrated. On the other hand, when you do things that fulfill the needs of the sign your Moon is in, you feel renewed energy. For instance, if you have the Moon in a water sign (Cancer, Scorpio and Pisces), being near large bodies of water is very soothing.

The Moon rules Cancer and is exalted in Taurus. Cancer is fundamentally an emotional sign, and these people wear their heart on their sleeve. Cancerian thought processes are more influenced by intuition than logical methods. They cherish their home and family, the two most important things in the world to them, and enjoy nurturing people and pets. Cancerians are nostalgic and sentimental, loving to take photos, and hating to throw anything away. Taureans are homebodies, and their first priority is family. They can be very hospitable, loving to host people at their house, and feed them! They are warm, nurturing and affectionate. Taureans like to do tangible things to show their love, such as buying a pretty little gift, or a tasty treat for someone.

The Moon vibrates with number 2 in numerology. Number 2 people are empathetic and excellent listeners; they care very much about developing close, meaningful one-on-one relationships. Harmony and teamwork are valued more than independence and competition. Number 2 people have a skill for matching people with tasks that best suit their personality, so that the finished product represents everyone's best work. Being too accommodating to other people's needs, at the expense of their own needs, is something they must guard against.

JUPITER AND NUMBER 3

Jupiter is the hugest planet, containing more mass than the other planets combined. This appearance is very fitting because Jupiter is the planet of expansion. Jupiter represents luck, blessings, good fortune, generosity, happiness, prosperity, optimism, cheer, philosophy, foreign places and cultures, broadening consciousness levels, wisdom, higher education, and religion.

Jupiter is the planet of rewards, many of them unearned. During key Jupiter transits, people come into our lives and promote us, influential people take interest in us, we may have an opportunity to visit a foreign place of interest, material prosperity comes more easily, and we may obtain new knowledge that allows for a breakthrough into a higher consciousness level.

Jupiter rules Sagittarius, so its traits are best expressed through that sign. Sagittarians are optimistic and cheerful. They need their freedom, both mentally and physically, and love adventures. Expanding their consciousness by learning new ways of doing things is what they enjoy doing. Philosophical by nature, they spend time contemplating the deeper questions of life. There is the constant seeking for experiences to deepen their wisdom.

Jupiter vibrates with number 3 in numerology. Number 3 people love to laugh, and have a good time. Socializing and attending parties is a joy for them. They believe in the goodness of people, choosing to give the benefit of the doubt. Articulate, they express their message clearly both orally and in the written form. Their philosophical, religious or spiritual bent may compel them to go in search of wisdom, to further themselves along the path. At the same time, they have to work on their tendency to brush aside other people's viewpoints, if not in agreement with their own.

SATURN, URANUS AND NUMBER 4

Saturn has been called the most beautiful planet because of its seven rings. The seven rings can also be descriptive of the rings or hurdles that Saturn makes you jump through in life! Indeed Saturn is a bringer of obstacles, delays, and difficult circumstances. On the positive side, Saturn's experiences can be character-building. If the situations are handled correctly, they can be used to develop patience, determination, and endurance. Make no mistake, the experience will not be experienced as easy at the time, but Saturn doesn't give us these situations for no reason. *The tough experiences always contain valuable lessons, if we are receptive.* Because Saturn is persistent, if we don't learn the lesson the first time, similar situations will be presented until we get it.

Saturn symbolizes restriction, austerity, tradition, hierarchy, structure, social status, hard work, achievements, and reputation. There are rules and regulations, and things have to be done a certain way. Saturn urges you to build a firm foundation, instead of relying on shortcuts. Therefore, Saturn transits are important for the bedrock of long-lasting success.

Saturn rules Capricorn and is exalted in Libra. Capricorn is the disciplinarian of the zodiac; they are ambitious and like to work hard for what they have. They tend to be reserved and formal in their approach. Status and respect is important to them, and they enjoy being in authoritative positions. Libra, symbolized by the scales, likes balance in all areas of life, and seeks justice for wrongdoings. Saturn does not let people get away with their bad behaviour, what you sow, you shall reap. Libra usually seeks to be fair, balanced, and just in their decisions, and takes care to look at both sides equally.

Saturn vibrates with numbers 4 and 8 and each number emphasizes a different facet of Saturn. Number 4 people may identify more with either Saturn or Uranus, but most of the time are a mixture of both. Saturn's influence on number 4 is methodical, reliable, and disciplined. These are the pillars of society: the hard workers that ensure all of the fundamentals are laid down so that society operates efficiently. Structure, regulations and a hierarchy are preferred. Traditional, they will usually continue with the way things have always been. If it isn't broken, why fix it? Number 4 is excellent at following through on plans, and they are unlikely to abandon a project half way through. However, these people sometimes take on too much responsibility. They need to learn how to balance their time, so that they have enough time to relax and take care of themselves.

Uranus was the first planet to be discovered after ancient times, and the first to be discovered using the telescope. It has a very eccentric tilt on its axis, over 90 degrees from the perpendicular. Again we find a connection between its physical and psychological characteristics! Uranus is the planet of eccentricity, creativity, unconventional interests, revolution, upheaval, shocks, surprises, new technology, rebellion, and shake-ups. People with a prominent Uranus are independent and want to stand out from the crowd. This can manifest physically, through distinct appearance or mannerisms, or psychologically-- with offbeat interests.

Uranian people want to introduce new trends. Nothing ever stays the same with Uranus; when it makes an important transit, our lives are changed suddenly and dramatically. We feel that out of the blue, the rug was pulled out from under us. A positive Uranus transit could bring a sudden windfall, sharp rise in status, or streak of good luck. In any case, Uranus urges us to clear out what was not working and make room for new constructive ways of living. Uranus represents us as a collective and usually when there are big social changes on a world scale, it is making important transits.

URANUS AND THE NUMBER 22

Uranus also vibrates to master number 22. In 22, we find visionaries and trailblazers. Because they have the practicality and work ethic of the 4, they are able to construct a feasible plan of action for making their vision become a reality. Representative of the spirit of invention and exploration, they see what isn't working and think up creative new ways to fill those voids. They like to venture into unknown territory because they feel there are always new exciting discoveries to be made. Very passionate about bringing to the forefront inequalities in society, and the needs of underprivileged or disadvantaged groups, they are crusaders for societal change.

CELEBRITY CASE STUDY: ROSA PARKS

Rosa Parks (born February 4th) is an excellent example of living up to the full potential of an Aquarius number 4. She was a prominent civil rights activist who played a crucial role in transforming race relations in America. On December 1st, 1955 in Montgomery, Alabama, on the ride home from work, she sat in the section in the bus designated for Blacks. The bus was full that day, and some White passengers were standing. As a result the bus driver asked four people, including her, to give up their seat. Three passengers gave up their seats, but Rosa did not, responding, "I don't think I should have to stand up."[56] This simple act of refusing to give up her seat was a catalyst for change. She later commented that she wasn't physically tired, but was tired of giving in.[57] She had to endure a legal trial for asserting her rights.

As a child in Pine Level, Alabama, she remembered having to walk to school, whereas White children could choose to take the bus. She commented "I'd see the bus pass every day, but to me, that was a way of life; we had no choice but to accept what was the custom. The bus was among the first ways I realized there

---

56 http://www.biographyonline.net/humanitarian/rosa-parks.html
57 http://www.history.com/topics/black-history/rosa-parks

was a Black world and a White world."[58] This experience was a prime motivator in causing her to take a stand as an adult.

As a result of Rosa being arrested, the Montgomery Bus Boycott was organized, and resulted in thousands of Black people walking or carpooling, starting with the day of Rosa's trial (December 5th, 1955). Rosa stayed strong even while losing her job, and experiencing harassment. There was an attempt to fight back by arresting Black citizens for boycotting, cancelling insurance for Black taxi's, burning Black churches, and bombing Martin Luther King Jr.'s and E.D. Nixon's homes, but the Boycott stood strong. A Black legal team took the issue of segregation on buses to court. The racial segregation laws were declared unconstitutional in June 1956. The city of Montgomery appealed the decision, but the U.S Supreme court upheld the previous decision. The city was forced to end segregation on the buses and the boycott officially ended on December 20th, 1956.[59]

Number 4 is influenced by both Saturn and Uranus and we can see that mixture in Rosa. In high school, she withdrew to fulfill her duty (Saturn) of taking care of her sick grandmother and mother. Four years later, characteristic of Saturn's desire for accomplishment, she completed her high school degree. The strong desire for justice is credited to both Saturn and Uranus. Recall that Saturn is exalted in Libra, a sign symbolized by the scales and concerned with restoring balance, equality, and justice.

Since Rosa was born during the month of Aquarius, Uranus's influence became very strong. Aquarius and the number 4 are influenced by Uranus, which is revolutionary in seeing potentials that other people do not at that time. While the other three passengers could not envision any other society in that they were not second class citizens, Rosa was tired of living within this structure of oppression. Instead of going along with the established protocol, she wanted to encourage people to take a stand for what they believed was right. Her refusal to go along

---

58 http://www.awb.com/dailydose/?p=699
59 http://www.biography.com/people/rosa-parks-9433715

with the crowd, and instead run that extra mile to distinguish herself, is characteristic of the originality and inventiveness of Uranus/Aquarius/4. She had a vision for herself and generations to come of a better society in which all people were treated equally regardless of their skin color. This combination is about shaking up the status quo to make room for progressive ideas that enhance the quality of life for everyone.

In 1999, Rosa was awarded the Congressional Gold Medal. She lived a long life, and when she died, she became the first woman in American history to lie in state at the U.S. Capitol. Although people under this combination are sometimes rewarded during their lifetime, it is often after death where their efforts have the most long-lasting impact. As a result of her bravery, countless African Americans have had opportunities and freedoms that would not have been possible without her bold act of defiance and fierce spirit.

MERCURY AND THE NUMBER 5

Mercury is the fastest planet in the solar system, having an orbit of 88 days. The Romans named the planet Mercury after the messenger of the gods because it is the planet of communications. The sign Mercury was in when you were born governs your thought processes (style, function, and speed), and the way you communicate your messages to the world.

Mercury is easily influenced by other planets that it aspects; the other planet will color the way you think and communicate. For example, Mercury in conjunction with Mars produces people who are straightforward in expressing themselves. They say what they mean and mean what they say. Mercury in conjunction with Uranus produces people whose thinking is offbeat and eccentric. These are visionaries, seeing ideas and products that are far ahead of the times. Saying things for shock value may be something they enjoy because they relish seeing how people will react to controversial statements.

Mercury rules Gemini and Virgo and is also exalted in Virgo. Each of these signs enable Mercury to function to its best ability. Both Gemini and Virgo produce objective, logical thinkers, able to separate fact from feeling. In Gemini, Mercury produces a quick-witted thinker who can be articulate and engaging. You will often see Gemini people using hand gestures when speaking; this is because Gemini rules the hands. Communication is their life blood: they love talking about a wide variety of subjects, although they may not study each in particular depth.

In Virgo, Mercury produces someone who has an excellent analytical mind, often excelling in technical subjects. They are excellent at details and anything requiring precision. Virgo is not as expressive as Gemini and communicates in a quieter, less animated way. Virgoans do not exaggerate; instead, they stick to the facts and figures. They are also more concrete and earthy in their speech topics, whereas Gemini is an air sign who enjoys more abstract discussions.

Mercury vibrates with the number 5 in numerology. Number 5 people are excellent communicators, and can be very persuasive when they want to be. Their charm and sense of humour is apparent to those around them. Blessed with an ability to engage their audience, they like to express themselves both orally and in writing. They also love learning about foreign cultures. Flexibility, adaptability, and change characterize their approach to life, and they need intellectual stimulation to keep things exciting. They must take caution with regards to starting multiple projects and not finishing them.

VENUS AND THE NUMBER 6

Venus was named after the Roman goddess of love and beauty. It is the brightest planet and the only celestial body besides the Sun and Moon that people can see during the day and night; thus, it also picked up the names Morning Star and Evening Star. Venus represents beauty, aesthetic appreciation, charm, grace, and sophistication. People with a prominent Venus love to be pampered with luxuries and creature comforts. Venus governs pleasurable social functions, entertainment, leisure, parties, artistic performances, and musical performances.

Venus also is the planet of love and governs romance, intimate relationships, and marriage. Venus represents who we are attracted to and our general social nature. The aspects Venus makes influence what types of partners we tend to attract and how we behave in relationships. For example, Venus in conjunction with Mars makes a person extremely passionate, and also direct in chasing someone they are interested in. They are also likely to believe that love involves some degree of suffering. Venus in aspect to Neptune produces the highest amount of idealism in romance, at times resembling a fairy tale. These people are empathetic and capable of unconditional love but they are also most likely to get disappointed when their reality does not match up to expectations.

Venus rules Taurus and Libra. Venus in Taurus is the best expression of appreciation for beauty and creature comforts. They take great pride in their very well-decorated home. Taurus is sensual and delights in the pleasures of the five senses, relishing in fine materials and gourmet meals. Taurus rules the throat, and these people often have pleasant voices and/ or singing talent.

Venus in Libra focuses more on Venus as the planet of love in relationships. Librans are partnership-oriented. They function well as part of a team, and can be uncomfortable spending too much time alone. Very sociable, they love to attend parties and other functions. Romantics at heart, they enjoy going out on dates, and keeping the freshness of love alive even after many years of marriage. They also have a fine appreciation of beauty, and are usually well-dressed.

Venus vibrates to the number 6, and number 6 people are very interested in family. They like to have a beautiful home filled with many luxurious items, and they enjoy indulging the senses.

Excellent hosts, they are skilled at making people feel right at home. Number 6 people are compassionate and seek to express their love in tangible ways; often they are attracted to professions involving helping, or taking care of people. The influence of Venus also enables them to be successful small business owners, especially if the business centers on a Venusian theme, such as music, art, love, romance, jewellery, clothing, entertainment, perfume, chocolates and sweets.

NEPTUNE AND THE NUMBER 7

In the 17th century, Galileo originally described the planet Neptune as a star. It wasn't until 1846 that Neptune was discovered as a planet. This is very fitting of nebulous Neptune, as its nature is very vague, and it governs intangible concepts. Neptune represents dreams, fantasies, subtle realms, otherworldliness, mystery, spirituality, enlightenment, compassion, artistic expression, metaphysics, meditation, mysticism and merging with God. On the other hand, Neptune also represents substance abuse, addiction, lethargy, depression, alcoholism, escapism, forgery, the inability to handle real world responsibilities, deception, scandal, and disillusionment.

Neptune rules Pisces. Pisces is the most otherworldly sign, and Pisceans may have a soft, dreamy, gentle look to them. Very compassionate, Pisces people empathize with people down on their luck, and always try to help, even if they don't really have enough time or resources. They love to daydream and have a rich imagination. Often talented artistically, they may have an attraction to sculpture, painting, dancing, or other work created with the hands. Their intuition is very strong; in fact, many psychics have a dominant Pisces/Neptune/12th house focus. Pisceans have a strong urge to merge with the divine, and often utilizes methods such as meditation, and other devotional practices to help them do so.

Neptune vibrates with the number 7, the most metaphysical number. Number 7 people have a marked need for solitude and silence, to contemplate truths, and the bigger questions and mysteries in life. They love to study interesting subjects and write about them. Spending time in nature allows them to reconnect with the splendour, and to relax and go deeper within. Although not people for idle chatter, they can be excellent conversationalists on topics that really mean something to them.

NEPTUNE AND THE NUMBER 11

Neptune also vibrates with master number 11. People born on the 11th are idealistic, compassionate, and intuitive. They are spiritual beings, who enjoy helping others to reconnect with the divine. Others may find them inspirational and a catalyst for their personal growth. From a young age, they have interests that are atypical, and most likely advanced for their age; people usually sense that they are old souls. They are highly intelligent, and may have a special interest in esoteric and occult subjects.

SATURN AND THE NUMBER 8

Saturn vibrates to the number 8. The number 8 highlights Saturn's need to achieve something long-lasting, by sacrificing pleasure now for glory later. Discipline and persistence are used to pursue goals, rise to the top, and receive accolades. Because Saturn is the only influence on number 8, it is a karmic number. It has challenges, obstacles and tests to be conquered, perhaps more so than the other numbers. As a result number 8 people can be highly resilient; truly believers in the philosophy that what doesn't kill you makes you stronger. Indeed they are very difficult to keep down because they will keep trying until they succeed. Like number 4, the number 8 represents hard work, but in this case is more directly linked with power, status and material rewards. Number 8 has luxurious tastes, and it is important to them to have nice vacations, beautiful clothes, the latest technological gadgets and so forth.

CELEBRITY CASE STUDY: BENJAMIN FRANKLIN

Benjamin Franklin (born January 17th) was one of the founding fathers who drafted the Declaration of Independence, and the Constitution of the United States. He was very hardworking, ambitious, and enterprising.

Although disciplined and diligent, people born under this combination can find themselves climbing an uphill battle. As a result of this, they become very resilient, and are able to bounce back stronger than before. Franklin is quoted as saying, "Do not fear mistakes. You will know failure. Continue to reach out."[60]

Although his career is remembered for all of its impressive accomplishments, he would have never known success, had he not learned from his failure. He began a magazine that failed, invented an alphabet that cut out several letters we now use, and leaked important letters, in what is now known as "the Hutchinson affair". Despite this, he never let his lack of education make him feel inferior to others, and that probably pushed him even more to make a success of his life.

At the age of 17, Benjamin worked as an apprentice printer, and even borrowed some money to set up his business. He had done a lot of preparation, so when opportunity came, he excelled. He lived by his saying "by failing to prepare, you are preparing to fail."[61] He did very well running his business. On top of this, he bought the Pennsylvania Gazette, and turned it into a huge success. Poor Richard's Almanac, which he published under a pseudonym, was distinguished by his memorable aphorisms such as "a penny saved is a penny earned" and "A small leak will sink a great ship,"[62] characteristic of this combination's proclivity towards frugality.

Capricorn/Saturn/8 is always striving to create structure in society and lay down strong foundations for organizations. In

60 http://www.brainyquote.com/quotes/quotes/b/benjaminfr119119.html
61 http://www.brainyquote.com/quotes/quotes/b/benjaminfr138217.html
62 http://www.goodreads.com/author/quotes/289513.Benjamin_

the 1730s and 1740s, Franklin started America's first lending library, launched the American Philosophical society, and brought together a group of people to form the Pennsylvania Hospital. He wanted to do something for fire prevention so he started Philadelphia's Union Fire Company, and also helped found the Philadelphia Contribution for Insurance against Loss by Fire.[63] [64] [65] He is fondly remembered, and his image endures today as the face of the American $100 bill. Saturn will always reward you when you don't take shortcuts, fulfill your duties, and put in your best effort.

MARS, PLUTO AND THE NUMBER 9

The planet Mars represents drive, ambition, how we express anger, desires, passion, and sexual attraction. For example, a woman with her Mars in Cancer will get turned on if she feels nurtured and well protected. A man with his Mars in Aries will be daring in pursuing his goals; he is a fighter and won't give up easily. Look at a person's Mars sign to see how they will react if you irritate them-- will they do a slow burn (Taurus), give you the silent treatment (Cancer, Pisces), scream at you (Aries, Leo), or will they skip being mad and instead get even (Scorpio)?

Mars rules Aries. Aries is the sign of the warrior, they will not hesitate to speak up for what they believe is right, and if they have a problem with you, they will tell you. Going for what they want with all guns blazing; they thrive on competition and hate to lose. Mars is exalted in Capricorn where there is ambition and willingness to endure to overcome obstacles. Goal-oriented: they will work hard to achieve positions of authority, status and wealth.

Mars vibrates to the number 9. Number 9 people are warriors, they like to fight for what is right, especially in getting justice for underprivileged groups. They are humanitarian in nature

63 http://www.ushistory.org/franklin/info/
64 http://www.britannica.com/biography/Benjamin-Franklin
65 http://www.biography.com/people/benjamin-franklin-9301234

THE WISDOM OF ASTRONUMEROLOGY VOLUME 1

and like to volunteer their time and/or money to causes they find worthwhile. These people make excellent leaders, matching people to tasks that best suit them. Number 9 also vibrates to Pluto. Pluto is termed a dwarf planet but astrologers worldwide know that it packs a powerful punch. Pluto represents death, rebirth, transformation, sex, regeneration, esoteric subjects, in-depth investigations, intensity, obsessions, compulsions and power. Pluto aspecting any planet natally will give it an obsessive quality-- with Mars it lusts after power and control, with Venus it gives a compulsive and extreme tone in romance.

Pluto rules Scorpio. Scorpio is the sign that is hardest to read in terms of facial expression and body language, these people are very good at covering up what they truly feel or think. Exuding intensity and mystery, they want to know all about others but do not like revealing themselves. Blessed with accurate intuition, they can pick up on things that most other people miss. These people have a lot of depth in all areas of their life, if they study a subject they want to know it inside and out. Scorpio people crave power and will go to great lengths to get it, however they cannot stand being dominated. If they feel backed into a corner, their enemies better watch their backs!

Pluto represents a different side to the number 9 than Mars. Here it is the profound insights, the mysticism and healing power of 9. Number 9 people are interested in connecting with the divine, and are philosophical by nature. They seek to understand the truths of the universe, and the more complex processes of human behaviour. This is the teacher, who after being a long-term student, has developed their knowledge and wants to communicate it to the world.

Chapter 7

Aries Numbers 1-9

Aries Number 1 (March 28th, April 1st, April 10th, April 19th)

Original, pioneering, and courageous, you are one of the most naturally talented leaders in the zodiac. The Sun, which corresponds to the number 1, is exalted in Aries, meaning that it is able to have its most powerful expression. In many ways, you are bold, and not afraid to take risks that could potentially make your life more exciting and fulfilling. Whether or not you intend to, something about you (appearance, work, ideas, thoughts, or talents) causes you to stand out from the crowd. Your innate self-confidence, action-orientation, and belief that you can do anything you are determined to do, greatly helps you achieve the success you desire. Healthy competition with others gives you an adrenaline rush and causes you to perform to your personal best.

In terms of career, the need for independence, creativity, and autonomy are most important; therefore, roles that allow you one or more of these needs are where you will do your most productive work. You like to take the lead and create your own opportunities, rather than waiting for other people to give them to you. Although you may face setbacks early on, if you rely on your resilience and faith in yourself, you can run a very successful business.

It is also essential for you to feel a sense of mental and/ or physical challenge in your career, so medicine, policing, firefighting, journalism, broadcasting, business management, psychology, the military, law, human rights, politics, skilled trades, sports, coaching, martial arts, fitness, and higher education may hold a special interest.

Skilled creatively, drama, music, writing, or fashion may also be a passion of yours.

In any field you enter, you are likely to be the first to do something, devise an influential theory or invention, or set a record.

In romance, when a lover captures your heart, you are willing to go to great lengths for them. At the same time, you highly value your independence of thought and personal freedom. Going on adventures together strengthens the bond between you. By example, you teach your family the value of being one of a kind. They also appreciate your warrior spirit and willingness to stand up for them when they need it. Although you are naturally self-reliant, letting family help you through difficult times draws you closer.

Celebrities

Lady Gaga, multi-award winning singer, songwriter, and actress. She was honoured as Billboard's 2015 Woman of the Year (March 28th)

Abraham Maslow, psychologist who developed the theory of innate needs, resulting in self-actualization (April 1st)

William Booth, Methodist preacher, and founder of Salvation Army (April 10th)

Mukesh Ambani, billionaire and business magnate. He resides at Antilia, the world's most expensive private residential property 66 (April 19th)

ARIES NUMBER 2 (MARCH 29TH, APRIL 2ND, APRIL 11TH, APRIL 20TH)

Idealistic and imaginative, but strong-willed and independent, you are able to use these complementary skills to make a lasting mark on the world. This combination is particularly auspicious for entrepreneurial pursuits as you have an intuition about what people desire, and have the courage and practicality needed to run a large enterprise.

You have a very strong interest in other people, and your natural tendency is to take the lead. Thus you are frequently a popular leader, one who understands, and accommodates, the needs and goals of his or her group members.

Your surroundings have quite an influence on you, and you are sensitive to the auras or vibrations of other people and places. For this reason, you should take care where you spend your time, and which people you allow into your inner circle.

If you were born on April 11th, you receive the benefits of this master number. You are gifted with a powerful ability to further the interests of organizations, causes, thought systems, and people you believe in. With your idealism, diplomacy, skill of negotiation, and innate interest in others, you are able to persuade people why they should believe in what you are saying, and inspire them to take action. You can also bring together people or groups who have been at odds, and assist them to come to a win-win resolution. Naturally self-reflective, there is likely to be an interest in esoteric studies, mysticism, metaphysics, spirituality, philosophy or religion, as you go in search of wisdom and deeper truths. There is a need for periodic solitary rest times, which you should take to go deeper within, and recharge your batteries.

In terms of career, you do well in roles allowing for interaction with other people, such as counselling, sales, advertising, marketing, teaching, politics, medicine, business management, social work, mediation, or charity work. You may wish to communicate your vision creatively through literature, broadcasting, journalism, visual and performing arts, filmmaking, or photography. Positions requiring diplomacy, tact, and negotiating, as well as bringing people together, are also where you may excel.

In romance, you are attracted to people with self-confidence and a personal vision for their life. Lovers appreciate your sensitivity, idealism, and warmth. Although you can be quite flexible in professional environments in considering other people's viewpoints for negotiations, this may not translate to your own family. You have to be more willing to make compromises with family and make more of an accommodation to suit their wishes. You encourage imagination and dreaming big in your children; perhaps this is why they often have the courage to follow their passion later in life.

Celebrities

Sam Walton, founder of Walmart and Sam's Club (March 29th)

Hans Christian Andersen, writer, playwright, and poet, cultural icon (April 2nd)

Mary White Ovington, suffragist, journalist, and co-founder of the NAACP (April 11th)

Napolean III, first President of the French Second Republic, and the Emperor of the Second French Empire (April 20th)

ARIES NUMBER 3 (MARCH 21ST, MARCH 30TH, APRIL 3RD, APRIL 12TH)

Independent, optimistic, and creative, you are one who blazes your own path in life, rather than trying to fit into the established hierarchy. There is often a particular message you feel compelled to put out into the world, and you are unwilling to compromise on its authenticity. There is a natural confidence to you; you are not dependent on others to verify the worth of what you create. This is unusual in today's society, and a great gift of yours. Although you may brainstorm with others, ultimately you do your best work alone, because you like things done according to your creative vision. But one area to work on is curbing your tendency to be brutally honest; sometimes tact can go a long way in preventing hurt feelings.

In terms of career, you are a creative powerhouse, so self-expression is vital in the roles you take on. In anything you do, there is a need to feel a sense of aliveness and meaning. If you are not given a chance to place your personal stamp of originality on your paid work, try to maintain a hobby that allows for this. You are a free-spirited thinker that doesn't like to be tied down or micro-managed. For this reason, careers that allow for a lot of personal space and autonomy suit you.

Careers in education, broadcasting, healthcare, mediation, healing, working with animals, working with children, foreign relations, fitness, wellness, politics, science, justice, religion, spirituality, yoga, the occult, beauty, fashion, international business, the military, sales, music, acting, graphic design, and literature may be of interest.

In romance, you need a lover who shares your enthusiasm and zest for life! Lovers are attracted to your sense of adventure and confidence. Although your natural tendency is to be independent, being vulnerable with family members allows a chance for increased trust and intimacy. There is a strong need to see your family making the right decisions and doing well in their various pursuits; however, combining your suggestions for improvement with compliments, allows other people to more easily accept your advice without becoming defensive.

Celebrities

Rosie O'Donnell, multi-award winning comedienne, actress, author, television producer, television personality, and lesbian rights activist (March 21st)

Vincent van Gogh, Post-Impressionist painter and cultural icon (March 30th)

Jane Goodall, multi-award winning primatologist, ethologist, anthropologist, UN Messenger of Peace, and founder of the Jane Goodall Institute (April 3rd)

Herbie Hancock, multi-award winning pianist, keyboardist, bandleader, and composer. Recipient of the 2013 Kennedy Center Honors (April 12th)

Aries Number 4 (March 22nd, March 31st, April 4th, April 13th)

Original and unconventional, you have faith in yourself to stay true to your heart. There is an inspirational part of you that is able to encourage and motivate people when things are not going their way. Perhaps this is due to the lack of recognition for your talents you faced earlier in life. You learned to be tenacious, because you knew one day things would be better.

You have a natural sense of shrewdness and an ability to observe other people in detail, picking up on subtle nuances that other people miss. This skill makes you a particularly good writer or commentator and can be very helpful in many situations where the ability to read people is involved. Your general approach of getting right to the heart of the matter, rather than beating around the bush, earns you respect.

If you were born on March 22nd, you receive the benefits of this master number. Correcting social inequalities and working to advance the rights of the oppressed and marginalized is likely an interest of yours, and you have the power to be a catalyst for constructive change. This ability also extends to your work and relationships. With the brilliance and intuition of the 22, and the enthusiasm and vigor of Aries, you are able to see hidden talents in other people. You inspire them to hone those skills and fulfill their dreams. In anything you do, there is an emphasis on doing it the right way. There are no shortcuts or get-rich-quick schemes. You will devote yourself fully to your pursuit until it is finished to your high standards.

In terms of career, your skills of problem solving and investigation can be used in business management, academia, psychology, politics, law, science, math, technology, engineering, architecture, and research.

Because of your communication skills, literature, broadcasting, journalism, counselling, poetry, and creative writing are beneficial for you. Music, drama, dance, and feng shui are also a good use of your talents.

You may like working with your hands, so massage therapy, body work, landscaping, painting, and physical rehabilitation may be well-suited.

Innovation is your strong suit, and you instinctively know how to build on existing structures, or change outmoded structures to make room for new growth. You need to have intellectual stimulation, otherwise you will get restless and will not be motivated to perform your best.

In romance, you need a lover who appreciates your leadership ability and courage. You desire someone who is willing to step outside the box and wants to see people, places, and situations with fresh eyes. As long as each of you gives the other plenty of freedom, and agree to disagree when there are differing viewpoints, things will run smoothly. With your children, you strive to give them the very best experiences, but remember that they need to make their own mistakes in order to learn and grow.

Although relinquishing control may be difficult, doing so will result in more open communication lines between you.

Celebrities

Andrew Lloyd Webber, multi-award winning English composer, and impresario of musical theatre (March 22nd)

René Descartes, philosopher, mathematician, and scientist (March 31st)

Maya Angelou, multi-award winning author, poet, dancer, actress, and singer (April 4th)

Frank W. Woolworth, founder of F. W. Woolworth Company, and the operator of variety stores known as "five-and-dimes" (April 13th)

ARIES NUMBER 5 (MARCH 23RD, APRIL 5TH, APRIL 14TH)

A highly talented and persuasive speaker, you have a natural talent for knowing exactly the right words to say, and when to say it, to have the most lasting impact. Your message gets across so that other people know you mean business! Mental and physical freedom is very important to you, as your curious mind loves to get immersed in exciting new fields of study. You also like to travel to as many places as your budget will take you.

Change and multitasking are two themes in your life. Although you are perfectly capable of singular concentration when needed, doing two or more things at a time is natural for you and sometimes you can at times work better that way. In the midst of changing external circumstances, your flexibility and optimism allows you to make lemonade out of lemons.

In terms of career, communications is a major talent, so any role where you are needed to get a particular message across suits you. A sense of security is beneficial in your career, to be able to do your best work, and to balance out the many changes in other areas of your life.

With your natural affinity for young people, you may consider working with them in some capacity.
Or perhaps your interest in human behaviour and motivation may lead you to the occult, metaphysics, psychology, history, political science, and sociology.

Your skill in logic, analysis, research, and investigation may lead to a career in math, science, education, finance, engineering, forensics, law enforcement, technology, or sales.

In romance, it may take you a while to find the partner you want to commit to, but when you do, you will give it your all. Lovers are attracted to your intellect and curiosity. You desire someone who is on the same wavelength as you, and with whom you can have thought-provoking discussions with. Although you love discussions, it may be harder for you to share your deeper emotions, as you may tend to intellectualize them. Allowing yourself to feel what your family members are feeling, and just being with them silently in times of hardship, allows for a much deeper trust and connection.

Celebrities

Chaka Khan, Grammy award-winning singer and songwriter (March 23rd)

Booker T. Washington, educator, author, orator, and advisor to presidents of the United States on race relations (April 5th)

Julie Christie, multi-award winning actress and activist (April 14th)

ARIES NUMBER 6 (MARCH 24TH, APRIL 6TH, APRIL 15TH)

There is a great store of artistic talent in you and it would be a crime to let it go undeveloped! The need for self-expression is high as there are so many innovative ideas floating around in your head. You also love to physically design things, such as delicious meals, clothing, beautiful pieces of art, a nice garden, and other decorations for your home. People admire your spontaneity, and your ability to have a sensual appreciation of the little wonders of life.

You have an urge for discovery of the unknown, for knowledge and wisdom, mysteries, and other esoteric subjects. Once your curiosity is aroused you will go to great lengths to get to the truth. Your determination and passion often means that you will unravel the deeper meanings behind what is already known.

In terms of career, you are multitalented and will probably be doing more than one thing at a time. For your love of research, analysis, experimentation, observation, and discovery, you may try careers in science, law, literature, academia, astronomy, foreign relations, culinary arts, journalism, and writing.

Your designing side may find full expression in the beauty/makeup industry, luxury goods/services, retail, jewellery, or interior decoration fields.

Your artistic needs may be satisfied in the visual and performing arts, filmmaking, fashion, or photography industries.

Your nurturing side may be put to use in healthcare, hospitality, rehabilitation, working with children, working with animals, working with special needs and disabled persons, or charity work. With the entrepreneurial potential of Aries, starting a business around any of the aforementioned areas is also auspicious.

In romance, lovers appreciate your optimism, simplicity, and preference to keep things open and honest. You have a policy of saying what you mean, and meaning what you say, so you need a lover who is straightforward, but diplomatic. Family members appreciate that you often catch things that they miss, and that you strive to be objective in your dealings. However, when relating to your family, it is best to put your natural tendency to analyze and observe away, and instead pay more attention to your intuition. Your children admire your innovation and sense of style.

Celebrities

Tommy Hilfiger, multi-award winning fashion designer, and founder of the lifestyle brand Tommy Hilfiger Corporation (March 24th)

James Watson, molecular biologist, geneticist, and zoologist. Best known as one of the co-discoverers of the structure of DNA. Winner of the Nobel Prize in Physiology or Medicine in 1962 (April 6th)

Leonardo da Vinci, painter, sculptor, architect, musician, mathematician, engineer, inventor, anatomist, geologist, cartographer, botanist, and writer (April 15th)

ARIES NUMBER 7 (MARCH 25TH, APRIL 7TH, APRIL 16TH)

There is a significant part of you that craves solitude. You greatly enjoy the peace of deep reflection, and contemplation on life's mysteries and philosophical questions. A free-spirited thinker, you observe, analyze, and experiment to base your theories on your personal experience, rather than tradition. Your spiritual or religious side is likely to be highly developed, or if not so inclined, you nevertheless devote a lot of time to the deeper questions of life. Your dreams are very real and sometimes prophetic, you would greatly benefit from recording them for later reflection. Idealism runs very strong and there is frequently a humanitarian, or social cause to which you invest a great deal of your passion and energy.

In terms of career, you have an advantage in that you are combining the visionary potential of the 7, with the practical ambition of Aries, allowing you to turn your dreams into reality. Your strong interest in the occult, metaphysics, healing, humanitarian causes, spirituality, philosophy, mysticism, and foreign travel, may lead to a career involving these areas.

Artistic pursuits such as painting, poetry, literature, architecture, creative writing, drawing, filmmaking, photography, drama or music may appeal.

Work in nature, with animals, or near bodies of water may also suit you.

In romance, lovers appreciate your independence and self-reliance. You need a partner who gives you an abundance of personal space, but with whom you can build a mutually supportive relationship with. Be slower to accept so many time commitments as it relates to your family. You need to spend more time on each one, rather than wearing yourself thin trying to do too much. Although your personal beliefs on many topics are likely to be very strong, you must take care not to enforce your opinions on others. Your ability to lighten heavy situations is appreciated by your partner and children.

Celebrities

Gloria Steinem, multi-award winning feminist leader, journalist, and social activist. She received the Presidential Medal of Freedom in 2013 (March 25th)

Ravi Shankar, musician and composer of Hindustani classical music. Winner of the *Bharat Ratna*, India's highest civilian honour (April 7th)

Charlie Chaplin, comic actor, composer, and filmmaker (April 16th)

ARIES NUMBER 8 (MARCH 26TH, APRIL 8TH, APRIL 17TH)

Confident, independent, and entrepreneurial, your ambition takes you far. Getting right down to business is your style, and you don't waste any time. Goal-oriented, you go for what you want with full force, and even if you fail, your resilience guarantees a strong comeback. You are street smart and shrewd; it is very difficult to pull one over on you. There is a strong sense of justice and you can be a great fighter for the needs of the oppressed and disadvantaged. Despising power abuses, you will do whatever you can to draw attention to these matters in the hope of changing them. However, one drawback of yours is your tendency to take things too seriously-- focusing on the glass half full, will greatly assist your ability to get ahead.

In terms of career, your innate toughness, self-discipline and authoritative presence help you to get into leadership positions. You are not content being a follower, and if you work for someone else, you'll need a lot of personal space and freedom to succeed.

You work well under pressure, and can stay calm when other people are getting anxious and upset. Therefore jobs dealing with crisis such as law enforcement, mental health, medicine, firefighting, paramedics, emergency services, and working with at risk or dangerous populations may draw you in.

You have great physical stamina, so sports, roles requiring physical endurance, the military, martial arts, dance, or the skilled trades may interest you.

Your excellent technical skills and logically oriented mind may lead you to business management, administration, accounting, real estate, engineering, technology, computer science, research, science, or math.

If creatively inclined, you may want to try literature, writing, poetry, or the visual and performing arts.

In romance, lovers appreciate your loyalty and willingness to stick it out through the good and bad times. Since you have a tendency to take things seriously, someone with a good sense of humour can help you see the lighter side of life. As a parent, you are determined to help your children succeed professionally. However, by relaxing your expectations, you are allowing them to go through their precious stages of self-discovery. This will make them more resilient and put them in a better position to handle life's challenges with grace.

Celebrities

Robert Frost, poet, and four time Pulitzer Prize winner (March 26th)

Diana Ross, multi-award winning singer, actress, and record producer. Winner of the Grammy Lifetime Achievement Award in 2012 (April 8th)

John Pierpont Morgan, financier, banker, philanthropist, and art collector (April 17th)

ARIES NUMBER 9 (MARCH 27TH, APRIL 9TH, APRIL 18TH)

This is one of the most harmonious placements, because number 9 corresponds with Mars, the ruling planet of Aries. You are independent, action-oriented, and a warrior. Not one to shy away from battle, you will move forward with courage and will power. Whatever your goals are, your self-motivation and power of endurance gives you a strong boost in accomplishing them. However, you do have a tendency to go to extremes, and the art of compromise is one you will have to consciously work on to improve relations with those around you.

There is a lot of physical energy that needs to be expended through constructive outlets like sports, martial arts, or intense exercise. Otherwise, pent-up physical energy may lead to aggression, stress, or anger. You may have an interest in pushing your body to new heights of excellence and/or admire those who are able to do so. Overall, you need to watch a tendency to be impulsive and to take unnecessary risks, taking your time and proper precaution can save you heartache down the road.

In terms of career, the military, sports, law, politics, medicine, the healing arts, international business, engineering, science, math, education, the skilled trades, firefighting, rehabilitation, forensics, health studies, massage therapy, fitness, wellness, or law enforcement may capture your interest.

If more creative, music, fashion, drama, graphic design, comedy, and poetry are good expressions of your talent.

You like a sense of excitement and don't do well in jobs requiring lots of routines and predictability. Since you like things done a particular way, you tend to do better as a leader or working alone.

There may be a humanitarian or philanthropic side to you, and you may use your inner warrior to fight for the needs of disadvantaged or oppressed people.

In romance, lovers are attracted to your passion, honesty, and originality. You desire someone who is confident and possesses inner strength. Growing up, there may have been a lot of obstacles on your road to success, or your parents may have been excessively strict. Fortunately, that is probably how you developed your considerable resilience. However, your family may need more diplomacy and understanding than you received from your parents, or other authority figures. By showing your forgiving side, your children open up to you.

Celebrities

Mariah Carey, multi-award winning and best-selling singer, songwriter, and record producer (March 27th)

Marc Jacobs, multi-award winning fashion designer (April 9th)

Conan O'Brien, multi-award winning television host, comedian, writer, producer, musician, and voice actor (April 18th)

CHAPTER 8

TAURUS NUMBERS 1-9

TAURUS NUMBER 1 (APRIL 28TH, MAY 1ST, MAY 10TH, MAY 19TH)

Gifted with a strong presence, people notice your charm, sensuality, and personal style. You possess an instinctive understanding of timing, and if you follow this intuition, it won't fail to put you in the right place at the right time. Due to the influence of the 1, honesty, self-reliance, and directness characterize your approach. Fortunately you also exhibit the tact and relationship skill of Venus to balance it out.

Easily one of the most determined and persistent individuals of the zodiac, you rarely give up once you set out to accomplish something. Perhaps this is why you succeed in circumstances in which most other people would fail, quit, or lose hope. Further, you have the charisma and public speaking skill to inspire people experiencing similar circumstances to yours; to use your test as testimony and to advocate for the needs of an underprivileged group.

One challenge for you is your stubbornness, which is almost as strong as your tenacity! Do be willing to give careful consideration to others' opinions concerning information that runs counter to your position, even if you ultimately stick with your beliefs.

In terms of career, teaching and communicating are major strengths that position you as well-suited to make use of careers in education, broadcasting, lecturing, writing, editing, law, advocacy, journalism, and interviewing.

Interest in the physical body may lead you to medicine, kinesiology, alternative healing methods, massage therapy, or the wellness and fitness industries.

Your eye for beauty and creative skill may lead you to a career in music, fashion, graphic design, interior design, filmmaking, real estate, dance, retail, personal grooming, and the beauty/makeup industries.

The entrepreneurial skill of the 1 may be used in Taurus-governed domains to set up a business offering luxury goods/services, jewellery, body products, sweets, and home decorations.

In romance, lovers are attracted to your sensual and affectionate nature, and entrepreneurial spirit. You are a calm and soothing presence in times of need. You need a lover who understands your need for independence, but who is also very family-oriented, and cares to create a stable home environment. Children love your imagination and ability to tell an engaging story. They appreciate that you encourage them in whatever they pursue, and give them the freedom they need to discover life on their own terms.

Celebrities

Penélope Cruz Sánchez, model and first Spanish American Actress to win an Academy award, and to receive a star on the Hollywood Walk of Fame (April 28th)

Wes Anderson, multi-award winning film director and screenwriter (May 1st)

Dr. Wayne Dyer, #1 New York Times bestselling self-help author and motivational speaker (May 10th)

Malcolm X, Muslim cleric and human rights activist (May 19th)

TAURUS NUMBER 2 (APRIL 29TH, MAY 2ND, MAY 11TH, MAY 20TH)

Number 2 blends with Taurus very well because the Moon--which corresponds to the number 2--is exalted in Taurus. Home and family are your two main priorities in life. In fact, family may often rely on your nurturing and caring personality to help when needed.

You enjoy building meaningful bonds, especially with your children. If you don't have children, then the children of those closest to you.

You possess a great diversity of talents so you may find the activities and roles in your life constantly evolving.

You pay a great deal of interest to how you come across, and may often tend to notice subtle things about others that most would miss. Also, you have powerful insight into human motivation, and if you paid more attention to your intuition about people you'd rarely go wrong!

If you were born on May 11th, you receive the benefits of this master number. The areas of beauty, sensuality, and luxury might be one focus for your creativity and intuition. You know what aesthetic combinations look the best, what appeals to people, and what will create memorable experiences for them. These skills can be of great help in an entrepreneurial pursuit. There may be a talent in music and singing/song writing. Your work can touch many people, and certainly will be unique. Generally, your imagination is vivid, and when combined with Taurean tenacity and practicality, you can turn your visions into practical reality. Originality is a strength of yours, so much so that other people may perceive you as somewhat odd or outrageous at times.

Realizing that you don't have to fit in, and being true to yourself despite what others think, is essential to maintaining your self-confidence.

In terms of career, your interest in the motivations of other people may lead you to psychology, research, education, federal investigations, forensics, detective work, politics, history, sociology, counselling, therapy, or psychiatry.

You enjoy helping or supporting others, so medicine, social work, spirituality, rehabilitation, healthcare, the healing arts, customer service, or charity work may appeal.

Your eye for beauty and an artistic bent may incline you toward fashion, retail, interior decoration, importing foreign goods, jewellery, luxury goods and services, or the personal grooming industries. There is creative talent, which can be expressed through filmmaking, music, drama, visual arts, or culinary arts.

In romance, you are relationship-oriented and value stability and security. Lovers find your caring, sensual, and dependable nature very alluring. You are attracted to people who invest positive energy into how they present themselves to the world. You must watch a tendency towards mood swings with family members, and your resulting tendency to be blunt when upset. Although you may forget about it later, other people might not. Often, you are the glue that keeps the family together--and although they may not always say it, they really appreciate all the supportive work you do to keep the home running smoothly.

Celebrities

Jerry Seinfeld, multi-award winning comedian, actor, writer, and producer (April 29th)

Donatella Versace, multi-award winning fashion designer, and current Vice President of the Versace Group (May 2nd)

Salvador Dalí, surrealist painter, sculptor, scenographer, filmmaker, jewelry designer, and writer (May 11th)

Cher, multi-award winning actress, best-selling singer, entertainer, and fashion icon (May 20th)

TAURUS NUMBER 3 (APRIL 21ST, APRIL 30TH, MAY 3RD, MAY 12TH)

You have an aura of dignity and authority, and frequently find yourself in a position of leadership in some facet of your life. Regardless of your inner state, you present a calm face to the world and are able to represent yourself very well.

Coming under the influence of two benefic planets (Venus is the ruler of Taurus and Jupiter corresponds to number 3), you have good personal taste and are fortunate to receive a good deal of blessings on your life. You derive great pleasure from sensual luxuries and can be generous with your family and friends; if everyone has a great time then so do you. You are also good at coming up with initiatives to improve the quality of life for others.

In terms of career, your willpower, high intelligence, and work ethic can carry you far. Security and stability of employment are important to you, as is financial independence.

You may be attracted to careers in literature, visual and performing arts, public relations, fitness, nutrition, luxury goods/ services, interior decorating, animation, filmmaking, real estate, culinary arts, dramatic arts, massage therapy, landscaping, architecture, nursing, education, tourism, child care, social work, writing, law, politics, international business, psychology, or counselling.

In romance, lovers are attracted to your optimism, generosity, and intelligence. You are attracted to people who are thoughtful and caring. You aim to create a secure, stable and loving environment for your family, and they depend on you for guidance and support. However, one thing you have to watch for is a tendency towards stubbornness. Especially if your family members have a tendency towards changeability, give them room to explore their unique twists and turns throughout life.

Celebrities

Queen Elizabeth II, British royalty (April 21st)

Dhundiraj Govind Phalke, producer, director, and screenwriter, known as the Father of Indian cinema. The Dadasaheb Phalke Award is India's highest award in cinema. (April 30th)

Bing Crosby, best-selling singer and multi-award winning actor. Recipient of the first Grammy Global Achievement Award in 1963 (May 3rd)

Florence Nightingale, social reformer and statistician. Founder of modern nursing (May 12th)

TAURUS NUMBER 4 (APRIL 22ND, MAY 4TH, MAY 13TH)

Responsible, dependable, and nurturing, you are a pillar of your community. You are one who believes that actions speak louder than words, and you do what needs to be done without a lot of fanfare. There are great reserves of willpower within you that you can choose to tap into when you are working towards your goals.

Experience and instinct is much more important to you than academics or theory, you believe things as they happen. Although you have the Taurean stability, the 4 influence means that there is a bit of the rebel in you, and are more willing to take risks. Because of this you may achieve a wider scope of success than others. There may be something about your appearance that causes you to stand out from the crowd. Usually there is an earthy, sensual presence that can be used to make a statement with few words; often you can convey what you really mean through body language alone.

If you were born on April 22nd, you receive the benefits of this master number. True to the master builder capacity of the 22, there is a great ability within you to build tangible products, buildings, organizations, and systems that enhance the quality of life for those around you. With the Taurus influence, you may want to focus your scope on a topic within this sign's domain such as the family unit, music, entertainment, luxury services, beauty, the care of the physical body, or the home. Naturally brilliant, unconventional and future oriented, you catch on to innovative ideas ahead of others. Combined with Taurus's practicality and concentration, you can really turn your vision into a commercial success. On the other hand, you often have social justice concerns and can use your unique voice to make a lasting difference for people in need.

In terms of career, you crave a sense of stability in your work, and financial independence is high on your checklist. For this reason, you may like careers in finance, business, accounting, economics, engineering, medicine, law, or politics.

You can be a very talented teacher and you have a skill for advising others, therefore you may want to go into education, spirituality, healing arts, healthcare, counselling, or working with young people.

You may enjoy communicating your knowledge or helping others express their knowledge to a larger audience via broadcasting, lecturing, media, creative writing, editing, or publishing.

The humanitarian side of you may enjoy charity work, social work, or human rights.

Creatively, you may enjoy music, singing, painting, acting, interior decoration, or fashion design.

In romance, you can be one of the most loyal and enduring lovers of the zodiac; once someone captures your heart you would go to the ends of the earth for them. Lovers appreciate your sensuality, practicality, and family orientation. Although you an excellent source of guidance for your children, one area to watch for is being overprotective. Letting them discover the ups and downs of life firsthand is an essential part of growing up and expanding their horizons. Your family appreciates that you are an excellent provider and stay true to your word.

Celebrities

Kamla Persad-Bissessar, current Prime Minister of Trinidad and Tobago (April 22nd)

Audrey Hepburn, multi-award winning actress, fashion icon, and humanitarian (May 4th)

Stevie Wonder, multi-award winning musician, singer, songwriter, record producer, and multi-instrumentalist (May 13th)

TAURUS NUMBER 5 (APRIL 23RD, MAY 5TH, MAY 14TH)

Your words can be transformative catalysts for those around you. People take note of what you say, because of your thought-provoking or inspirational message. Highly intelligent, your ideas are ahead of the times, and people sense you are ushering in a new wave of innovative ideas. However, it may take some time before they fully catch up to you.

You may be skilled at allowing other people to form better connections with each other, either through staying in touch or improving the flow of intimacy and trust between them. Alternatively, you could lead people to go deeper within themselves for greater self-understanding and healing. In whatever you do, the versatility and persuasive skill of the 5, combined with the Taurean endurance and willpower, allows you to follow through on turning your dreams into reality.

In terms of career, you are fortunate to be born under a combination that is particularly favourable for material comfort. Therefore you tend to rise in your career into positions of higher status.

You are well able to handle several different goals and careers at the same time, and can succeed at all of them. Careers involving communication suit you best; for example writing, literature, media, broadcasting, sociology, lecturing, journalism, sales, teaching, coaching, or public speaking. Creatively, visual and performing arts, dance, and fashion may interest you.

Your interest in discovery may lead to careers in science, medicine, healing arts, philosophy, metaphysics, the occult, or spirituality.

You may also excel in traditionally Taurus governed areas like culinary arts, personal grooming, exercise, entertainment, luxury, or the beauty industry. Because you are very innovative, you could easily start a business based on one or more of your passions. You could be a pioneer and carve out your own particular niche.

In romance, even if you have the occasional doubt, you usually have the right words to say to convey to your lover how you really feel. Sensual and affectionate, bonding with him or her is very high on your list of priorities. You need a partner who gives you freedom, and plenty of intellectual stimulation. One challenge for you is that you have to watch for not extending your excessively high standards to your children. Although you are an excellent motivator, be more accepting, and less critical, when they fall short of the mark. Your advanced thinking inspires your family to look beyond what is known, and venture into the unknown.

Celebrities

William Shakespeare, poet, playwright, and actor, cultural icon (April 23rd)

Karl Marx, philosopher, economist, sociologist, journalist, and revolutionary socialist (May 5th)

Mark Zuckerberg, billionaire, co-founder, chairman, and chief executive of Facebook (May 14th)

Taurus Number 6 (April 24th, May 6th, May 15th)

The combination of Taurus and number 6 is a harmonious one, because Venus as ruler of Taurus corresponds to 6. Therefore your sense of beauty, harmony, and luxury is among the most highly developed of the zodiac. Very physically oriented, you derive great pleasure from goods and services designed to pamper the physical senses. There is a need for you to be in pleasant or beautiful surroundings, otherwise your mood is adversely affected.

You may find success and personal enjoyment in traditionally Taurus governed domains such as beauty, decoration, music, singing, entertainment, luxury goods/services, finances, investments, real estate, personal grooming, culinary arts, home, and family.

Having exceptional taste, your residence and wardrobe receives many compliments, and you intentionally present a sophisticated image. Naturally magnetic and charming, entertaining others comes easily to you, and you enjoy having family and friends come over and spend quality time.

The unconscious mind may play a big part in your life, either in attempting to understand other people's motivations, or perhaps your own. Maybe it is your work or interests that revolve around the unconscious. Alternatively, you may be the one to bring to public awareness what is in the collective unconscious of those around you (saying or doing things that others are thinking about, or would like to do, but don't want to express themselves publicly).

In terms of career, status, stability, and financial reward are important. You are determined to rise to the top. You may like business, politics, science, real estate, psychology, social science, investments, accountancy, medicine, science, healthcare, or education.

There is a creative side to you that could excel in visual and performing arts, fashion, and graphic design.

Generally, you have a good speaking and writing style and could feel compelled to share your opinions, thoughts and feelings with others; therefore careers or hobbies involving communication are good for you.

You may also do a job that will give you material comfort, while pursuing your passion on the side (in the event that it doesn't pay well).

In romance, you can be affectionate, caring, and sensitive towards your lover. Your partner appreciates your protectiveness and commitment towards family. Although at times your guidance is appreciated, one of your challenges is dropping the need to control what your family does. They must feel free to make their own decisions. Your family appreciates your loyalty during the difficult times, and find that your well-reasoned direction in times of crises is helpful.

Celebrities

Barbra Streisand, multi-award winning singer, songwriter, actress, and filmmaker (April 24th)

Sigmund Freud, neurologist and founder of psychoanalysis (May 6th)

Pierre Curie, physicist and a pioneer in crystallography, magnetism, piezoelectricity and radioactivity. Winner of the Nobel Prize in Physics in 1903 (May 15th)

Taurus Number 7 (April 25th, May 7th, May 16th)

Possessing a vivid imagination combined with a down-to-earth nature, your inner life is rich, while still efficiently fulfilling your duties in the outer world. You have a unique style that could manifest in your appearance, ideas, mannerisms, behaviour, or relationships. This style evolves over the years, and typically you stand out from the crowd more as you get older.

You feel that life is your best teacher and you prefer learning on your own instead of formally. There may a special interest in poetry, metaphysics, spirituality, the occult, mysticism, or other esoteric subjects. Your intuition is strong and you should pay particular attention to your dreams and hunches, for they usually contain an important message.

There is probably a creative gift that you have which should be expressed, for example music, singing, drama, dance, or fashion.

Home and family is very important to you and you devote much of your time to strengthening bonds. A beautiful and harmonious home gives you peace. Generally, you have a strong appreciation for beautiful things and pleasures of the senses. Therefore pampering your body, mind, and spirit is essential to cultivating inner joy.

In terms of career, you may be capable of sticking with one career your whole life if circumstances require it. You value stability, security, and financial independence in whatever you do.

Careers in literature, poetry, journalism, writing, publishing, education, psychology, filmmaking, spirituality, non-profit organizations, business management, communications, social work, counselling, healthcare, science, or entertainment, may interest you.

In romance, you are capable of making many sacrifices for your spouse and children. You appreciate when your family gives you cards and thoughtful gifts on special occasions, and acknowledges your efforts in running the home. You need a partner with whom you feel you are mentally and spiritually on the same wavelength. Your kindness and generosity towards those in need inspires your family to follow suit.

Celebrities

Ella Fitzgerald, multi-award winning jazz singer and actress (April 25th)

Rabindranath Tagore, poet, writer, and painter. Winner of the Nobel Prize in Literature in 1913 (May 7th)

Liberace, multi-award winning pianist and entertainer (May 16th)

Taurus Number 8 (April 26th, May 8th, May 17th)

Strong-willed, determined, and ambitious, you certainly are a force to be reckoned with! Other people rely on the quality of your work, and the dependability of your word. Your mind tends to be logical, serious, and analytical. You believe in evidence and results, not theories and fantasies.

Honest and outspoken, you tend to say what is on your mind, which can have both good and bad consequences for you. Your opinions and ideas are quite resistant to change. One challenge for you will be to integrate new information as it comes in to your belief system, and to accept that people and situations are not as clear cut as they seem.

In terms of career, you are conscientious and are willing to put in the hours to achieve what you set out to do. Status conscious and desirous of material wealth, you aspire towards roles that bring you admiration and respect.

You may be attracted to careers in business management, finance, history, economics, accounting, real estate, investments, medicine, law, politics, engineering, fitness, wellness, comedy, nutrition, literature, science, writing, editing, journalism, social work, human rights, or religion.

If creatively inclined, music, singing, visual arts, drama, or yoga may be of special interest.

You prefer roles where you can get right down to business, because you hate wasting time, and having superfluous discussions. Having a naturally authoritative presence, you may start your own business.

In romance, you care about the little details that make a romantic gesture just perfect. You strive to provide your family with the very best money can buy and push your children hard to succeed in their endeavours. They appreciate your honest nature and action orientation. Going on foreign trips and socializing with people from different cultures, backgrounds and lifestyles will broaden your outlook as a family.

Celebrities

Carol Burnett, multi-award winning actress, comedian, singer, and writer (April 26th)

Jean Henri Dunant, businessman and social activist. Founder of the International Red Cross, and one of the first Noble Peace Prize winners in 1901 (May 8th)

Edward Jenner, physician and scientist who was the pioneer of smallpox vaccine, and the father of immunology (May 17th)

TAURUS NUMBER 9 (APRIL 27TH, MAY 9TH, MAY 18TH)

Self-confident, courageous, and having great strength of will, you go after what you want with all guns blazing. Even when you fail, there is great capacity to learn from your mistakes and become wiser. Since you may have experienced quite a few hard knocks, you are in a position to empathize with, and help those who are facing similar issues. Your ability to relate to people from a diverse range of backgrounds helps you in all your pursuits. You are a warrior and can use your skill to improve the conditions of the disadvantaged, or to raise awareness for societal injustices or power abuses.

Your body is important to you, and you are likely to take care of it well through eating right, exercising, pampering yourself, and being well-groomed. There is a need for you to burn off excess stress through fitness, sports or other intense activity. Otherwise that stress is likely to turn into anger and aggression and be detrimental to your relationships. You may be drawn towards activities that test the limits of the body or that challenge it in some way. Your physical strength may draw you to martial arts, sports, the military, the skilled trades, construction, or fitness.

In terms of career, roles requiring persuasion, advocacy, activism or raising of societal issues fits you well. Humanitarian efforts, human rights, politics, law, sales, advertising, social work, sociology, psychiatry, or psychology may capture your attention.

Your ability to teach or advise others may lead to careers in counselling, religion, education, healthcare, or the healing arts.

There may be a special talent for music, singing, painting, dance, and drama.

You may excel in traditional Taurean careers such as beauty, finance, entertainment, luxury goods/services, and culinary arts.

In romance, you are passionate, generous, and affectionate. You need a partner who is adventurous but also values the stability of home and family. You inspire your family with your desire to improve the world and the quality of life for those around you. You also teach your children to stay firm on matters of ethical or moral importance. Although your strong beliefs can be an advantage in certain situations, recognizing when to change your course of action may be something you need to learn. Participating in charity work as a family brings you closer together.

Celebrities

Samuel Morse, painter and inventor, inventor of the electric telegraph (April 27th)

Billy Joel, multi-award winning and best-selling pianist, singer-songwriter, and composer (May 9th)

Pope John Paul II, served as Pope from 1978 to 2005, made a saint by the Roman Catholic Church (May 18th)

Chapter 9

Gemini Numbers 1-9

Gemini Number 1 (May 28th, June 1st, June 10th, June 19th)

Combining Gemini's skill for communication, and the independence of the number 1, you are a thought leader in your field. Your mind is characterized by independence, logic, and analysis. You tend to form your opinions based on first-hand experience rather than what has been traditionally taught. The quest for innovative ideas and ways to share them with the world is important to you.

Always ready to state your views and naturally competitive, you don't shy away from debate; in fact you thrive on it! Your skill for understanding opposing sides of a situation helps you craft more convincing arguments for the points you make.

A career which allows you autonomy is essential, as is variety, because you need diversity and excitement in whatever you do. You may find yourself in different careers over your life, because your spirit craves adventure, freedom, and novel stimuli.

Careers involving communication such as media, literature, writing, publishing, journalism, negotiations, mediation, public relations, sales, politics, marketing, advertising, education, counselling, and psychology may be good fits for you.

Music, drama, photography, fashion design, filmmaking or drawing may be a creative passion.

Your analytical skills may do well in science, math, logistics, engineering, investigations, or research.

In romance, you are a thoughtful and committed partner, but you need plenty of space to pursue your interests. Finding another free spirit who enjoys exchange of information, and healthy debate is important.

People sense that you are forever young; in fact you may have a special affinity with young people because you are young at heart. Your children appreciate your ability to understand where they are coming from, and to listen to them nonjudgmentally. The only thing you have to watch for is that your natural tendency to speak your mind bluntly should be combined with diplomacy. In this way, your family is more likely to consider your well-intentioned advice.

Celebrities

Gladys Knight, Grammy award-winning recording artist, songwriter, businesswoman, humanitarian, and author (May 28th)

Marilyn Monroe, cultural icon, multi-award winning actress, model, and singer (June 1st)

Hattie McDaniel, actress, singer-songwriter, and comedienne. First African American to win an Oscar in 1940 (June 10th)

Lou Gehrig, baseball player and first MLB player to have his uniform number retired (June 19th)

GEMINI NUMBER 2 (MAY 29TH, JUNE 2ND, JUNE 11TH, JUNE 20TH)

Your love of learning is the feature that is most prominent in you; you are like a sponge, soaking up information on every subject that interests you, and there are many! You are the eternal student, going through life with an imaginative and receptive mind, willing to consider many viewpoints and ideas in forming your philosophies. Because you are open-minded, non-judgemental, and empathetic, people seek you out for guidance in times of need.

It is important to you to play a part in correcting social inequities. Your willingness to take a stand to effect the change you want to see, even if there is some personal risk to you, is admirable.

If you were born on June 11th, you receive the benefits of this master number. You are spiritual by nature, so careers involving meditation, yoga, healing, spiritual teaching, esoteric studies, and metaphysical studies are all fruitful. You are very optimistic, enthusiastic and determined. By example, you can inspire people with your willingness and ability to push established traditions to make significant breakthroughs in thought and action. You are a trailblazer who introduces to society genuinely fresh ways of viewing the world.

In terms of careers, you have a strong skill for working one-on-one with people, thus counselling and therapy are good options. You generally do your best in professions that are people-oriented and that take care of others. You must be allowed to talk with people in order to thrive in your career, so professions requiring too much solitude are not for you (unless you were born on June 11th, and in that case you have a strong need for solitude to recharge yourself).

Other fields that may capture your interest are psychology, social work, science, research, public relations, journalism, education, music, humanitarian work, medicine, healthcare, yoga, rehabilitation, law, the government, drama, fashion, or fine arts.

In romance you highly value intimacy, and you enjoy talking with your partner about your thoughts, feelings, dreams, and desires--lovers are attracted to your compassion and intelligence. You must find a partner who is comfortable having lengthy discussions about soulful topics. There may be a special affinity with children in general, and it is especially important to you to maintain a close relationship with your own children. You are a good disciplinarian, but they still think of you as a friend.

Celebrities

John F. Kennedy, 35th President of the United States. Recipient of numerous awards including the Presidential Medal of Freedom in 1963, and the Pulitzer Prize for Biography or Autobiography in 1957 (May 29th)

Wayne Brady, Emmy Award winning actor, singer, comedian, and television personality (June 2nd)

Jacques-Yves Cousteau, multi-award winning oceanographer, naval officer, explorer, conservationist, filmmaker, innovator, scientist, photographer, author, and researcher. Recipient of both the U.S. Presidential Medal of Freedom in 1985 and the Commander of the Legion of Honour in 1972 (June 11th)

Nicole Kidman, multi-award winning actress and film producer (June 20th)

GEMINI NUMBER 3 (MAY 21ST, MAY 30TH, JUNE 3RD, JUNE 12TH)

A fascinating storyteller with an ability to keep an audience engaged for a long time! You are likely known as an excellent conversationalist with a great sense of humour. Able to relate well to people of all walks of life, you love to learn about new cultures. You especially love to talk about your travels, which you do quite regularly if circumstances allow.

Upbeat and jovial, you like to attend social functions, and really enjoy meeting new people. But there is also a deeper, more philosophical side to your nature that enjoys discussing the more mysterious sides to life and creation. You may enjoy meeting with a group of like-minded people to do this.

In terms of career, you have a strong need for self-expression, intellectual stimulation, diversity, and creative thought. You may have more than one career at a time or switch careers several times as your restless nature is always seeking adventure and variety. Persuading other people to understand your point of view is a natural talent.

Sales, marketing, retail, writing, editing, research, math, science, education, law, politics, religion, metaphysics, the occult, event planning, healthcare, rehabilitation, acting, comedy, psychology, psychiatry, mediation, drawing, painting, music, or literature may appeal.

You may have an entrepreneurial streak, and starting a business centered on communications, technology, social media, or publishing is particularly favoured.

In relationships, sense of humour and appreciation for adventure are high on your list of desirable characteristics. You desire someone that you can discuss important ideas but also joke around with. However, be mindful of differences in thoughts and beliefs of your partner. Even though your powers of persuasion are strong, they should not be used to try to convert your loved ones to your belief system. Your family loves your vibrant and youthful spirit.

Celebrities

Henri Rousseau, Post-Impressionist painter (May 21st)

Bob Evans, founder of Bob Evans Restaurants. Honored three times by the National Wildlife Federation for more than 40 years of preserving wildlife (May 30th)

Dr. David R. Hawkins, multi-award winning psychiatrist, consciousness researcher, and best-selling author (June 3rd)

Anne Frank, author of The Diary of Anne Frank and one of the most discussed victims of the Jewish Holocaust. Anne was named among the heroes and icons of the 20th century on Time Magazine's list of The Most Important People of the Century (June 12th)

GEMINI NUMBER 4 (MAY 22ND, MAY 31ST, JUNE 4TH, JUNE 13TH)

Your ideas are very original because you tend to see situations from a different angle than most others. Frequently this can work for you as you can use your considerable communication talent to introduce subtle nuances in interpretation and policy. Science and technology is particularly appealing as you combine your research orientation with unique vision. In the spirit of discovery, you may invent new items or ways of doing things.

You may be attracted to unusual interests or people, as you have a bit of an unconventional streak to you. You have your own set of values which may often go against what is dominant in society at the time. However, you have a healthy respect for society's structure, and are hard-working, determined, and persistent in reaching your goals. Humanitarian and global concerns are important to you, and often you donate time and money in raising awareness for your favourite causes.

May 22nd is a master number and brings with it mental brilliance, and ideas far ahead of their time. You may find yourself using Gemini's gift for communication in advocating for groups that are oppressed, disadvantaged or marginalized. In whichever role you find yourself, your ideas are certainly out of the box and cause people to re-think old ideas. Your concentration and devotion is particularly strong when absorbed in a goal you are passionate about. Your family is your top priority, and you greatly appreciate the bonding experience, especially with your children and grandchildren.

In terms of career, you have solid technical skills and excellent logical reasoning skills so any profession requiring this type of precision works well. You tend to have a serious demeanour, an eye for detail, and are a good organizer.

Teaching, sales, marketing, advertising, writing, editing, publishing, journalism, literature, languages, speech pathology, or social justice may interest you.

Your analytical skills can work for you in math, science, information technology, engineering, software design, and computers.

Yoga, music, the occult, healing arts, filmmaking and drama may also be a passion.

In romance, you admire a lover who is intelligent, dynamic, and creative. Partners are attracted to your inventiveness, and willingness to stand out from the crowd. You need someone who respects your need for freedom and exploration. One of your challenges is that you may at times be too slow to give affection, so you need a partner who is affectionate and sensitive to balance you out. Your family appreciates your adventurous spirit and willingness to encourage their "far out" ideas.

Celebrities

Harvey Milk, politician and gay rights activist. He was awarded the Presidential Medal of Freedom in 2009 (May 22nd)

Clint Eastwood, multi-award winning actor, film director, producer, musician, and politician. He was the recipient of both the Commandeur de la Légion d'honneur in 2009, and the American Film Institute Life Achievement Award in 1996 (May 31st)

Angelina Jolie, multi-award winning actress, filmmaker, and humanitarian. She was the recipient of the Jean Hersholt Humanitarian Award in 2013, and was awarded an honorary damehood of the Order of St Michael and St George in 2014 (June 4th)

John Forbes Nash, multi-award winning mathematician with fundamental contributions in game theory, differential geometry, and partial differential equations (June 13th)

GEMINI NUMBER 5 (MAY 23RD, JUNE 5TH, JUNE 14TH)

Your combination is the most harmonious as Mercury ruler of Gemini, vibrates to the number 5. Persuasive, intelligent, and humorous, communication is one of your strongest skills. You love discussion, debating, and brainstorming. Learning new things and meeting interesting new people is a way of life.

Forever the student, you are on the lookout to gain knowledge, experience, and skills in subjects that interest you. If circumstances allow, you'll want to travel to as many foreign places as you can, as you greatly enjoy learning about different lifestyles and cultures. If you don't travel physically, you are certain to travel mentally through books and movies that transport you to a different place and time.

Change is the only constant in your life; fortunately, you are flexible and are able to make the most out of a sudden change in plans.

In terms of career, you have a logical, analytical mind and could excel in research, problem solving, and investigation. You may be drawn to math, science, technology, inventions, engineering, accounting, financial services, investing, business management, real estate, public relations, construction, tourism, foreign relations, law, corrections, forensics, politics, the military, and medicine.

Languages, translating, public speaking, teaching, sales, songwriting, filmmaking, interviewing, broadcasting, journalism, media, literature, comedy, editing, writing, advertising, or marketing may draw your interest.

You have a high need for intellectual stimulation, and positions requiring repetitive tasks won't satisfy you. Multitasking is a great strength of yours. Your versatility means you can excel in many areas, although you have a tendency to not spend too much time on each one.

In romance, you are an enthusiastic, energetic, and loving partner but need a lot of freedom both physically and mentally to explore your interests. You need someone who you can have good conversation with, and who is spontaneous enough to go with the flow. Lovers are attracted to your intelligence, sense of adventure, and wonderful sense of humour. You love to instill in your children a sense of inquisitiveness, namely that that there are always mysteries to be solved, and deeper reasons for the inner workings of things. Engaging in activities designed to stimulate exploration and invention are a great way to spend time as a family.

Celebrities

John Bardeen, physicist and electrical engineer, co-inventor of the transistor, and revolutionized the electronics industry. He is the only person to have won the Nobel Prize in Physics twice (May 23rd)

Suze Orman, NYT best-selling author, financial advisor, motivational speaker, and award-winning television host (June 5th)

Che Guevara, major figure of the Cuban Revolution Marxist revolutionary, physician, author, guerrilla leader, diplomat, and military theorist (June 14th)

GEMINI NUMBER 6 (MAY 24TH, JUNE 6TH, JUNE 15TH)

There is no shortage of natural charm and magnetism in you, and your easygoing, warm presence attracts many friends and admirers. Also noticeable is your eye for beauty; you particularly love unusual and distinctive pieces that spark discussion.

You are attracted to subjects that seek to understand human behaviour such as psychology and psychiatry. Peeling back the layers to people and constantly discovering new sides to their nature and motivation comes naturally.

Responsible and dutiful, once you make a promise, others can count on you to keep it. Although you must take care to not bite off more than you can chew.

In terms of career, your artistic talents and ability to beautify people and surroundings can be utilized in many ways, possibly even through running your own business. With your eye for beauty, you may enjoy the retail, landscaping, architecture, fashion design, interior decoration, real estate, or the luxury goods/ services industries.

Number 6 is a natural entrepreneur, and Geminis are natural communicators, so businesses centering on communications are a good expression of your talents (publishing, editing, public relations, lecturing, broadcasting, and writing).

Medicine, kinesiology, fitness, wellness, rehabilitation, and nursing may be a good match for you.

Music, acting, drawing, painting, and writing may capture your attention as well.

In romance, you are faithful and loyal. You need a partner who is completely devoted to home and family, and is willing to make the necessary sacrifices to maintain a happy home life. Lovers are attracted to your compassion and desire to assist people in need. You like to keep romance alive long after you are married, so a partner who makes a mutual effort to do so is very much appreciated. Your family loves your thoughtfulness and sensitivity.

Celebrities

Queen Victoria, British Royalty (May 24th)

Paul Giamatti, multi-award winning actor (June 6th)

Erik Erikson, developmental psychologist and psychoanalyst (June 15th)

Gemini Number 7 (May 25th, June 7th, June 16th)

Your love of reading and writing is readily apparent to all those who know you, and your quest for knowledge and wisdom is everlasting. You express yourself best via the written word, as you appreciate your solitude and time to record your reflections. Due to your rich imagination, you may also express yourself well through the visual and performing arts.

A lifelong learner, you take your studies very seriously, and deeply contemplate the information you are absorbing. Naturally intuitive and observant, you notice details and subtle nuances that others miss. You are a very analytical thinker, and can problem-solve very well; in fact you may have a special talent for solving mysteries or puzzles.

Living near the water has a soothing and calming influence on you. Similarly, being in nature does wonders to uplift your spirit.

In terms of career, you need a position that gives you the opportunity to constantly learn new information. You would feel stifled if you were stuck in a routine that didn't allow for discovery.

Careers that may be a good fit are science, technology, math, literature, linguistics, feng shui, the occult, psychology, politics, history, photography, medicine, journalism, publishing, editing, media, social work, counselling, and human rights.

In romance, you have a fundamental need for honest, authentic communication, and you feel that problems can be solved by talking them out. Lovers are attracted to your intelligence and sense of adventure. You need a partner that understands your need for autonomy and solitude as you don't like the feeling of being smothered or constricted. Your children appreciate your generosity and willingness to help in times of need.

Celebrities

Ralph Waldo Emerson, essayist, lecturer, and poet. He led the Transcendentalist movement of the mid-19th century (May 25th)

Liam Neeson, Academy award, Golden Globe and BAFTA nominated actor, appointed Officer of the Order of the British Empire (OBE) by Queen Elizabeth II in 1999 (June 7th)

Stan Laurel, comic actor, writer and film director, most famous for his role in the comedy duo Laurel and Hardy. He was the recipient of the Lifetime Achievement Academy Award in 1961 (June 16th)

Gemini Number 8 (May 26th, June 8th, June 17th)

A very skilled networker with an eye for acting on career opportunities, you are always cognizant of climbing to the top of your field. Hardworking and precocious from a young age, you've always had two feet fixed firmly on the ground while working through your challenges. You may have developed a thick skin and street smarts because of this.

You are strong-willed, and enjoy positions of authority, wealth, and power. This may translate into being a workaholic due to the high standards you set for yourself. Unlike most Geminis, you don't scatter your energies on many projects; rather, you tend to focus on one goal at a time until you achieve it.

In terms of career, you need your accomplishments and abilities to be positively recognized. Your mind tends to be organized, logical, and governed by analysis, thus professions requiring those skills would fit well. Regardless of your specific field, your tremendous work ethic, and ability to bounce back from adversity will take you far.

Careers you may find appealing are business management, computer science, engineering, law, healthcare, media, sports, literature, languages, accounting, sales, food/movie/book critic, administration, math, science, medicine, research, music, forensics, policing, firefighting, working with the elderly, or journalism.

In romance, lovers are attracted to your sense of humour, strength of will, and determination. You admire partners who are loyal and honest. You must watch for a tendency to be judgemental in word or action; cultivating diplomacy and tolerance go a long way in harmonious relationships. Despite busy schedules, making time for family dinners or special activities builds greater levels of emotional closeness. Your family appreciates that you are push them to put in 110% of their effort into whatever activity captures their passion.

Celebrities

Stevie Nicks, best-selling singer and songwriter. She was the recipient of the Grammy Hall of Fame Award in 2003 (May 26th)

Sir Francis Crick, molecular biologist and co-discoverer of DNA molecule. He was awarded the 1962 Nobel Prize for Physiology or Medicine (June 8th)

Venus Williams, tennis player who was ranked World No. 1 in singles by the Women's Tennis Association on three separate occasions. She is the winner of multiple Olympic gold medals (June 17th)

Gemini Number 9 (May 27th, June 9th, June 18th)

You are outspoken and value simplicity of speech. You hate beating around the bush, and will push others to state their point right up front. Your warm demeanour and fun spirit gives you an affinity for interacting with young people. The appreciation is mutual as you both learn a lot from each other.

You must watch for a tendency to be impulsive in all areas of life; taking time before you speak can save you regret or hurt feelings later. Your temper can flare up quickly, but you do have a tendency to forget about it relatively fast.

Blessed with tremendous reserves of energy, you are eager to have new experiences and adventures. For ultimate contentment, you will have to focus on those experiences that give you the strongest sense of life purpose.

In terms of career, you have a warrior spirit, combined with confidence, and articulate expression. This can be used in advocacy for underprivileged groups. This may lead you to social services, teaching, counselling, the legal field, politics, social activism, or charitable work.

Whichever field you pursue, your enthusiasm and passion is evident to those around you, and will allow you to fulfill your ambitions. Other areas you may enjoy are healthcare, labour relations, astronomy, metaphysics, yoga, international business, rehabilitation, music, mechanics, sports, firefighting, tourism, culinary arts, fitness, wellness, literature, and mediation.

In romance, you are attracted to lovers who are inspiring, upbeat, and view life with a sense of gratitude. You enjoy the simple pleasures of life, and need a partner who takes the time to appreciate the little things. Your family appreciates your thoughtfulness, devotion and sense of adventure. Your children love that you encourage them to not be afraid of making mistakes, and instead view them as building blocks on the road to success.

Celebrities

Henry Kissinger, multi-award winning diplomat and political scientist, secretary of state. He was offered the Nobel Peace Prize for his work on the Paris Peace Accords (May 27th)

Johnny Depp, multi-award winning actor, producer, and musician. He was listed in the 2012 Guinness World Records as the highest-paid actor (June 9th)

Roger Ebert, film critic, journalist, author and screenwriter. He was the first film critic to win the Pulitzer Prize for Criticism in 1975 (June 18th)

CHAPTER 10

CANCER NUMBERS 1-9

CANCER NUMBER 1 (JUNE 28TH, JULY 1ST, JULY 10TH, JULY 19TH)

Patriotic and home-loving, you are proud of your roots, and current country of residence. You love to incorporate the traditions of your country of origin into your daily life, and share them with all those around you. Your childhood memories are very vivid in your mind, and perhaps more than other people, continue to affect the way you are motivated now.

A fierce protector of your loved ones, you will move heaven and earth should anyone mistreat them. You make a great parent because your children feel that they can talk to you about anything. At the same time you understand their need for learning through trial and error.

In terms of career, you have a skill for understanding the changing tastes of the public, and have a knack for designing products or introducing services that appeal to the masses. For this reason, entrepreneurship, especially in services or products designed to enhance comfort or to indulge the senses, like food, hospitality, and tourism, are favourable.

You are able to handle positions of leadership because you combine emotional intelligence with ambition. People enjoy working for you because you know how to make them feel valued. However, you can at times take suggestions for improvement as signs of personal criticism, which most often they are just honest attempts to help you improve.

If you prefer working in a structured environment, a government position is a good way to show your national pride. Other careers you may enjoy are music, drama, visual arts, filmmaking, comedy, media, writing, psychology, science, administration, customer service, fitness, wellness, engineering, research, medicine, nursing, the occult, metaphysics, and financial services. In whatever career you choose, the home/work life balance is an important one.

In romance, you are a curious blend of traditional and modern. You have a healthy respect for customs but love to spice them up! Since your moods are easily changeable and you can switch frequently from being active to passive, you need a partner who helps keep participation in decision-making relatively equal. You must state what is on your mind in a diplomatic way so that resentments do not have a chance to build up. Your family loves that you encourage them to be proud of their heritage.

Celebrities

Mel Brooks, multi-award winning director, actor, comedian, and songwriter. He was the recipient of the American Film Institute Life Achievement Award and the British Film Institute Fellowship (June 28th)

Princess Diana, British royalty (July 1st)

Nikola Tesla, inventor, electrical engineer, mechanical engineer, physicist, and author (July 10th)

Edgar Degas, artist famous for his paintings, sculptures, prints, and drawings. He was one of the founders of Impressionism (July 19th)

CANCER NUMBER 2 (JUNE 29TH, JULY 2ND, JULY 11TH, JULY 20TH)

This combination is most harmonious for Cancer, as its ruler Moon corresponds to the number 2. Intuitive, empathetic, and sensitive, you are able to understand and soak up the emotions of those around you. Primarily feeling-oriented, you are guided more by your gut instincts than by hard facts.

You are a nurturer, deriving great pleasure from taking care of family, friends, and pets. Your memory is very strong, and you may have a special place in your heart for your childhood, the country you grew up in, and old friends.

If you were born on July 11th, you receive the benefits of this master number. In your case, your intuition borders on psychic abilities, and you often have knowledge without knowing where it came from. Following these insights can be of great assistance to you in your daily life. Charming and diplomatic, your people skills are highly developed, and you can successfully interact with almost anyone. You may be a source of encouragement in other people's lives by highlighting the best in them. Interpersonal relationships, especially with family, who are the center of your world is the area where you derive your greatest pleasure from.

In terms of career, you have an innate understanding of public trends, moods and desires. You can use this skill to start a successful business, especially around Cancerian domains such as food, hotels, water, travelling, antiques, children, or families. Positions that involve making other people feel "at home" are ideally suited to you.

You may enjoy working with the elderly, children, animals, or special-needs populations. You may use your people skills in psychology, psychiatry, counselling, social work, rehabilitation, or healthcare.

You also may have a talent for positions dealing with buying and selling homes/properties/ commercial buildings, therefore real estate may attract your attention.

Creatively, you may gravitate towards filmmaking, fashion, photography, graphic design, literature, poetry, dance, writing, drama, and music.

In terms of work settings, you may enjoy places near the water or historical places. You may also choose a career in aviation.

In romance, you are sentimental, and enjoy collecting memorabilia and antiques, as well as taking plenty of photos to preserve special moments. In fact, there are probably hundreds of pictures of your children, especially your first-born child! Since you are imaginative, you encourage your children to think creatively and rely on what their heart tells them is right. Your family appreciates that you are the glue that holds everyone together, and that you support each person's unique talents from behind the scenes.

Celebrities

Antoine de Saint-Exupéry, aristocrat, writer, poet, and pioneering aviator (June 29th)

Hermann Hesse, poet, novelist, and painter. He was the winner of the Nobel Prize in Literature in 1946 (July 2nd)

Giorgio Armani, multi-award winning fashion designer, and billionaire (July 11th)

Giselle Bündchen, supermodel, actress, producer and Goodwill Ambassador for the United Nations Programme (July 20th)

CANCER NUMBER 3 (JUNE 21ST, JUNE 30TH, JULY 3RD, JULY 12TH, JULY 21ST)

You are endlessly fascinated with cultures; the one you were born and raised in, the one you live in now, as well as other cultures globally. You love foreign travel and are an avid collector of mementos representing your memories abroad.

The human condition is a subject you are passionate about learning and understanding. When you combine this with your natural shrewdness, you are very skilled at assessing the motivations of others. You believe that what makes a person "offbeat" is much more interesting than what is "normal" and are very interested in people who are outside of society's boundaries in one way or the other.

Generous and sympathetic, you are not afraid to go deep within to meaningfully comfort others in difficult situations, even though you may be slow to let others see your deeper emotions and comfort you. Home and family is very important to you as is having fun, so you love to entertain others at home and are likely a very popular host or hostess. Family values are something that you instill in your children from a young age.

In terms of career, you would do well in sports, visual and performing arts, sciences, history, tourism, yoga, education, astronomy, philosophy, psychology, nursing, massage therapy, the skilled trades, creative writing, and law.

You love to talk to people and find out their unique life stories, so coaching, counselling, and advising suit you.

You may enjoy working in the family business or going into business with family members. There may also be an ancestral gift running down the family line that you are meant to partake in, whether for a career or hobby.

In romance, you appreciate someone who is open-minded and willing to embark upon adventures with you. At the same time, you are fully committed to family life, and you need your partner to be a devoted spouse and parent who can create a sense of stability at home. Although you are ever-ready to comfort those you love in times of need, you must let your partner in on your true feelings, and lean on their shoulder once in a while.

Celebrities

Prince William, British Royalty (June 21st)

Michael Phelps, swimmer and Olympic gold medallist. With a total of 22 gold medals, he has set a record for most gold medal wins in history. (June 30th)

Tom Cruise, multi-award winning actor and filmmaker (July 3rd)

Henry David Thoreau, author and philosopher, cultural icon (July 12th)

Ernest Hemingway, author and journalist. He was the recipient of the Nobel Prize in Literature in 1954 (July 21st)

CANCER NUMBER 4 (JUNE 22ND, JULY 4TH, JULY 13TH, JULY 22ND)

A sensitive, deep thinker, you are known in your circles as original, and perhaps a bit unusual. Your thoughts and ideas are ahead of the time, so not everyone understands where you are coming from. Yet, you are practical, and willing to fulfill all mundane responsibilities that come your way.

You are very dutiful towards your parents and the elderly in general, admiring them for their wisdom and any sacrifices made. You never forget your roots and you are proud of your cultural background as well as your country of residence. Your interest in the workings and problems of the nation you live in is strong.

If you were born June 22nd or July 22nd you receive the benefits of master number 22. You can see the extraordinary in the ordinary. Passionate, emotional, and idealistic, you give 110% effort to everything that captures your interest, nothing halfway for you. Your imagination and intuition is very strong, which makes for a highly developed interior life. However, there may be sudden, unexpected ups and downs in your external life circumstances, and one of your greatest challenges is towards equanimity. One of your particular concerns may be participating in social justice or humanitarian causes, as you feel very sharply the plight of those less fortunate than yourself. With your practicality and vision, you can come up with unique ways to get them the help they need.

In your career, you do particularly well in politics, law, history, drama, social science, interviewing, fashion design, literature, humanitarian work, computer science, social work, media, administration, childcare, teaching, public relations, photography, and technology.

Whatever your career, you have a knack for seizing opportunities to advance you further on your desired goal. Your success may be due to taking risks at the right time that other people are perhaps too afraid to take. This is not to say that they all turn out well, but even in the event they don't, your ability to learn from your errors is very good.

In romance, you are one of the most faithful and loyal partners there is. Once someone captures your heart, they know you will stick it out through thick and thin. You need someone who reciprocates this devotion to you with all their heart and soul. Although you are prone to quickly changing emotions, you must make an effort to get your partner to understand the reasons behind them for long-term relationships to run smoothly. Your family admires your creativity, ambition, and work ethic.

Celebrities

Meryl Streep, multi-award winning actress. She holds the record for Academy Award nominations among both actors and actresses. Meryl was the recipient of the Presidential Medal of Freedom in 2014 (June 22nd)

Calvin Coolidge, 30th United States President (July 4th)

Wole Soyinka, playwright and poet. He was the first African to receive the Nobel Prize in Literature in 1986 (July 13th)

Oscar de la Renta, multi-award winning fashion designer. He was awarded the Gold Medal of Bellas Artes and the La Gran Cruz de la Orden del Mérito Civil in 2000 (July 22nd)

CANCER NUMBER 5 (JUNE 23RD, JULY 5TH, JULY 14TH)

With the Moon and Mercury influencing you, your life is characterized by changeability and love of adventure. You have a profound understanding that nothing is permanent, and this too shall pass. This philosophy helps you in difficult circumstances as you realize that better times are ahead. You are either mentally or physically on the move, always wanting to explore life to the fullest by trying out several different things. While this adaptability serves you well when the situation calls for it, it can cause uncertainty in those around you as to what you plan to do. Since this type of sampling is a natural tendency, you don't have to feel guilty about it, but perhaps give a brief explanation to put your loved ones at ease.

In your career, you require diversity and excitement as routines can quickly cause you to feel unfulfilled. Interaction with people is preferred because you do your best in people-oriented careers, and particularly those with a nurturing component.

You definitely have a way with words and know how to choose them to have the right emotional impact, this skill can be used in many ways: lecturing, public relations, public speaking, broadcasting, writing, editing, telecommunications, and sales for example.

The fields of tourism, hospitality, media, literature, education, science, math, nursing, rehabilitation, music, customer service, administration, medicine, healing arts, spirituality, and philosophy may hold special appeal.

In romance, you are a charming conversationalist, always with engaging stories to tell. You are a natural flirt, and enjoy the process of meeting new people. However, when it comes time to settling down, you place high value on intimate connection with your partner. You must have someone who understands your tendency for change in all areas of your life. Someone who expects you to stick with one thing will only make you unhappy. At the same time, you benefit from someone who encourages diversity, but also helps you focus on things more in-depth.

Celebrities

Alfred Kinsey, biologist, sexologist, and author (June 23rd)

Hazrath Inayat Khan, Sufi poet, teacher, and Indian classical musician (July 5th)

Pema Chödrön, Buddhist nun, teacher, and best-selling author (July 14th)

CANCER NUMBER 6 (JUNE 24TH, JULY 6TH, JULY 15TH)

Your warm, compassionate, magnetic, and gentle ways are what people find most attractive about you. Always willing to lend a sympathetic ear, people seek you out for heartfelt advice. Your family and home life is of utmost importance to you and there is no end to the sacrifices you will make for your family's happiness. Your home is a major source of pride and you love to decorate it with charming antiques. You may even have a large assortment of keepsake items, because you are sentimental you equate throwing them out with throwing out the memory. Entertaining others is natural for you and people really look forward to these occasions. This is because you are the perfect host/ hostess, always anticipating needs before they are said.

In your career you can use your desire to be of service to others in a wide variety of ways, it is important to you to feel you are helping people in some way. You may decide to use the entrepreneurial skill of the 6 to start a small business centered on a Cancerian domain such as food, home, imagination, education, children, families, story-telling, or hospitality. You are successful because you add a personal touch and instinctively know what your customers desire.

You are nostalgic and may decide to do something allowing you to help others preserve their cherished memories, such as photography, making videos, or painting.

Gentle and contemplative, you may offer spiritual guidance in counselling people. You may have a fondness for the news and historical archives since they document important stories for a point in time so that they can be looked back on later.

In romance, you are a true romantic! You are attracted to nurturing personalities who give you a sense of security and comfort. Your partner will appreciate your thoughtfulness and sensitivity. Well into your marriage, you seek to keep the romance alive, so you need to find someone who will equally match your efforts. Your family loves your imagination, and talent for storytelling; creating home videos, scrap books, and letters is a wonderful way to spend time together.

Celebrities

Roy O. Disney, co-founder of the Walt Disney Company (June 24th)

Tenzin Gyatso, 14th Dalai Lama, and best-selling author.
He was the recipient of the Nobel Peace Prize in 1989
(July 6th)

Arianna Huffington, co-founder and editor-in-chief of The
Huffington Post and best-selling author (July 15th)

CANCER NUMBER 7 (JUNE 25TH, JULY 7TH, JULY 16TH)

Artistic, imaginative and fanciful, your inner world is rich with
vision. Your intuition is so strong that you feel what other people
feel without them saying a word. You have an abundance of
empathy and seek to be of assistance whenever you can, often
siding with the underdog.

You are a very talented writer and your ability to capture
profundity of emotion is second to none; people are completely
immersed in your narrative. Perhaps this is because you pour out
so much of your soul into your creative pursuits. If you choose
to express your artistic side through another avenue, such as
drawing, poetry, painting, dancing, acting, or music, the result is
the same, in that the work provokes a deep and a wide range of
emotions from people.

The subconscious mind holds a particular interest of yours as
you seek to uncover its workings in yourself and those around
you.

Careers which allow you to express your artistic gifts are
preferred. Even if you work in a more technical field, you still
should express your creative side through hobbies for your
fulfillment. Your depth of emotional understanding, and interest
in the subconscious mind could be beneficial in transformational
healing or energy work. When you speak, your intention and
message is quite effectively communicated to your audience.

You may find that social justice, humanitarian work, nursing, education, literature, writing, publishing, or science are good fits for you.

In romance, you are passionate, caring, and affectionate. Your partner appreciates the honesty through which you share your thoughts and feelings, even if you don't always use many words to express yourself. You need a lover who matches your depth and range of emotion, and is able to support your dreams. Your family loves your enthusiasm, drive, and originality. You are able to help them sort out their ideas, and express themselves with clarity and effectiveness.

Celebrities

George Orwell, novelist, essayist, journalist and critic. He was ranked second on a list of "The 50 greatest British writers since 1945" by The Times in 2008 (June 25th)

Ringo Starr, songwriter and drummer for the Beatles. He was one of only 21 people to have been inducted into the Rock and Roll Hall of Fame twice (July 7th)

Ginger Rogers, multi-award winning actress, dancer, and singer. She was the recipient of the Women's International Center's Living Legacy Awards in 1995 (July 16th)

CANCER NUMBER 8 (JUNE 26TH, JULY 8TH, JULY 17TH)

Combining your Cancerian intuition for what appeals to the public with number 8's skill for business and acquiring power, you have the potential to create an original empire! Your business skills are sharp and shrewd, and you are not easily fooled or intimidated by anyone. Hardworking and disciplined, you have the skill to run large organizations.

Your desire for perfection is very strong as you believe if you are going to do something, you might as well do it right. Do keep in mind though that most people do not have this same desire, and those around you may get tired trying to live up to your standards. But people admire your stamina, endurance, and drive.

In your career, you have excellent business sense and ambition, which can be applied to virtually any field. You set a goal and work tirelessly to achieve it. Because of this, you may find yourself in a powerful position with material rewards. Regardless of your specific job, you need a good deal of independence and autonomy, otherwise feelings of dissatisfaction may surface.

Careers that may hold special appeal include music, drama, hospitality, foreign relations, law, politics, psychology, labour relations, the occult, religion, culinary arts, home remodeling, dentistry, medicine, massage therapy, graphic design, technology, accounting, real estate, customer service, finance, and computer science.

In romance, you tend to show your love in practical ways. You want to give your family the very best opportunities, and see to it that they are well taken care of. In doing this, you may work very long hours and your family may long to spend more quality time with you. Be sure to give them the precious gift of your time. While you may be able to do things your own way at work, with personal relationships, you must work on the art of compromise. Your family appreciates your ambition, detail orientation, and persistence.

Celebrities

Ariana Grande, multi-award winning singer and actress (June 26th)

John D. Rockefeller, business magnate and philanthropist, richest person in United States history (July 8th)

Angela Merkel, first female Chancellor of Germany and physical chemist. She was named most powerful woman in the world for the seventh time by Forbes in 2015 (July 17th)

CANCER NUMBER 9 (JUNE 27TH, JULY 9TH, JULY 18TH)

You are one of those people who seemingly never ages, as you remain young at heart! You have a talent for working with young people because you remember so well what it was like to be their age. Consequently, you can understand them in a way that perhaps no other adult really can.

Early in life, you may have had more than your fair share of disappointments. Later in life, these tests become your testimony, and you help people overcome the same troubles that you did. Because of this, with your own children, you encourage them to stand up for what they believe in, and to do their best to help those who have been a victim of injustice. One thing that really bothers you is inequality. You are very sensitive to the needs of those through no fault of their own have been given a tough hand in life, and you do your best to help wherever you can in this regard. If you are a member of a disadvantaged or marginalized group, you could be a spokesperson in raising awareness. You believe that everyone should be given a fair chance, and you try to come to your own conclusions about people regardless of what everyone else says or thinks of them.

In terms of career, one of your skills is your tenacity, especially when it comes to defending those whose rights have been violated. You also like solving mysteries and uncovering the truth. For this reason law, politics, social work, psychology, forensics, and research are good choices.

You may be inclined to use your skill for working with children in a number of roles including teaching, counselling, or other business centered on children.

Other areas of interest may include drama, literature, languages, photography, writing, firefighting, corrections, painting, rehabilitation, and healthcare.

Regardless of your specific field, your determination and strength of will is admirable and will help you go where you desire to be.

In romance, you are very loyal, and once you have a family, you will do anything to protect them. Although you will go to great lengths to defend others, others may not see your need for protection, because you have such a strong exterior. Being vulnerable with your partner will greatly increase intimacy. You are able to inspire your family by showing great reserves of endurance and strength of will.

Celebrities

Helen Keller, political activist, lecturer, and author. She was the first deafblind person to earn a Bachelor of Arts degree (June 27th)

Tom Hanks, multi-award winning actor and filmmaker, one of the highest-grossing actors in film history (July 9th)

Nelson Mandela, former President of South Africa, multi-award winning anti-apartheid revolutionary, politician, philanthropist, and best-selling author. He was the recipient of the Nobel Peace Prize in 1993, and received the United States Presidential Medal of Freedom in 2002 (July 18th)

Chapter 11

Leo Numbers 1-9

Leo Number 1 (July 28th, Aug 1st, Aug 10th, Aug 19th)

This is the most harmonious combination for Leo, as its ruler Sun corresponds with number 1. You are an original, inventive, and independent thinker who is very comfortable in the spotlight. Self-confidence in your abilities is high, and you expect good things to happen to you. Naturally dominant, positions of authority and leadership come naturally to you as you shine the brightest when in charge.

In whichever activities you pursue, you have a deep-seated need for self-expression. You like to show the world what you can do, not so much for monetary gain, as for the satisfaction of being honored. However, you must watch for a tendency to become dependent on other people's attention and approval. Since you are ambitious and determined to get ahead, and you stay optimistic about the future, success usually comes to you sooner rather than later.

In terms of career, you have a need for roles that give you authority, autonomy and freedom of expression. Having any type of audience is ideal. Because you are dominant, you are not satisfied with behind the scenes positions, or positions in which you have to frequently answer to others. Careers in which you receive plenty of recognition for your talent and a chance to move up the ladder to positions of leadership are best.

You do well in careers that allow for creative expression such as drama, entertainment, management, music, designing, fashion, writing, publishing, poetry, philosophy, healing arts, or teaching.

Owning your own business comes most naturally, as you are inventive, enterprising, and well able to convince others why your product or service is the best.

You may also thrive in careers having an element of healthy competition, such as sports, the military, politics, law, martial arts, dancing, debate, or business management.

In romance, lovers are attracted to your warmth, charisma, and generosity. You are attracted to people who are creative, adventurous, and original. Your family admires your no guts, no glory philosophy, and ability to take risks that propel you further ahead in life. One area for you to consider is your lack of desire to make compromises. Your children need to be told reasons for why they cannot do certain things, or why they are being punished. Being more egalitarian greatly improves the flow of trust between you.

Celebrities

Terry Fox, athlete, humanitarian, cancer research activist, and youngest person to have been named a Companion of the Order of Canada. He was winner of the Lou Marsh Award as Canada's top sportsman in 1980 (July 28th)

Yves St Laurent, celebrated fashion designer, awarded the rank of Grand Officier de la Légion d'honneur in 2007 (Aug 1st)

Jimmy Dean, best-selling and Grammy award-winning country music singer, television host, actor, and businessman (Aug 10th)

Orville Wright, inventor, and aviation pioneer. He built the world's first successful airplane, and is credited with the first successful human flight (Aug 19th)

Leo Number 2 (July 29th, Aug 2nd, Aug 11th, Aug 20th)

You are a great leader because of your knack for putting people in positions where their skills are best able to be utilized. Because of this, they perform better, and collective goals tend to be accomplished more efficiently. Even in your personal life, you have an innate understanding of those around you, and are able to promote greater self-awareness in others through discussion.

Loyalty is one of your most cherished features, once you give someone your friendship, they know they can count on you in the good times and the bad. You have a strong desire for self-reflection which also extends to reflection on current events and the world we live in. You may benefit from writing these experiences in a book, or sharing them via some form of broadcast.

If you were born on August 11th, you receive the benefits of this master number. Spiritually inclined, you may participate in activities that provide greater connection to God and that help elevate the consciousness of humanity. Leadership positions within an organization devoted to spirituality and consciousness raising are well-suited to you. Your ability for self-analysis is very high as you constantly go within to find the root of your motivations, drives and behaviour. Because of this, your ability to progress on the spiritual path is immeasurably helped. You not only seek to find the truth about yourself, but in all areas of life, you promote transparency. You like to bring dark or distressing subjects to the open, so they can be transformed for the good of all.

As a Leo 2 person, your skills of negotiation, tact, and social understanding can be put to good use in any area requiring compromise: foreign relations, unions, tribunals, arbitration, or mediation. You are able to see both sides of the coin and enhance interpersonal understanding. You are a skilled commentator of current events on a global level, and can illuminate new perspectives.

Drama, entertainment, journalism, broadcasting, entrepreneurial pursuits (especially in hospitality, tourism and luxury goods/services), counselling, business, sports, technology, humanitarian work, social justice, politics and law may capture your interest.

In romance, you are cheerful, and like to show your love for your partner in demonstrative ways; you may also expect them to do the same for you. Lovers appreciate your intelligence, curiosity, and well-developed communication skills. You crave a deep level of intimacy, and will put a lot of effort into making your relationships work well. Your family values your warmth, generosity, and fairness. You encourage them to cultivate a sense of discovery, always seeking to learn more about themselves and the world around them.

Celebrities

Peter Jennings, multi-award winning journalist and sole anchor of ABC's World News Tonight from 1983 to 2005. He was inducted into the Order of Canada in 2005 (July 29th)

James Baldwin, multi-award winning author, activist, playwright, poet, and social critic (Aug 2nd)

Viola Davis, multi-award winning actress and first African-American actress to win outstanding lead actress in a drama series at the Emmy awards. She was listed by Time as one of the 100 Most Influential People in the World in 2012 (Aug 11th)

**Connie Chung, multi-award winning journalist, news
reporter and anchor. First Asian, and the second woman to
anchor a major U.S. network newscast (Aug 20th)**

LEO NUMBER 3 (JULY 30TH, AUG 3RD, AUG 12TH, AUG 21ST)

Creativity and charisma are your greatest strengths. Blessed with
an endless imagination and skill for performance, you love being
in front of an adoring audience. Although popular, you enjoy
doing your creative pieces solo. Regardless of your background,
there is an unmistakable regality about you that is greatly admired.

You are also very strong-willed and the fastest way for someone
to get you to do something is probably to tell you why you
couldn't do it! It is hard to keep you down for long because
at your core you are very optimistic and enthusiastic, always
knowing that the rainbow is going to burst through that cloud of
sorrow, and that something better is just around the corner. You
enjoy uplifting people in times of need.

In terms of career, you have a need for authority and prestige.
Background roles are not suited to your personality. It is usually
not about the wealth or power so much as the desire to be
prominent in one way or the other. This is not confined to the
performing arts; any role in which there is some type of audience
(students are an audience for teachers for example) makes you
happy.

Whatever field you enter has to allow you a certain degree
of limelight because you need your voice to be heard and your
talents to be publicly displayed (although people born on August
12th can sometimes have a conflict within themselves that
vacillates between accepting center stage and wanting to fit in
to the crowd.) Regardless of social status, your impression of
dignity helps you gain favour with people in power.

In romance, you are a take charge person who is not afraid to boldly go after the man or woman of your dreams. You especially like the fun and flirtation of dating. But there may be a tendency to be overly dependent on flattery, especially when younger. Engaging in creative activities as a family brings many wonderful memories. Your children appreciate that you encourage them to stay true to their passion.

Celebrities

Arnold Schwarzenegger, 38th Governor of California, actor, director, model, producer, author, businessman, investor, philanthropist, and bodybuilder. He was a former Mr. Universe, and seven time Mr. Olympia contest winner (July 30th)

Martha Stewart, businesswoman, best-selling author, and multi-award winning television personality. Founder of Martha Stewart Living Omni media (Aug 3rd)

Pete Sampras, tennis player, holds the ATP record of six year-end No. 1 rankings, former ITF world No. 1 champion (6x) (Aug 12th)

Wilt Chamberlain, basketball player, businessman and author. He holds numerous NBA records in scoring, rebounding and durability categories (Aug 21st)

LEO NUMBER 4 (JULY 31ST, AUG 4TH, AUG 13TH, AUG 22ND)

Whatever your start in life, you may find yourself put in higher levels of authority as you grow up. A major part of this is due to your work ethic and determination.

You also have considerable artistic talent and vivid imagination which can be expressed in many ways. You can be a little flamboyant and at the very least have an unconventional approach to life that other people find intriguing, although they may not totally understand you. You want to challenge people who accept everything as it is because someone else said so, or are resistant to change because they conclude that is the way it has always been.

You are fascinated with the human condition, and may be inclined to reflect on the good versus evil parts frequently. Morality and ethics may be of special interest.

Throughout life, there may be very sudden and unexpected shifts in direction which change the course of your destiny or you may find your status dramatically changed overnight.

If you were born August 22nd the tendency towards sudden and unexpected shifts in direction throughout life is amplified. Your mind is original and brilliant, but people may not always understand your message. Regardless of how conventional you may appear, you are a free spirit, always very independent in thought and action. Warm and generous, the sight of suffering and inequality shakes you to the core, and you do your best to help in whatever capacity you can. You may use your speaking or performing talent to draw attention to causes that capture your heart.

In terms of career, positions of authority gravitate towards you, as your motivation to succeed propels you to the top. You may have more than your fair share of trials and obstacles in the first part of life, especially in regards to trouble with authority. Fortunately, with your resilience and endurance, these only make you more prepared for success as you get older.

You crave autonomy and have a lot of resistance to following orders, thus it is ideal to be self-employed. There is a noted interest in justice, equality and different cultures. This may manifest as a career in politics, humanitarian concerns, international human rights, law, or social justice, as you seek to protect people from systemic discrimination.

You may choose to express your artistic side through writing, poetry, song, filmmaking, dance, drama, painting, and culinary arts.

Your strong communication skills can be used in entertainment, broadcasting, speech pathology, interviewing, and publishing.

In romance, you are passionate and loyal, but crave your freedom. You need plenty of time to pursue independent interests. If you are granted this space, you are more likely to have a successful relationship. You are attracted to intellectual and socially aware partners who understand the importance of being a global citizen. Even though you may be devoted to your career, your children appreciate that you always make quality time for them.

Celebrities

JK Rowling, best-selling and multi-award winning novelist (Harry Potter series) (July 31st)

Barack Obama, Harvard educated lawyer and first African-American President of the United States. Recipient of the Nobel Peace Prize in 2009 (Aug 4th)

Alfred Hitchcock, multi-award winning film director and producer. He was appointed a Knight Commander of the Most Excellent Order of the British Empire by Queen Elizabeth II in 1980 (Aug 13th)

Giada De Laurentiis, chef, writer, entrepreneur, Emmy Award winning television personality, and host of the current Food Network television program Giada at Home. She was inducted into the Culinary Hall of Fame in 2012 (Aug 22nd)

Leo Number 5 (July 23rd, Aug 5th, Aug 14th)

Your desire for change, variety, and adventure is likely to take you to places around the world, as you greatly enjoy learning about different people and cultures. You have a flair for dramatic communication, which is especially useful in the performing arts, motivational speaking, and sales.

Blessed with an ability to touch people's emotions and inspire them on a heart level, your work resonates widely. This is partly because you are willing and able to expose the elephant in the room, to say and do what needs to be done in order for people to really make the inner shift towards positive change.

Your own emotions are very powerful but sometimes you can intellectualize them. This can be detrimental to you as emotions become repressed and unconscious, setting the stage for outbursts later. You must feel what you feel without thinking too much. When you do this, you find yourself calmer and more at peace.

In your career, variety is the spice of life, you hate feeling tied down to roles and places. You may be attracted to positions involving a foreign component. Your depth of emotion, interest in listening to people's stories, and talent for getting them to take a deeper look at themselves, can be used in psychology, psychiatry, the healing arts, coaching, counselling, or therapy.

You may be attracted to sales, public speaking, literature, theater, media, entertainment, yoga, journalism, advertising, business, fitness, massage therapy, nutrition and working with children/adolescents.

In romance, you have a wonderful sense of humour, and enjoy having stimulating discussions. You are attracted to people who live life from the heart. With your flair for drama, you have to ensure that your emotions are not running wild in arguments, as your partner may not easily forget your stinging words in the heat of the moment. If you have a partner who can handle your considerable emotional intensity and need for spontaneity, you can have a successful relationship. Your family appreciates your ability to give them your full attention, and to be really present for them.

Celebrities

Max Heindel, astrologer, occultist, author, and founder of the Rosicrucian Fellowship of the U.S. (July 23rd)

Kajol, multi-award winning Bollywood actress, social activist, recipient of the Padma Shri, the fourth highest civilian award of India, and the Karmaveer Puraskaar for her work with widows and children (Aug 5th)

Halle Berry, multi-award winning actress, Revlon spokesmodel, former fashion model, and 1st runner-up in the 35th Miss USA Pageant (Aug 14th)

LEO NUMBER 6 (JULY 24TH, AUG 6TH, AUG 15TH)

Romantic, sensual, and affectionate, life is nothing without love. You are magnetic, and once in love, you commit with all your heart and soul. You radiate warmth and generosity to your family and friends, and they greatly enjoy spending time with you. Your family is very important to you and you protect them at all costs, spending time with them is one of your greatest pleasures in life. Always young at heart, children are attracted to you and you to them.

You also like to keep busy well after retirement, because there are always places to go, people to see and new things to discover! In this way you keep your inner glow all throughout your life. Bored relatively easy with mundane routines, you are on the search for extraordinary moments that take your breath away. This proclivity could lead you on pathways never before explored.

In terms of career, you have many talents to choose from. You may express your nurturing side through a role that allows you to take care of others in some way (food, hospitality, children, seniors, assisted living, rehabilitation, medical, and nursing). You may also be interested in the relationship industry (couples counselling, matchmaking, and enhancing intimacy).

There is a definite eye for beauty which can be put to use in personal grooming or any industry concerning appearance, arts, or interior decoration.

There is considerable creative talent which can be expressed in many ways. You enjoy a certain degree of public recognition for your work, and perform better when you receive attention.

Naturally suited for leadership positions, you find yourself in positions of authority or you could have your own business. However you must take care to be more democratic in listening to other people's ideas. Your ability to take significant risks that others wouldn't is often effective in catapulting you to the next level.

In romance, your charisma and enthusiasm attracts many admirers. You may have multiple relationships throughout life. However, once you are in a partnership, you are 100% committed. There may be a tendency at times to break relationships rather suddenly, and your partner may be quite surprised at your change of heart. If you find that a relationship is no longer working, you must have an honest discussion so that future problems are somewhat alleviated. Your family loves your affectionate, warm, and beautiful glow when you are around them.

Celebrities

Jennifer Lopez, multi-award winning actress, singer, dancer, producer, author and fashion designer. Presented with the prestigious landmark 2,500th star on the Hollywood Walk of Fame in 2013 (July 24th)

Andy Warhol, artist, leading figure in the visual art movement known as pop art, and cultural icon (Aug 6th)

Julia Child, multi-award winning chef, author, and television personality (Aug 15th)

LEO NUMBER 7 (JULY 25TH, AUG 7TH, AUG 16TH)

Idealistic and ambitious, you go after your dreams with everything you've got! Regardless of what it looks like at the moment, if you know you are capable of something, you won't stop until you've given it your best. Even if you don't win, you learn something through the experience and use that lesson in your future ventures.

You may have an interest in philosophy, mysticism, spirituality or other esoteric topics; these are good avenues to follow in your quest for unlocking life's mysteries and secrets. Your interest in faraway places could lead to extensive travel, where you have an experience that transforms your life in some way.

In terms of career, you are a skilled detective, effective at getting to the truth of the matter, and uncovering secrets, puzzles, and mysteries. You may use this in forensic work, the legal system, or in research among others. Naturally provocative, you may be the one to reveal the secrets/scandals behind your company or behind a social issue that the public has a right to know.

With your colorful inner world, you may enjoy writing, especially fiction and fantasy. In the performing arts, you are capable of playing roles that are night and day from your personality and/or physical appearance. Like all Leos, you need a certain degree of attention and recognition but the 7 reveals a side to you that needs extended periods of solitude to reflect on your life.

In romance, you are intuitive in finding out your partner's wishes, and are thoughtful and considerate. You need a lover who can complement your high energy with a sense of stability. You'll find increased intimacy when you let him or her disagree with you without feeling the need to convince them you are right. Talking to your family about your dreams and goals on a regular basis enhances understanding and support. Your children appreciate your forward thinking and open-mind when listening to issues of importance to them.

Celebrities

Walter Payton, football player, nine-time Pro Bowl selectee, elected into the Pro Football Hall of Fame in 1993 (July 25th)

Charlize Theron, multi-award winning actress, producer and fashion model (Aug 7th)

Madonna, multi-award winning singer, songwriter, record producer, dancer, actress, and businesswoman. Recognized as the best-selling female recording artist of all time by Guinness World Records (Aug 16th)

LEO NUMBER 8 (JULY 26TH, AUG 8TH, AUG 17TH)

Authoritative and commanding, you take the lead in many of the social circles that you are in. People listen to what you say because of your considerable knowledge, skill, and commitment to truth. Although at the same time, you could benefit from being more diplomatic.

Enterprising and ambitious, you are capable of pouring immense amounts of work and discipline into a role or project. Once you have decided on a course of action, you will finish it to the very best of your ability. When your goal is satisfied to your liking, you move on and do it all over again.

In your career, your ability to debate is pronounced, as you have both the knowledge and communication skills to effectively promote your position. You are good at pointing out current ways of thinking or social issues that are in need of change, and promoting new and efficient ways of looking at old problems.

You have a desire for power and a comfortable lifestyle, and you can have success with your entrepreneurial pursuits. Even if you lose the first couple of times, ultimately one of your businesses is likely to be highly successful if you persevere.

You may be attracted to the business management, legal, health, fitness, wellness, medical, math, engineering, accounting, real estate, skilled trades, finance, or science fields.

In relationships, you are attracted to goal-oriented people who know what they want, and go after it. Lovers are attracted to your intelligence and determination. Your family benefits from your desire to give them the best the world can offer, but you have to create a good work-life balance to spend quality time with them as well. You need to watch out for a tendency to be too dominant with your family, if you take a more easygoing approach, things are likely to run more smoothly.

Celebrities

Carl Jung, psychiatrist and psychotherapist, founder of analytical psychology (July 26th)

Roger Federer, Olympic gold medal winning tennis player. He was named the Laureus World Sportsman of the Year for a record of four consecutive years (Aug 8th)

Robert De Niro, multi-award winning actor and producer. Recipient of the American Film Institute Life Achievement Award in 2003 (Aug 17th)

LEO NUMBER 9 (JULY 27TH, AUG 9TH AUG 18TH)

Highly energetic, your zest for life is inspiring to those around you! You have a global perspective, and are interested in helping create fair outcomes for those less fortunate or disabled in some way. Sympathetic, you are committed to giving people a hand up, not a hand out; helping them preserve their dignity even at their lowest points.

Your simplicity allows you to connect with young people, and really understand where they are coming from. You often act as a mentor, giving advice freely and assisting in making major life decisions. At the same time, you tend to give advice to adults when it is not necessarily requested or appreciated. Being more mindful of this inclination can help you differentiate the circumstances in which people may be the most receptive to advice.

You are drawn to adventure, and new experiences, always having that spirit of exploration which may lead you down some unusual paths.

In your career, you are drawn to the process of learning, perhaps you may work at an institute of education. With your interest in children and in human behaviour you may be interested in child psychology, like the famous developmental psychologist Jean Piaget (b. Aug 9th).

Giving advice and guiding others is a strength that can be used in some type of counseling, therapy or mentorship.

Like all Leos, you have a preference to be in a leadership role or at least one with a great deal of autonomy. While other people of your sign can be too autocratic, you understand the position of the everyday man and woman, and keep their concerns in mind when making decisions.

You have lots of physical vitality and strength so you may be attracted to a physically based profession or one that focuses on bodily movement like sports, rehabilitation, kinesiology, or dancing. Whatever field you are in, you desire recognition for your best performance to shine through.

In romance, you are attracted to partners who feel deeply, and are compassionate towards others. You enjoy spending time with your family, and in turn they always feel that you are there to give them sound guidance. The only area to watch for is to not take it personally if they don't take your advice. There are times when they have to go their own way. You encourage honesty from your children, and because you accept them for who they are, they feel comfortable sharing important matters with you.

Celebrities

Martin Ennals, human rights activist, Secretary-General of Amnesty International, helped to found the British human rights organisation ARTICLE 19 and International Alert (July 27th)

Dr. Jean Piaget, developmental psychologist, philosopher, and author (Aug 9th)

Robert Redford, multi-award winning actor, film director, producer, businessman, environmentalist, philanthropist, and a founder of the Sundance Film Festival (Aug 18th)

Chapter 12

Virgo Numbers 1-9

Virgo Number 1 (Aug 28th, Sept 1st, Sept 10th, Sept 19th)

You may be more desiring of power, recognition and status than the typical Virgo. At the same time, there are some who still prefer a behind the scenes, lower key approach. Regardless of whether you are more ambitious or easygoing, you are concerned with your public image. You are interested in carefully grooming yourself and ensuring that anything or anyone associated with you presents their best appearance. The combination of logic and analysis with creativity makes you quite an unusual thinker; one who is gifted with the ability to devise inventive solutions to problems.

You are a skilled communicator but are more likely to use a straightforward approach than an eloquent one. You believe in telling the truth in a no frills kind of manner, this way you keep it real, and people admire that about you. Highly practical and sometimes conservative, you don't tend to waste your time on pie in the sky ideas, rather you want a concrete plan of action.

In your career, you can excel at professions requiring scientific, mathematical, statistical or factual analysis due to your strong intellect. You may also choose to use your organizational ability, practicality, and eye for detail in business management or administration.

Editing, writing, nursing, rehabilitation, assisted living, comedy, psychology, audiology, and medicine might be areas of interest.

If you are more creative, the arts that allow you to work with your hands and/or display your skill publicly are particularly suited to you. Music, fashion, and drama may also capture your attention.

You thrive against adversity and enjoy challenging yourself everyday, however if you are facing too many losses or making too many compromises, you must learn to recognize when to change course.

In romance, lovers are attracted to your ambition, creativity, and loyalty. You cherish the qualities of authenticity and sincerity; these are probably some of your most desired characteristics in a partner. You are generally honest, but if your partner is not straightforward with you, there will be issues that are harder to work out. Your family benefits from your desire to encourage their ideas, but at the same time give truthful, constructive feedback.

Celebrities

Shania Twain, multi-award winning singer and songwriter, best-selling female artist in the history of country music (Aug 28th)

Dr. Phil McGraw, psychologist, #1 NYT best-selling author, and multi-award winning TV show host (Sept 1st)

Karl Lagerfeld, multi-award winning fashion designer, artist, and photographer. Head designer and creative director of Chanel and Fendi (Sept 10th)

Jimmy Fallon, multi-award winning comedian, television host, actor, musician, writer, and producer (Sept 19th)

VIRGO NUMBER 2 (AUG 29TH, SEPT 2ND, SEPT 11TH, SEPT 20TH)

You are blessed with an unusual combination of practicality and logically oriented intellect, with wonderful intuition and imagination. This combination allows you to make the most out of any situation that comes your way.

You are careful with what you say, and you think of your impact on other people when you do things. People appreciate your thoughtfulness and consideration. Although some people of this combination like a central role in work or other circles, many enjoy working behind the scenes or working within teams. Even if you are in a public role, it is probably not because you sought it out, but rather was a natural consequence of your particular skill. You are content to help other people achieve their dreams without requiring public credit for it. Whichever side of an argument you are on, you are able to see the other person's perspective and listen. Other people feel that they felt heard, even if you don't ultimately agree with them.

If you were born on September 11th, you receive the benefit of this master number. Idealistic and enthusiastic, you have a strong desire to make this world a better place than it was before you were here. You desire that your life be impactful and consciousness raising. With your mental brilliance and excellent communication skills, you shine in whatever role you set your heart on. Writing is a strong gift of yours, you are able to explain complex concepts in a plain way that everyone can understand. By helping people find their inner greatness, your own greatness shines through.

In terms of your career, you are able to succeed in a wide variety of fields: international business, engineering, math, science, technology, literature, dance, social work, medicine, politics, book/film/music critic, publishing, the skilled trades, speech pathology, and the fine arts for example.

You are a quick learner and easily adapt to changing roles or circumstances. Because you are conscientious and will make sure you get the job done right, you become a valued addition to any workplace.

Although your natural inclination would be to give critical appraisal of performance and projects, you are diplomatic and are especially fond of the sandwich approach; putting your criticism in between two compliments. In this way, people appreciate your feedback and seek to improve where they can.

If you are inclined to start a business, it will benefit from your attention to detail, ability to critically analyze situations, and your sensitivity to the public's needs and desires. With these talents, you can cater to a specific niche that has not been filled yet.

In relationships, your ability to listen and sympathize goes a long way in honest, meaningful conversation. You are attracted to people who let their actions speak louder than their words, as you pay more attention to what people do more than what they say. Lovers are attracted to your ability to push past personal boundaries, and set the bar higher and higher for yourself. Your children appreciate your approachability and sensitivity to their needs.

Celebrities

Michael Jackson, King of Pop, best-selling and multi-award winning singer, songwriter, record producer, dancer, and actor (Aug 29th)

Salma Hayek, multi-award winning film actress, director, and producer. She was awarded the Chevalier of Ordre national de la Légion d'honneur in 2012 (Sept 2nd)

D. H Lawrence, novelist, poet, playwright, essayist, literary critic, and painter (Sept 11th)

Upton Sinclair, author, and Pulitzer Prize for Fiction winner in 1943 (Sept 20th)

Virgo Number 3 (Aug 30th, Sept 3rd, Sept 12th, Sept 21st)

Optimistic but at the same time analytical and realistic, you instinctively approach life with a knack for taking the right risks. Since you like to have fun and joke around, people may not always see your tough determination that helps you achieve success. You are great at pushing people to be their best; because you have high expectations for others, people rise to meet them.

A quality that stands out about you is your love for learning; not necessarily academics, which you may do well in, but also a curiosity to learn more about the world and different types of people.

Wellness and nutrition may be a special interest. You always like to keep yourself looking your best. Because you are more prone to high levels of stress, regular periods of solitude are helpful to relax and contemplate.

In terms of career, with your interest in the physical body and science, the medical, rehabilitation, and nursing fields may be a good fit. You may also like health studies and kinesiology.

Your interest in law and justice may lead you to a career in the legal field. Business, math and engineering are also good options for your analytical ability and attention to detail.

If you are more artistic, singing and playing an instrument is an especially good choice but you also may excel at other visual and performing arts.

With your ability to motivate people, counseling, coaching, therapy, writing or professional speaking are good selections.

In romance, you appreciate someone with a good sense of humour, and is goal-oriented and self-reliant. Your partners can sometimes be confused between your alternating periods of affection and becoming withdrawn. The latter is usually due to overload of work and stress without an outlet for release. You need someone who understands this dichotomy within you. Your family appreciates your natural curiosity, sense of wonder, and willingness to explore new frontiers.

Celebrities

Cameron Diaz, multi-award winning actress, producer, and author (Aug 30th)

Ferdinand Porsche, automotive engineer, and founder of the Porsche car company (Sept 3rd)

Jennifer Hudson, multi-award winning and best-selling singer, actress, author, and spokesperson (Weight Watchers) (Sept 12th)

Kareena Kapoor, multi-award winning Bollywood actress (Sept 21st)

VIRGO NUMBER 4 (AUG 31ST, SEPT 4TH, SEPT 13TH, SEPT 22ND)

Strength of intellect and ability to research, analyze, and investigate unusual topics are a hallmark of your nature. Although you may appear conventional, your originality and unconventionality is very strong, always being interested in things that are off the beaten path. You naturally have a different take on many subjects and stories, one that other people may not always understand.

Your powers of concentration are strong when you want to achieve something, and some may even call you a perfectionist. This attention to detail stands out among your peers, your passion very much in evidence. People around you know that when they ask you to do something, your work will always be of the highest quality.

If you were born on September 22nd, you receive the benefits of this master number. You have a natural mental brilliance, some may say genius, which stands out very clearly. If you apply your effort, you may become a thought leader in your field. You may be especially gifted in science, math, business, technology, analytics, aviation, language, health, strategy, and research. Your thinking is very much out of the box, as you dream up highly unusual plans that are far ahead of your time. Your combination of both abstract and concrete thinking allows you to envision ideas, and then work on their practical implementation.

In terms of your career, you are earthy, and need some type of structure as your foundation. Plans must be assessed for their practicality and ease of implementation. You are one for noticing details that other people miss, so any type of work that requires a lot of focus is good for you.

You probably have an interest in health, wellness, education, math, science, medicine, literature, speech pathology, rehabilitation, social work, drama, filmmaking, music, languages, business management, human rights, law, or technology, so careers in those fields may be a good fit.

With your passion and determination, you are also capable of turning one of your unusual interests or creative pursuits into a career. Regardless of what you do, you apply your unique touch of unconventionality that makes your work stand out.

In romance, you are a loving and loyal partner, and always there in times of need. You are attracted to people who care about other people, and find practical ways to show their love. Your partner benefits from your unique take on situations, and practical guidance. You will teach your family that serving others are a necessary part of living a meaningful and productive life. Always encouraging your kids to put in 100% effort into everything they do, they learn that the road to getting somewhere is more important than the destination.

Celebrities

Richard Gere, multi-award winning actor and human rights activist (Aug 31st)

Beyoncé Knowles, multi-award winning and best-selling singer, songwriter, and actress (Sept 4th)

Tyler Perry, multi-award winning actor, filmmaker, playwright, author, and songwriter (Sept 13th)

Charles B. Huggins, physician, physiologist, cancer researcher, and winner of the Nobel Prize for Physiology or Medicine in 1966 (Sept 22nd)

VIRGO NUMBER 5 (AUG 23RD, SEPT 5TH, SEPT 14TH)

This is a harmonious combination because Mercury is the ruler of Virgo, and Mercury also vibrates to number 5. Intelligent and possessing highly developed skills of communication, you are adept at getting your message across to the world in a relatable way. You usually don't feel the need to embellish, you feel the merit of your work speaks for itself. Your logical, analytical mind does very well with facts, figures, evidence, and research. The way for people to appeal to you is probably through your mind with a well-reasoned rationale.

You are capable of great concentration and may have a streak of perfectionism when focused on a goal that is important to you. Ensuring that you don't enforce your standards of perfection on others is necessary to maintaining satisfying relationships.

Variety and change are essential to you as you like to have multiple projects going at the same time.

In terms of career, you do well in math, science, languages, business, engineering, information technology, computers, foreign relations, business, advertising, literature, media, communications, editing, and writing. Your detail orientation, high standards, and refusal to take shortcuts ensures that your work is of the highest quality.

You may be good at positions requiring exacting precision such as dentistry, surgery or working with fine tools.

You have a naturally critical mind so positions that can use this talent constructively such as food or film critic, book reviewer, magazine editor, or publisher are ideal.

You have excellent organizational and administrative skills that can transfer to many roles such as event planning, office management, or administration.

When starting your own business, your focus, intelligence, and persistence helps you endure for the long term.

Music or visual arts requiring attention to detail, such as painting, drawing, and sculpture may be of interest.

In romance, you are attracted to thought-provoking and quick-witted lovers who you can carry on meaningful conversations with. Lovers are attracted to your versatility of knowledge, and determination to always do your best. Family is your number one priority and you seek to provide the very best learning opportunities for your children, encouraging them to study hard and pursue rewarding careers. They admire your intelligence and communication skills.

Celebrities

Harry F Guggenheim, businessman, diplomat, publisher, philanthropist, aviator, horseman, and founder of Guggenheim museum (Aug 23rd)

Jack Daniel, American distiller, and the founder of the Jack Daniel's Tennessee whiskey distillery (Sept 5th)

Ivan Pavlov, physiologist known primarily for his work in classical conditioning. He was the recipient of the Nobel Prize in Physiology or Medicine in 1904 (Sept 14th)

VIRGO NUMBER 6 (AUG 24TH, SEPT 6TH, SEPT 15TH)

A sense of beauty permeates all that you do. This extends from your grooming, to your possessions, to your places of residence, and to your projects and activities. You take great pride in presenting the very best of everything and people appreciate this attention to detail.

One of your admirable qualities is your independent and investigative mind. You base your opinions on personal experience and not what things look like, what other people said, or what seems to be true. Your love of knowledge and discovery is also a hallmark of your character. Your sense of exploration well into your older age keeps you young at heart.

You are very sharp in putting the factual pieces together, however you can sometimes miss things that come more intuitively. You also need to remember that unplanned surprises and shifts of direction are natural parts of life, so while you make your plans, they should only be in pencil.

Resourcefulness, common sense, patience, adaptability and a sense of service are natural skills, applying them to a career that relies on these talents would be best. Out of these, it is probably the sense of service that is most important, you really have a strong desire to help people, and will feel a sense of emptiness if this need is not met.

Careers you may gravitate towards include nursing, social work, sociology, history, administration, healing arts, science, medicine, humanitarian work, rehabilitation, counselling, the occult, metaphysics, public relations, the military, sports, and education.

You may also have a special skill for communications, particularly writing or speaking where your simple eloquence gets the message across so that a diverse audience resonates with what you are saying.

There may be a sense of the traditional when it comes to love and romance; this may come from your family upbringing, or be evident in your values, your courtship, your marriage, or the way you raise your family. However, you may be exercising your analytical mind in selecting a partner, and in that process letting go of relationships that could have been very satisfying for you. If you relax your expectations of what should be, both for your partner and your children, you will find much happier and authentic relationships. Your children admire your service-orientation, and this positively impacts their approach to life.

Celebrities

Paulo Coelho, multi-award winning, and best-selling novelist (Aug 24th)

Jane Addams, social worker, public philosopher, sociologist, author, and leader in women's suffrage. In 1931, she became the first woman to receive the Nobel Peace Prize (Sept 6th)

Prince Harry, British royalty (Sept 15th)

VIRGO NUMBER 7 (AUG 25TH, SEPT 7TH, SEPT 16TH)

Whether your role is public, or more behind the scenes, there is a need for solitude and personal contemplation. You are a world-class thinker who reflects on yourself, people around you, and global events. You may enjoy discussing your thoughts with those around you. Although not one for idle chatter, your considerable knowledge comes out when in discussion about things that really matter.

There is a natural air of dignity and sophistication to you that others may mistake for aloofness, but once they get to know you they will see your warm and caring personality.

Writing, speaking and research come naturally to you when it is on subjects that really capture your interest and passion. You may decide to write stories either for personal remembrance in a journal or perhaps to publish stories and commentaries.

Although you often excel at school, your love of learning about the world never ends, and you may enjoy some form of teaching. You may be attracted to professions which allow you a great deal of independence and autonomy to do things your way. Careers in education, politics, broadcasting, journalism, interviewing, international relations, tourism, dentistry, music, visual arts, psychology, and massage therapy may suit you.

Your natural competitiveness may find an outlet in some form of debate, or another role in which you promote and defend your ideas. This may lead you to careers in law, law enforcement, media, history, literature, social activism, and humanitarian work.

Your discipline, patience and persistence allows you to wait until the perfect time to present your work. You are one of those people who keeps going even after multiple failures or setbacks which allows your success to be even sweeter in the end.

In romance, you appreciate a partner who is able to connect with you on an intellectual level, and reflect on the world around you. At the same time you value silence, and can be with someone close to you without feeling the need to talk. Sometimes, you can be hesitant to be affectionate; being more conscious about showing your love through hugs and kisses improves the quality of your relationships. You inspire your family with your love of learning, encouraging them to follow their bliss.

Celebrities

Regis Philbin, TV talk show host, game show host, actor, singer and recipient of the Guinness World Record for the most time spent in front of a television camera (Aug 25th)

Queen Elizabeth I, British royalty (Sept 7th)

Karen Horney, psychiatrist, psychoanalyst, and author (Sept 16th)

VIRGO NUMBER 8 (AUG 26TH, SEPT 8TH, SEPT 17TH)

Serious, conscientious, and courageous, your dedication allows you to make a meaningful, long-lasting contribution in life. You set very high standards for yourself, and will persist until you achieve them. Some people may call you a perfectionist because of your careful attention to detail.

Few people can beat you in terms of effort, you give it everything you've got. Your younger years brought a lot of obstacles and setbacks, but as you persevered you grew tougher and gained a lot of wisdom. However, you do have to watch for a tendency to be overly skeptical or black and white, everyday is a new day and carries with it a sense of freshness and opportunity.

In your career, a sense of control and financial independence is important to you. The reason you work so hard is to be impactful, and you would like your impact to be positively recognized.

With a natural sense of justice, you may be drawn to law, politics, social activism, forensics, or corrections.

You may use your talent for numbers in math, real estate, accountancy, finance, technology, engineering, statistics, computers, or administration.

Medicine, healthcare, fitness, wellness, rehabilitation, audiology, dentistry, religion or working with animals may be good uses of your skill set.

Music, drama, painting, photography, dance, or filmmaking may draw your interest.

Because you experienced hardships growing up or were exposed to suffering, you may want to choose roles that help those who are struggling in some way, disabled or disadvantaged.

In romance, you may not be the hearts and flowers type but show your love by providing the very best for your family, and allowing them to do things you never got to do. They appreciate your dedication, but likely crave for more quality time spent with you. Make it a priority to create a realistic work/life balance so that you are able to enjoy the fruits of your labour. You teach, by example, the importance of being a global citizen; emphasizing that it is critical to help people all around the world suffering hardships.

Celebrities

Mother Teresa, Roman Catholic religious sister, missionary and cultural icon. She was the recipient of the Nobel Peace Prize in 1979 (Aug 26th)

Ruby Bridges, Civil Rights activist and author. She was the recipient of the Presidential Citizens Medal in 2001 (Sept 8th)

Narendra Modi, 15th and current Prime Minister of India, ranked fifth on Fortune magazine's annual list of 'World's Greatest Leaders' in 2015 (Sept 17th)

VIRGO NUMBER 9 (AUG 27TH, SEPT 9TH, SEPT 18TH)

You love sharing your knowledge and skills to make other people's life journey a little easier, especially those who have had many tough breaks in life. You speak and act with integrity, and are straightforward in your dealings. For this reason, people enjoy learning from you and listening to your heartfelt advice.

There is a sense of intrigue about you, because even if you have many friends or are in the public eye, your private inner world is seen by very few. You don't feel the need to share everything about yourself even with those closest to you, and certain experiences from the past may never be shared. The good thing is that you respect other people's needs for privacy and can keep confidences.

The abundance of physical energy that you possess should be expressed constructively through sports, exercise, martial arts or some other physical outlet, otherwise you tend to build up stress.

In your career, you need adventure and variety, because you can easily become bored and dissatisfied with routine. You dislike listening to people who don't capture your attention towards the beginning, or who speak in circles.

Travel appeals to you, and you are lucky when in distant lands, therefore incorporating this element into your profession is beneficial.

You are a dynamic speaker who can get the point across, so that the audience takes it to heart. For this reason, communications based careers suit you well.

If you are in business, you have almost a sixth sense about what your target audience desires in a product or service. With your ability to take risks you could be very successful in these enterprises.

Other fields capturing your interest may include fashion, sports, journalism, math, science, medicine, administration, metaphysics, and business management.

In romance, you are able to pick up on the intention behind the words, so are able to tune into what your partner is really thinking and feeling. You are attracted to people who make you laugh, and view life less critically. You partner can help you to flow along with the natural tide of life and not get too caught up in the details. By example, you inspire your children to take risks that add vitality to their lives, and seek out challenges that will lead to increased self-understanding.

Celebrities

Tom Ford, multi-award winning fashion designer and Academy Award nominated film director (Aug 27th)

Colonel Sanders, philanthropist, author, founder of Kentucky Fried Chicken (Sept 9th)

Ronaldo, football player and United Nations Development Programme Goodwill Ambassador. He is one of only four players to have won the FIFA World Player of the Year award three times or more (Sept 18th)

CHAPTER 13

LIBRA NUMBERS 1-9

LIBRA NUMBER 1 (SEPT 28TH, OCT 1ST, OCT 10TH, OCT 19TH)

There is an interesting duality to you, because on the one hand you are diplomatic, peace loving, and have a desire for partnership, but on the other hand you can be competitive, assertive, and enjoy doing things on your own. Perhaps in reconciling these tendencies, you have an unusual strength that most others don't, and are more easily able to adapt to changing circumstances.

You can be a popular leader because you know what it is like to be a part of the group. You care for people and have an interest in developing bonds on a personal level. On the other hand, as a team member, you know the challenges facing a leader, so you offer more constructive feedback. You are sensitive as to how your role impacts the larger goal of the group. A natural combination of shrewdness and charm enables you to succeed at getting other people to help you achieve your goals.

In your career, you have a special talent for the arts, but can apply your considerable creativity to whatever field you find yourself in. Drama, music, fashion, painting, writing, poetry and dance are particularly attractive.

You may enjoy landscaping, architecture, graphic design, feng shui, or interior designing.

You have a gift for interacting with people, and this should be used to your advantage in a role that requires a lot of one-on-one contact.

There may be an attraction to justice, politics, mediation, international diplomacy, law, business management, or education.

In any role you take, you have a gift for fighting for what you believe in, even if it goes against the majority.

In romance, your ability to give and take in relationships is very good, as you have an innate sense of balance and fairness. However, you do have to make an effort to not keep mental track of what is given and received, because it may undermine the intimacy of your relationship. Your children appreciate your explanation for rules and discipline when they have done something wrong, rather than just saying "because I said so." Participating in charitable activities as a family strengthens bonds, and introduces your children to broader issues of justice in the world.

Celebrities

Sheikh Hasina, current Prime Minister of Bangladesh, recipient of the Indira Gandhi Prize, M.K. Gandhi Award, and Mother Teresa Award (Sept 28th)

Julie Andrews, multi-award winning actress and singer, author, made a Dame by Queen Elizabeth II for services to the performing arts, recipient of the Kennedy Center Honors in 2001 (Oct 1st)

Laurence Tribe, lawyer and professor of constitutional law at Harvard (Oct 10th)

Sunny Deol, multi-award winning Bollywood film actor, director, and producer (Oct 19th)

Libra Number 2 (Sept 29th, Oct 2nd, Oct 11th, Oct 20th)

Harmonious, peace loving, and easygoing, you are a wonderful listener, and love to hear life stories. You are people-oriented, and genuinely interested in getting to know others at a soul to soul level. There is a need for balance and harmony in your life, thus you are interested in resolving conflict. You are willing to cooperate with people to get the best resolution and you prefer situations that create a win-win rather than a win-lose. Your natural charm and grace help you win friends and get support for your endeavours.

An interesting thing about you is that you can be quite sharp with your words when wanting to convey a thought or feeling. Even though you may appear soft or calm on the outside, you are very gritty on the inside. Fortunately, if people don't anger you to a certain point, they will never experience the formidable enemy you could be.

If you were born on October 11th, you receive the benefits of this master number. Idealistic and enthusiastic, you have a strong desire to uplift and encourage people, pushing them to discover their highest potential. You look at people for what they could be, than what they are, and inspire them to meet your expectations. Another talent is your mediation skills- in conflict situations, you are able to enhance understanding between opposing parties. One drawback is that because you like to focus on what is pleasant, you may not be as sympathetic when listening to other people's problems. When you allow yourself to be vulnerable, you pave the way for soul level connections that will inspire you and transform your life.

In terms of career, you would do well in a role where you can hear other's stories, create meaningful connections, and be helpful. Because relationships mean so much to you, you may work in a role focused on enhancing intimacy, such as a marriage therapist, author of books on relationships, or in another business focused on enhancing intimacy. Counseling or nurturing professions allow you to express your supportive side.

You may be attracted to stock markets, sales, customer service, culinary arts, speech therapy, hairdressing, administrative work, law, broadcasting, media, massage therapy, body work, psychology, dentistry, teaching, writing, advertising, skilled trades, or comedy.

At work, you are capable of working well within teams or partnerships. If you work alone, you strive very hard to please your customers and get repeat business, it is due to this extra personal effort that you succeed.

In romance, you are sweet and sentimental, always keeping mementos and photos to capture those special moments. You need a partner who is affectionate, loyal, and sensitive. Although you are not hesitant to express displeasure if someone wrongs you, you can be hyper- sensitive when taking other's criticisms. Being more open to constructive criticism builds trust with family members. As a parent you are very interested in all aspects of your child's life; they are grateful that you create an atmosphere that is safe to be honest and open.

Celebrities

Bryant Gumbel, multi-award winning news anchor (Sept 29th)

Mahatma Gandhi, cultural icon, lawyer, leader of Indian Independence Movement, and best-selling author. He was named Man of the Year in 1930 by Time magazine (Oct 2nd)

Thích Nhất Hạnh, Zen Buddhist monk, teacher, best-selling author, poet, and peace activist (Oct 11th)

Mickey Mantle, professional baseball player, seven-time World Series champion. He was inducted into the National Baseball Hall of Fame in 1974 (Oct 20th)

LIBRA NUMBER 3 (SEPT 30TH, OCT 3RD, OCT 12TH, OCT 21ST)

Positivity and faith are two of your greatest strengths. Regardless of the situation, you view it as glass half full, and encourage those around you to count their blessings. This doesn't mean that you don't understand grief and suffering, for you probably understand it all too well, but rather that you view challenges as opportunities for self-development. You don't want the painful experiences to needlessly repeat without having some sort of good come out of it.

There is a side to you that is sociable, fun, and lighthearted; you probably enjoy parties or functions that give you a chance to meet new interesting people in a relaxed environment. At the same time there is a philosophical approach to life, one which you enjoy sharing with others in meaningful discussion.

In terms of career, there might be an attraction to the arts and music. Whether you have a creative profession or not, your skill in these areas should be expressed as a hobby.

Your knowledge of current trends and events, excellent manners, and ability to network, are noted by all who come in contact with you, so you are an ideal person to represent the business for social functions and negotiations. Even if you have to make a tendentious statement or action, your natural charm makes it difficult for people to take a dislike to you personally (although they may still disagree with you professionally).

With your interest in social justice and human rights, the legal field, politics, social work, or humanitarian careers may suit you.

You may enjoy positions connected with leisure such as amusement parks, circuses, entertainment, restaurants, golfing, or massage. Other areas include jewellery designing, interior decoration, investing, broadcasting, and working with children.

In romance, your charm, humour, and generosity is appreciated by your partner. Sometimes you can be too tough (perhaps from difficult experiences in the past) and someone who can make you feel comfortable with your vulnerability is good for you. You need someone who can help you to relax and clear your mind. You teach your kids to seek out the truth, stand up for what they believe in, and to make sure their arguments are backed up with evidence before presenting them.

Celebrities

Elie Wiesel, Holocaust activist, New York Times best-selling author, professor and Nobel Laureate (Sept 30th)

India Arie, Grammy award-winning singer-songwriter, musician, and record producer (Oct 3rd)

Hugh Jackman, multi-award winning actor and Academy Awards host (Oct 12th)

Benjamin Netanyahu, current Israeli Prime Minister and author. Recipient of the American Enterprise Institute's highest honour, Irving Kristol Award in 2015 (Oct 21st)

LIBRA NUMBER 4 (OCT 4TH, OCT 13TH, OCT 22ND)

You have the admirable combination of charm and toughness. The charm covers the toughness, such that a pleasant smile allows you to be firm in your position, disagree when necessary, and even make controversial statements, all while staying in favour with the other person!

The fact that other people may underestimate your fortitude is something you can use to your advantage. Very little escapes your attention and you use this information to advance your position, while on the surface remaining pleasant. Perhaps because of this, you almost never judge a book by its cover, understanding there is always more to people than meets the eye. There is a skill with strategy, as you have a way of gaining information but revealing very little when the situation calls for it.

You are unconventional and original in thought and action, and are not afraid to stand by your convictions, remaining headstrong at the opposition. However, you shouldn't be rebellious just for the sake of it, and you need to carefully consider rational information that may go against your firmly held thoughts.

If you were born on October 22nd, you receive the benefits of this master number. Future oriented and visionary; your ideas are far beyond the times, and probably considered revolutionary. However, you present them in such a way so that others can get a glimpse as to how they can transform their lives. Your emotions are powerful, and your energy has a significant effect on others, you should be aware of this magnetism and use it to uplift people around you. Spirituality or religion is important to you, as you seek to go deeper and deeper within yourself for the answers to life's great mysteries. There is an inspirational quality to you that is excellent for leadership, as you show others how to tap into their inner reservoir of wisdom.

In your career, you are determined to do your job to the very best of your capabilities. Thus regardless of your social station at birth, you usually manage to rise higher. Your innate toughness gives you the stamina and determination to forge ahead long after others have given up. There are a variety of fields you may do well in, such as counselling, business, education, music, psychology, massage therapy, the occult, literature, public relations, event planning, social work, law, journalism, medicine, dentistry, information technology, science, math, and politics.

In romance, you may be attracted to partners who are visionary, or unconventional, or perhaps the relationship dynamic takes on those qualities. Lovers are attracted to your quick wit, and reservoir of interesting conversation. You teach your family creative approaches to problem solving and analysis. While they appreciate the confidence of your high expectations for their performance, you also must be diligent in conveying that you are pleased with them for trying their best. Your children admire your intelligence, and that you've always given them the same respect and attention you gave to adults.

Celebrities

Dr. Christiane Northrup, medical doctor, New York Times best-selling author, and leading authority in the field of women's health and wellness (Oct 4th)

Margaret Thatcher, first and only female United Kingdom Prime Minister in history, and longest-serving British Prime Minister of the 20th century. She was the recipient of the Presidential Medal of Freedom in 1991, and appointed a Lady Companion of the Order of the Garter in 1995 (Oct 13th)

Dr. Deepak Chopra, medical doctor, alternative medicine advocate, and New York Times best-selling author (Oct 22nd)

LIBRA NUMBER 5 (SEPT 23RD, OCT 5TH, OCT 14TH)

The ability to adapt to new information, people, and circumstances is one of your greatest skills. You possess a broad tolerance for different ways of thinking and acting. Your craving for excitement, adventure, and variety means that you may be constantly on the go, either mentally or physically. In fact foreign travel will figure prominently into your life and you may even move to a different country than the one you were born and raised in.

Fair outcomes, equal rights, and justice are important areas in your life and if you are in a position to expose power abuses or corruption, you will do so. You express your positions clearly to get right to the heart of the issue. There may have been more than your share of disappointments, and challenges throughout life, but such adversity had the effect of making you stronger and more courageous. You may be in a position to help others who faced the same problems as you through your personal example of triumph, sharing advice, and offering support.

In terms of your career, your strong interest in justice may lead to roles in the legal field, law enforcement, humanitarian organizations or social services, where you can help needy populations. It may also guide you into journalism, broadcasting, drama or filmmaking, where you can bring to life stories of people who have been victimized.

Singing, dance, and fashion design may be good outlets for your creativity.

You could also do well in the beauty industry, helping people look their best. Or perhaps interior decoration/ feng shui where you can help people create beautiful spaces.

In romance, you need a partner who is as mentally sharp as you and who enjoys discussing interesting topics. Honest communication and trust are likely your two biggest ingredients for a successful relationship. Your family admires your determination to rise above your challenges, and your desire to help those who don't have a voice take back their power. You encourage your children to stay strong through adversity, and to see how they can use their experience to make a difference in the lives of people who may gain strength through their life story.

Celebrities

Bruce Springsteen, multi-award winning and best-selling musician, singer, and songwriter. He was inducted into the Songwriters Hall of Fame and the Rock and Roll Hall of Fame in 1999 (Sept 23rd)

Ray Kroc, McDonalds entrepreneur. The Ray Kroc Awards are given to the top 1% of McDonalds restaurant managers on a national level (Oct 5th)

Ralph Lauren, multi-award winning fashion designer, philanthropist, and billionaire. He was the recipient of the Chevalier de la Legion d'honneur in 2010 (Oct 14th)

LIBRA NUMBER 6 (SEPT 24TH, OCT 6TH, OCT 15TH)

Your combination is the most harmonious for Libra, as ruler Venus corresponds to the number 6. One-on-one relationships are of particular importance in your life, and your major life lessons are sure to come from intimate relationships. Home and family are your number one priority as you seek to create a stable, loving atmosphere for your children to grow up in.

Your personal style is sophisticated, and you have an eye for beauty in people, places and things. Proportion, symmetry, color, and design are all things that come naturally to you. Your creative talents are marked, especially in culinary arts, dance, architecture, fashion, music, interior decoration, and graphic design.

You have a strongly developed sense of fairness and justice, and want to do your best to see that everyone has an equal chance at success. Although you can be diplomatic when you need to be, you are quite honest in letting people know what you really think and feel, even if you know your opinion is not widely shared and/or goes against traditional thinking. You may even share your thoughts via a public venue. Morals, ethics and societal/global issues could hold a special interest for you in this regard.

In terms of career, you may enjoy event planning, entertainment, science, medicine, social work, literature, law, fitness, wellness, retail, teaching, massage therapy, counselling, psychology, humanitarian pursuits, healing arts, yoga, feng shui, and writing. Generally once you overcome your tendency to be indecisive, success follows you wherever you go.

In romance, you are attracted to intelligent and thoughtful partners with a good sense of humour. Lovers are attracted to your magnetism, empathy, and sense of adventure. You are willing to make long-term commitments as long as you have your freedom. Since you have wanderlust, foreign travelling with family is an ideal way to discover the world and get those new experiences you crave. You encourage your family to expand their knowledge of the world through interacting with people from many different walks of life.

Celebrities

John Marshall, longest-serving Chief Justice, and the fourth longest-serving justice in U.S. Supreme Court history, emphasized the necessity for a judicial review (Sept 24th)

Florence B. Seibert, biochemist, and creator of the standard Tuberculosis test (Oct 6th)

Emeril Lagasse, celebrity chef, restaurateur, television personality, and best-selling cookbook author (Oct 15th)

LIBRA NUMBER 7 (SEPT 25TH, OCT 7TH, OCT 16TH)

You are a very deep thinker, and your mind is likely philosophical and abstract. Analysis and observation come naturally to you, as there is often reflection on interesting ideas, potentials and visions. Imaginative and intuitive, your creativity can be used in writing, filmmaking, and acting.

Sophisticated, cultured, and tasteful, your personal style is one that other people respect and admire. There is an innate understanding of beauty in all its forms; symmetry, balance or proportion could play a role in your life in some way.

Even though you may appear to others as likeable and easygoing, there is a side to you that is strong-willed and concerned about exposing the truth in people and society as you see it. You feel that if change is ever going to happen, it has to start with at least one person who isn't afraid to challenge the established tradition of power and authority. In this way, one of your life purposes is to shake things up and be a catalyst for positive social progress.

In terms of career, roles involving research, lecturing, analysis, observation, critical thinking, and writing, are ones you would do well in. Education, law, journalism, social justice, and politics may be a good use of your talent.

You may be drawn to a role within a spiritual or religious organization to express the more solitary and reflective side of your nature.

If creatively inclined, music and dance are a good way to express yourself.

Other areas of interest could be cosmetics, beauty, feng shui, yoga, healing arts, medicine, architecture, and landscaping.

In romance, your ability to understand that people are constantly evolving helps you relate to your partner as a fresh person everyday. You need a partner who also understands this about you, and gives you your freedom of thought and action. In your family, you must watch that your tendency to analyze does not make you overthink what people are saying to you. Trusting that they are being straightforward will make for healthier, happier relations. Your family admires your free spirit, and willingness to take healthy risks.

Celebrities

Will Smith, Academy award nominated actor and producer. Grammy-award winning rapper and songwriter (Sept 25th)

Bishop Desmond Tutu, first black Archbishop of Cape Town, and South African social rights activist. He won the Nobel Peace Prize in 1984 (Oct 7th)

Oscar Wilde, novelist, playwright, and poet (Oct 16th)

Libra Number 8 (Sept 26th, Oct 8th, Oct 17th)

This is a harmonious combination as Saturn is exalted in Libra, and Saturn corresponds to the number 8. Intellectual and serious, you are often concerned with global and political issues, and what you can do to bring awareness to them. There is a marked love for gaining knowledge, and then sharing what you have learned with others; you are a teacher at heart.

Because you are inclined to be influential, people may attack your point of view, but you are well-prepared with the facts to defend yourself in difficult situations. This stamina was probably acquired in your younger years where you emerged resilient and wiser from setbacks and failures.

One thing to keep in mind is that new information becomes available constantly and sometimes while your original position was rooted in solid factual basis, you need to recognize when it is time to shift your viewpoint. The good thing is that you do use your mistakes to learn and grow, and may even use your story to help others overcome their obstacles.

In terms of career, you may be drawn to professional careers reliant upon facts and research, such as law, medicine, dentistry, engineering, psychology, math, and science.

You are willing to devote many hours to your work, so pursuits which depend on practice and application such as playing instruments, dance, martial arts, or sports are where you can show off your technical mastery.

Your interest in social justice may lead you to careers in politics, education, journalism, or charitable organizations. If you are a writer, publisher, or lecturer, you will want to use your work to draw attention to larger societal issues needing attention.

Graphic design, healing arts, the occult, metaphysics, yoga, literature, technology, drama, music, fashion, sculpture, and painting may also hold special appeal.

In romance, you are passionate and intense. Initially admirers will be attracted to your charm and complexity. In married life, you have to take care that your devotion to work does not overshadow your family, and that you spend enough time building bonds with your children, especially when they are young.

Your family appreciates your sensitivity and empathy, and you encourage them to look for ways to help both in their community and on a global scale.

Celebrities

TS Eliot, poet and winner of the Nobel Prize in Literature in 1948 (Sept 26th)

Louise Hay, founder of Hay House publishing company and New York Times best-selling author (Oct 8th)

Arthur Miller, multi-award winning playwright and essayist. He was the winner of the Pulitzer Prize for Drama in 1949 (Oct 17th)

LIBRA NUMBER 9 (SEPT 27TH, OCT 9TH, OCT 18TH)

Enthusiastic and vivacious, you have a zest for life that remains with you until the very end. Eager to learn, explore, and discover, you are on a quest to know more, and do better. You are curious and inquisitive, and particularly interested in the study of human motivation and personal potential. The heights of personal accomplishment hold a fascination for you.

Well-suited to leadership, group members appreciate your sensitivity and interest in using their unique skills in the overall group mission. One thing to keep in mind is that being either physically or mentally magnetic, you are capable of exerting a strong influence on those around you, and you must be careful how you use this power.

In terms of career, your creative side may be drawn towards painting, drawing, poetry, music, and acting.

Since you have strong physical vitality, a role which uses this energy helps to work out excess stress (sports, martial arts, skilled trades) might be good.

Your interest in the human mind may draw you to psychology, psychiatry, counselling, coaching, or advising.

The talent you have for persuasion and correct word choice can help you in law, politics, teaching, government, business management, advertising, marketing, or sales.

Other areas capturing your attention may be jewellery making, retail, customer service, massage therapy, business administration, event planning, cosmetics, and hairstyling.

In romance, you are affectionate and always curious to learn more about your lover. You need someone who shares the same need for adventure and mental stimulation. Partners are attracted to your joyful spirit. One area to watch for is being sensitive to constructive criticism from family, as they have your best interests in mind. Your children appreciate your bright smile and warm encouragement. They respect that you teach by example, rather than by lecture.

Celebrities

Gwyneth Paltrow, multi-award winning actress, singer, and author (Sept 27th)

John Lennon, multi-award winning and best-selling singer and songwriter, co-founder of the Beatles (Oct 9th)

Pierre Trudeau, 15th Canadian Prime Minister and made a member of the Queen's Privy Council for Canada. He was awarded the Albert Einstein Peace Prize in 1984 (Oct 18th)

Chapter 14

Scorpio Numbers 1-9

Scorpio Number 1 (Oct 28th, Nov 1st, Nov 10th, Nov 19th)

Intense, steely and determined, once you set your heart on something, it's as good as yours. The adversity you face in your formative years toughens your strength of will, and persistence to prove any naysayers wrong. You are a formidable opponent because your ideas are always well-planned and researched.

Positions of leadership and power are naturally attracted to you due to your subtle dominance. At the same time, when you are in positions of authority, and even in your daily life, you must be more willing to listen to others and take into consideration their advice.

Regardless of your demeanour on the outside, reading your true emotion is a hard task. It becomes harder because you don't tend to say much that would reveal your feelings. Therefore most people can risk offending you if they don't know you are upset. Learning to recognize this is a major step in preventing feelings of betrayal. Forgiveness will be a major issue for you all throughout your life, both in forgiving others and in being forgiven.

In terms of career you may be attracted to positions relying on research, investigation and truth seeking, especially if part of it lets you unleash your warrior side. You enjoy solving mysteries, puzzles, and codes, these skills can be used in detective type work. Strategy is a skill of yours because you are able to elicit information but at the same time be very elusive when probed for information. Due to your work ethic and intelligence, there are few roles that you won't do well in. The exceptions are work that is too shallow, has too many rules or has too much supervision. You thrive on competition; even if not competing with others, you like to compete against your own personal best. You are fortunate to be born under a combination that is among the most auspicious for gaining status, wealth and power.

In romance, your emotional complexity is alternately loved and hated by your partner, they may appreciate your intensity, but at the same time not know where they truly stand with you. Being more open and vulnerable with your true emotions is something you need to gradually get more accustomed to. You need a partner who will help you loosen up and be more spontaneous. Likewise, spending time with children allows you to develop your sense of humour, and laugh at yourself more often.

Celebrities

Bill Gates, billionaire business magnate, philanthropist, investor, computer programmer, and inventor (Oct 28th)

Aishwarya Rai Bachchan, multi-award winning Bollywood actress, winner of the Miss World pageant, awarded the Padma Shri (fourth highest civilian honour) by the Government of India (Nov 1st)

Martin Luther, friar, priest, and professor of theology (Nov 10th)

Indira Gandhi, first, and only female Prime Minister of India. Recipient of the Bharat Ratna (highest civilian award of India) in 1971 (Nov 19th)

SCORPIO NUMBER 2 (OCT 29TH, NOV 2ND, NOV 11TH, NOV 20TH)

You are like a glacier, what people see is only the tip of the iceberg. Beneath your calm exterior lies tremendously powerful and intense emotions that drive your behaviour. Your ability to pick up on the thoughts and feelings of other people is like a sixth sense, and your imitation of them uncannily accurate. Your insight into human behaviour is penetrating, and hidden motives become all too apparent to you. At the same time, you rarely reveal how much you know, and would rather use this information to your advantage later on. Persuasion is a strong suit, and you are capable of letting other people think they are getting their way, when all along they are doing exactly what you wanted them to do!

If you were born on November 11th, you receive the benefits of this master number. In this case, your intuition is so amped up that people feel you understand them without even having to say a word. Your talent for reading nonverbal communication is unmatched, and you rely far more on this than anything they say. You can be very inspirational and charismatic as a leader of a cause you believe in. Because you are associated with it, the issue is able to garner a lot more awareness in the mind of the public, just due to the strength of the emotion in your speech. You are a natural healer, whether in the traditional or alternative sense. Because you are committed to your self-development and spirituality, and are not afraid of visiting the dark, hidden places within your soul, you are able to help others do the same.

In terms of career, positions involving psychology, motivation, behaviour, research, investigation, and analysis come naturally to you. If you go into business, your sensitivity to people's preferences can be used to design a highly appealing product or service.

Your understanding of the subconscious, and other hidden determinants of behaviour make you ideal for therapy or any other profession where talking to people about their problems is needed. You are able to be a catalyst for transformation and much needed change in their lives.

Other areas that may interest you are politics, government, foreign relations, drama, entertainment, filmmaking, metaphysics, the occult, police force, firefighting, sports, surgery, and the military.

In romance, you are prone to major mood swings, which are only heightened by their characteristic depth and passion. There is indeed a very thin line between love and hate for you. Your sarcasm can be very hurtful when you have the desire to wound someone. Therefore, you have to stop yourself before talking when angry. You need a partner who understands that your love stays constant, regardless of these emotional ups and downs. Your family is your main priority and you never stop making sacrifices for their wellbeing; it is obvious that you go to great lengths to protect them. Your children appreciate the complete fullness of your devotion as they get older.

Celebrities

Ellen Johnson-Sirleaf, Africa's first elected female Head of State (Oct 29th)

Shah Rukh Khan, multi-award winning Bollywood actor, producer, and television personality (Nov 2nd)

Leonardo DiCaprio, Golden Globe winning actor, film producer, and environmentalist (Nov 11th)

Joseph Biden, 47th Vice President of the United States, recipient of the George Arents Pioneer Medal—Syracuse University's highest alumni award (Nov 20th)

SCORPIO NUMBER 3 (OCT 30TH, NOV 3RD, NOV 12TH, NOV 21ST)

Sassy, magnetic, passionate, and intelligent, you take the world by storm! Your intensity, charm, and optimism help you take a lot on your plate, and be successful. However, you only take on projects that capture your heart because you want to put 110% into everything you do. There is a lot of stamina in pursuing your goals; you may fail along the way, but you are very resilient and just keep going.

Foreign travel may play an important role in your life, such that you have an intensely transformational experience in another country, which changes the course of your life direction.

You can be quite ruthless with your enemies, with your combination of strategy, sharp words and penetration, people should want to keep you on their side. However, the danger is that this may spill over into personal relationships when you are angry. Keeping the feelings of others in mind, and controlling your words and actions when upset, will improve your relationships.

In terms of career, you excel in a number of roles because of your high quality of work and dedication. You are capable of multitasking and succeeding at many projects or roles at the same time, although you may find it necessary to delegate tasks to people you trust.

You may express your talents through teaching, social work, psychology, medicine, law, business management, fashion design, politics, literature, publishing, philosophy, history, metaphysics, religion, research, investigations, the arts, healing, and broadcasting.

Whatever you do, you add a new, personalized twist. While you respect tradition, you are eager to look for ways to improve or build on established protocols.

In romance, your seductive presence, elegance, and mystery attract many admirers. Even if not conventionally attractive, there is a natural self-confidence in your appearance and you enjoy the physical expressions of love. You are attracted to people who are comfortable in their own skin, and self-confident in their abilities. You instill a sense of self-reliance, conscientiousness, and responsibility in your children from a young age, so that when they grow up they take pride in their work.

Celebrities

Ivanka Trump, multi-award winning fashion designer, entrepreneur, author, and former model (Oct 30th)

Anna Wintour, multi-award winning fashion designer and editor-in-chief of American Vogue (Nov 3rd)

Elizabeth Cady Stanton, suffragist, social activist, abolitionist, and leading figure of the early women's rights movement (Nov 12th)

Goldie Hawn, multi-award winning actress, comedienne, director, and producer (Nov 21st)

SCORPIO NUMBER 4 (OCT 31ST, NOV 4TH, NOV 13TH, NOV 22ND)

Provocative is your middle name! You love to make statements you know are contentious just to arouse a little excitement in your environment, and see people's reactions! The fighter in you is not afraid to say what others won't say, you stand firm behind your statements. Sometimes this can be good in exposing the truth, but other times you may fight just for the sake of it, or for shock value. You are capable of devoting intense concentration to whatever subject catches your attention, and this may include topics that are unconventional or mysterious in some way. Generally you are well-informed about what is going on globally and you enjoy discussing current events.

If you were born on November 22nd, you receive the benefits of this master number. Nov 22nd is described both for Sagittarius and Scorpio, so please confirm which sign you are. If you are a Scorpio number 22, your mind is very well-suited to getting to the heart of the matter, and you have an insatiable urge to uncover life's mysteries. Highly intelligent, persistent, and creative, people are often surprised at the lengths you will go to achieve your aims, your wild child rebel side comes out every so often! Your concentration is usually focused on one goal that captures your passion and you give it everything you have. Future oriented approaches to healing and transformation may be an interest and you can make important contributions in these fields. You may have a special skill for uncovering the root of people's problems, to really encourage them to go deep within and heal themselves. The subconscious mind, human rights, global events, power, control, and the heights of human accomplishment, may be topics that you spend a great deal of time thinking about.

In terms of career, you enjoy research, investigation, and work that requires probing deeper into the core of issues. You benefit from a sense of structure to better define your duties and obligations. If you are in a position of authority, you have to watch for a tendency to control your subordinates or exert undue influence on their work.

You may be attracted to journalism, media, politics, sports, religion, law enforcement, the occult, metaphysics, counselling, psychology, human rights, medicine, comedy, the Navy, the airlines, administration, or business management.

If creative, music, singing, acting, fashion, culinary arts, and the visual arts are good expressions.

In romance, you are loyal and devoted to the special lover that captures your heart. Forgiving and forgetting are likely to be major themes in your relationships but when you master this, you are able to have much more harmonious relationships. When raising a family, you have to keep in mind the old adage that your kids won't follow what you say but rather what you do. When they express an opinion or belief contrary to yours, listen to it without judgement and encourage them to stay true to themselves. In doing so you build mutual trust and respect.

Celebrities

Dan Rather, multi-award winning news anchor and journalist, inducted into the Television Hall of Fame (Oct 31st)

Matthew McConaughey, multi-award winning actor (Nov 4th)

Whoopi Goldberg, multi-award winning actress, voice actress, comedian, screenwriter, producer, author, singer, songwriter, DJ, talk show host, and political activist (Nov 13th)

Jamie Lee Curtis, multi-award winning actress and New York Times best-selling author (Nov 22nd)

SCORPIO NUMBER 5 (OCT 23RD, NOV 5TH, NOV 14TH)

There is great power of intellect combined with a shrewdness and way with words: you are well able to choose just the right words, and tone, to convey your message so that people take action. You prefer to cut right to the chase so that your message doesn't get obscured with unimportant details. Because of this your messages are targeted, and sometimes blunt. You are driven to expose what you perceive to be dishonest people or underhanded occurrences. Your mind is always "on," analyzing people, looking for hidden messages, motives and what you perceive to be the real meaning behind what other people say. This can be good because it is very hard to pull the wool over your eyes, but at the same time people close to you may wonder if you truly trust them.

Foreign travel is likely to play a fairly large role in your life, you may meet people who drastically change your outlook and sense of purpose. You may also travel in search of higher education or to take specialized training or courses. There is a sense of restlessness and craving for change and variety, for this reason you are likely to be involved with many projects, goals, and tasks at the same time.

In terms of career, you are changeable and will either take on multiple careers at once or change careers several times throughout life. You need to have intellectual stimulation and some degree of excitement and passion in your work, otherwise you lose motivation.

Careers involving communication in any form: broadcasting, media, entertainment, journalism, literature, publishing, editing, speaking, and writing are ideal.

Areas such as international business, medicine, alternative healing, yoga, dentistry, sports, law, education, research, computer technology, sales, advertising, marketing, psychology, travel, and publishing may hold special interest.

Drama, music, and the visual arts may appeal to your need for creative self-expression.

In romance, lovers are attracted to your intelligence, compassion, and eagerness to have a meaningful impact on the world. Because at times you tend to be more outer-directed, you need a partner who can encourage you to look deeper within yourself and do inner work needed to make personal progress. Your family members love that you take a very active role in each of their lives, and encourage them to pursue their unique talents, even if off the beaten path.

Celebrities

Michael Crichton, multi-award winning physician, producer, director, screenwriter, and best-selling author (Oct 23rd)

Bryan Adams, best-selling and multi-award winning singer, musician, producer, actor, social activist, and photographer (Nov 5th)

Charles, Prince of Wales, British Royalty (Nov 14th)

SCORPIO NUMBER 6 (OCT 24TH, NOV 6TH, NOV 15TH)

Your sense of responsibility, patience, empathy, and service is highly developed as you may have found yourself in the role of caretaker relatively early in life. Even as an adult you are still in charge of the wellbeing of family, relatives or others who need assistance. Elderly people and children are drawn to you, and you enjoy making their lives more joyful. You show your love through engaging in acts of service, and rarely will you let others down in this regard.

You make a great advocate for people in need. If you or someone you love is being taken advantage of, or treated unfairly, your inner warrior comes out with a vengeance. Even though you may be calm on the outside, opponents are likely to underestimate your kindness for weakness, and your fire will come out when they least expect it!

In terms of career, you have a talent for small details that others miss, and have a very strong drive to produce goods or services of the very highest quality. Luxury goods are über luxurious because of your attention to style and comfort. Because of this personal touch, customers are likely to come back to you. Businesses centered on fashion, food, and cars are particularly favoured.

You may use your nurturing side to take care of other people professionally, in the medical, social service, rehabilitation, veterinary medicine, or assisted living fields.

Your ability to encourage people can be put to good use in roles requiring motivational skills or getting back on track (self-help, losing weight, healthy living, counselling and recovering addictions). Energy, enthusiasm, and vitality run high, and you can use your impact on others to uplift and inspire.

Other areas of interest may include politics, broadcasting, sales, administration, writing, the occult, metaphysics, comedy, and the military.

In romance, you have a high capacity to be devoted and generous in all areas with your partner. You are attracted to compassionate and faithful partners. Lovers are attracted to your sincerity and sweetness. You instill a sense of responsibility and caring for others in your children from a young age so that when they grow up they desire to be of service in a meaningful way.

Celebrities

Kevin Kline, multi-award winning actor, inducted into the American Theatre Hall of Fame in 2003 (Oct 24th)

Maria Shriver, multi-award winning TV show host, best-selling author, journalist, activist, special anchor, and correspondent for NBC News (Nov 6th)

Jimmy Choo, multi-award winning fashion designer (Nov 15th)

Scorpio Number 7 (Oct 25th, Nov 7th, Nov 16th)

Very observant, analytical, and shrewd, your incisive comments are often right on target. You won't take anything anyone says, even so called experts, for the absolute truth. There is a desire to research, explore, and experience on your own in coming to your conclusions. You may be the first to point out a flaw in previously accepted fact or tradition that gets people to think more deeply. There is a distaste for anyone or anything you perceive to be superficial. People may misjudge you for being aloof, but you would really rather engage with people and activities you find meaningful. Naturally introspective, you may prefer to spend time alone in the process of self-development and discovery.

In terms of career, you need a significant time to be by yourself to think and reflect. If you are in a career requiring large amounts of time dealing with groups of people, you will need frequent periods of rest to recharge. Strategic thinking, investigations, problem solving, research and designing are your strengths.

Fields capturing your interest may include medicine, alternative healing, media, military, police force, federal investigations, philosophy, psychology, politics, history, metaphysics, healing, drama, music, science, research, government, writing, and publishing. Creatively, you can excel at the visual and performing arts, particularly working with your hands. You may also enjoy working or living near the water or in nature/outdoors.

In romance, you are attracted to people who are interested in finding about life's mysteries, and are more on the spiritual or philosophical side. Your partner appreciates your quest for going deeper and deeper in the process of learning, and discovering about yourself and the world. You convey to your family that passion and persistence for what they are doing are the most important ingredients for success, and they are grateful for your support.

Celebrities

Pablo Picasso, painter, sculptor, ceramist, stage designer, poet, and playwright (Oct 25th)

Madame Curie, physicist and chemist who conducted pioneering research on radioactivity. Winner of two Nobel Peace Prizes in Physics and Chemistry (Nov 7th)

Shigeru Miyamoto, game designer of Nintendo and Wii video games (Nov 16th)

SCORPIO NUMBER 8 (OCT 26TH, NOV 8TH, NOV 17TH)

The quest for power is a driving force to your personality, and the proper use of it is a lifelong lesson for you. Growing up, there were many tribulations. You might have felt misunderstood by family, relatives and others around you as there is an intensity and complexity that may be hard for others to fully grasp. Your sharp memory keeps tracks of all of these instances and pushes you to be stronger, to overcome, and to ultimately succeed. Your tenacity, self-control and strength of will makes you one of the toughest cookies in the zodiac!

There is an interest in the dark side of human nature or dark subjects that would be considered taboo or out of bounds by society. This interest can be used to address these themes and their relation to society. For example, director Martin Scorcese (b. Nov 17th) focuses on dark humour, crime, violence, gangs and conflict in his films and has been awarded numerous accolades for it.

In terms of career, you may be attracted to the military, sports, martial arts, entertainment, music, international business, law, engineering, technology, comedy, medicine, science, culinary arts, the occult, religion, teaching, the skilled trades, and rehabilitation.

You have a talent for staying calm under a lot of pressure so you do well under deadlines, fast pace and high-stress work, although you do need to stop overworking sometimes.

If in a leadership position, you have to curb a tendency to meddle in your subordinates' projects. You work well in a team, and are willing to listen to other people's points of view and meet them half-way. Your power of concentration is very good, and combined with your hard work and ambition, can lead you to the very top.

In relationships, you can be serious and intense. You need someone who is light-hearted and can make you laugh! You are attracted to people who are self-confident and authentic. As tough as you are on the outside, with your family you are warm and sensitive. There were many sacrifices for your children's happiness. Your family knows they can count on you no matter what.

Celebrities

Evo Morales, President of Bolivia, country's first president to come from the indigenous population (Oct 26th)

Mary Hart, television personality and long-running host of Entertainment Tonight, past winner of Miss South Dakota (Nov 8th)

Martin Scorcese, multi-award winning director, producer, screenwriter, actor, and film historian, and founder of the World Cinema Foundation. He was the recipient of the recipient of the American Film Institute Life Achievement Award in 1997 (Nov 17th)

SCORPIO NUMBER 9 (OCT 27TH, NOV 9TH, NOV 18TH)

Pluto is the ruler of Scorpio and it corresponds to number 9, therefore your combination is most harmonious among Scorpios. Powerful, intense, mysterious, and perceptive, your ability to get to the heart of the matter is right on target. In terms of ability to read people, and understand psychology and motivation, you are one of the best due to your sharp intuition.

You have a lot of inner strength, tenacity and courage, therefore people who underestimate your ability for attack are in for quite a surprise. Definitely a warrior, there has to be a vision you are fighting for.

Constructively, you may use this to advocate for the needs of the disabled, disadvantaged, or oppressed. As powerful as an enemy as you can be, fortunately, if people keep you on their good side, you are equally as loyal and trustworthy.

In terms of career, you have tremendous vitality, and with your determination to succeed, you can do well in many fields. You are capable of single-minded concentration when the situation calls for it. Of particular interest may be roles where you can exert physical energy, satisfy your need for intellectual stimulation or exercise your warrior spirit.

The military, policing, corrections, medicine (particularly surgery), healing arts, engineering, competitive or extreme sports, skilled trades, construction, martial arts, astronomy, social justice or debating may fit you well.

A natural psychologist, problem solver, and detective, positions that allow you to get to the truth, such as psychiatry, therapy, investigations, research, solving mysteries, crime, forensics, and law may hold your interest. You are authoritative and operate best in positions of leadership.

In romance, you seek a meeting of mind, body and soul; you give everything you have because either you are in, or you are out, nothing halfway. You are attracted to people who fascinate you and who may be somewhat of an enigma. Your family appreciates your intense devotion and all the sacrifices you make for them, especially when your kids are young. One challenge for you is to make more of an effort to control your mood swings. This will be helpful in preventing wounds, as you can be quite stinging with sarcasm when upset.

Celebrities

Theodore Roosevelt, statesman, author, explorer, soldier, naturalist, and reformer. He served as the 26th President of the United States (Oct 27th)

Chris Jericho, multi-championship winning professional wrestler, musician, media personality, actor, author, businessman, and first undisputed WWF Champion (Nov 9th)

Alan Shepard, naval officer and aviator, test pilot, and flag officer. He was one of the original NASA Mercury Seven astronauts, and first American to travel into space (Nov 18th)

CHAPTER 15

SAGITTARIUS NUMBERS 1-9

SAGITTARIUS NUMBER 1 (NOV 28TH, DEC 1ST, DEC 10TH, DEC 19TH)

Optimistic, hopeful and, self-confident you feel ready to tackle the world head on. You have a strong belief that you can do anything you set your mind to, and because our thoughts shape our reality, you are able to achieve your goals. You believe, if at first I don't succeed, I will try, try, and try again! You are willing to change strategies that are not working, and try alternate routes as the situation calls for.

Idealistic, philosophical, and a free spirit, you are constantly questioning established theories, reflecting on life's mysteries, and relying on your own experience in coming to conclusions. There is a natural curiosity and quest for wisdom that only grows stronger with age. Outspoken and honest, you have a strong desire to get your unique message out there. Your generosity with your time, money, and effort is appreciated by those close to you.

In terms of career, positions of leadership come naturally to you. The group is fortunate because you see their inner potential, and inspire them to achieve their personal best. You are good at overlooking little mistakes, and tend to give the benefit of the doubt. Although you can work as part of a team, you are better in positions that give autonomy and independence. If you work with others, you generally are straightforward with any potential problems and hope to resolve them through talking it out. You may be attracted to work outdoors, in nature or with animals/plants.

Writing, lecturing, teaching, publishing, education, law, business, languages, literature, music, and entrepreneurial pursuits are well-suited to you.

Your interest in metaphysics, religion, spirituality and philosophy may be expressed through working in an organization focused on these areas.

In romance, you are genuine, and honest, and are attracted to partners who are cheerful and funny, but with a philosophical bent towards life. Although you get mad, you don't tend to hold grudges because you feel that life is too short. This attitude, if also shared by your partner, can lead to a harmonious relationship.

Your family appreciates your sense of adventure, and willingness to try new things. Your positive energy, search for wisdom, and zest for life are an inspiring example for your children.

Celebrities

Berry Gordy Jr, multi-award winning songwriter and founder of Motown Records. He is the first living individual to receive the Songwriters Hall of Fame's Pioneer Award in 2013 (Nov 28th)

Woody Allen, multi-award winning actor, writer, director, comedian, and playwright (Dec 1st)

Emily Dickinson, poet and cultural icon (Dec 10th)

Jake Gyllenhaal, multi-award winning actor (Dec 19th)

Sagittarius Number 2 (Nov 29th, Dec 2nd, Dec 11th, Dec 20th)

There is a great sense of aliveness in you, you appreciate the wonder of the earth, and seek out moments that are awe-inspiring. You try your best to live in the moment, and have a sensual appreciation of the simple pleasures life has to offer. People fascinate you, and you love hearing stories from all over the world; especially of people who surpassed overwhelming challenges to be their personal best.

You possess a talent for encouraging deeper reflection and you can exercise this skill by getting people to think about how their strengths can be used to serve others. On the other hand, you also have a knack for pulling trigger points. This may cause some hurt feelings; you must learn to apologize more quickly after you have realized your error.

If you were born on December 11th, you are able to access the benefits of this master number. Born with a high degree of idealism and enthusiasm, you can inspire people to live their best lives. You have a lot of impact on those around you. Because you expect good things from people and situations, this is what you usually receive. There is a side to you that is religious, spiritual, mystical, or otherwise believes that there is more to this world than can be seen or heard. You may devote a significant amount of time to these pursuits of higher consciousness.

In terms of career, you may find the healing arts, medicine, teaching, social work, counselling, public relations, mediation, real estate, advertising, writing, publishing, tourism or hospitality fields rewarding.

A good motivator with a capability for inspiring people to see the positive in every situation, you may find yourself in the position of a professional coach or advisor.

You may study many subjects at the same time so that you know a little bit about many things rather than just specializing in one area.

In romance, you are thoughtful, and partners appreciate your honesty. However, learning not to push your family's buttons when irritated, and instead trying a more diplomatic approach will contribute to healthier relationships. You often are able to spot dormant potentials within your spouse or children that later turn into major talents. Be confident in telling them what you think their strengths are. Your children are grateful that you let them try things out for themselves, rather than doing everything for them.

Celebrities

CS Lewis, novelist, poet, academic, medievalist, literary critic, essayist, lay theologian, broadcaster, lecturer, and Christian apologist (Nov 29th)

Nelly Furtado, best-selling and multi-award winning singer and songwriter (Dec 2nd)

Rita Moreno, multi-award winning actress and singer (Dec 11th)

Harvey Samuel Firestone, founder of the Firestone Tire and Rubber Company, and one of the first global makers of automobile tires (Dec 20th)

SAGITTARIUS NUMBER 3 (NOV 30TH, DEC 3RD, DEC 12TH, DEC 21ST)

You are fortunate to be blessed with a double dose of good fortune, as the number 3 corresponds to Jupiter, Sagittarius' ruling planet. It is true as others may have noticed, that you are naturally lucky, and able to capitalize on opportunities at the right time. You are likely to be interested in higher education, philosophy, metaphysics, mysticism, publishing, psychology, motivation, fitness, foreign travel, spirituality, religion, law, justice, politics, the government and the arts.

Expansive, you seek to broaden your outlook and increase your consciousness level. Understanding the world from a global perspective is important, and interacting with people from different cultures or who have different lifestyles captures your interest. At the same time, you can be quite secretive when revealing yourself on a deeper level to others. There is a marked need for solitude, as often you do your highest quality work this way. You generally have a good sense of humour, but can be quite defensive when others criticize you.

In terms of careers, you are resourceful, and practice passionately until you have achieved the perfection you desired. You are one of the most persuasive people of the zodiac, intuitively knowing when and how to say and do things for the best effects! Thus any job involving communication, sales, advertising, or fundraising could be a good fit.

Your approach to solving problems is very well thought out, therefore careers or hobbies which require defeating an opponent such as competitive sport, dance, martial arts, debate, or the military may hold your interest.

You are a natural teacher so any career involving advising, guiding, writing, or speaking works well.

You may like jobs having to do with nature, the outdoors, animals, foreign travel, law, the government, humanitarian pursuits, or social justice.

In romance, you are generous and optimistic. You try your best to see the good in everyone, especially your family. Lovers are attracted to your intelligence and sense of humour. Because your own inner passion and interests dictate what you do, you don't feel the need for your ideas and work to be accepted by everyone.

You teach your children to follow their heart in deciding what to do as well. Because your views are very strong, one of your challenges is letting your loved ones form their own opinions based on their thoughts and experiences, without feeling the need to convert them to your system of beliefs.

Celebrities

Winston Churchill, Prime Minister of the United Kingdom, officer in the British Army, historian, artist and first person to be made an honorary citizen of the United States. Winner of the Nobel Prize in Literature in 1953 (Nov 30th)

Anna Freud, author and one of the founders of psychoanalytic child psychology (Dec 3rd)

Frank Sinatra, multi-award winning singer, actor, director, and producer (Dec 12th)

Jane Fonda, multi-award winning actress, writer, political activist, and fitness guru (Dec 21st)

Sagittarius Number 4 (Nov 22nd, Dec 4th, Dec 13th)

There is a spirit of innovation in you. Always with an eye to the future, you are able to spot trends ahead of everyone else. You crave freedom physically, mentally, emotionally, and spiritually. In that vein, attempts by others to control you are futile. Travelling and higher education holds great interest for you.

Unconventional people and philosophies fascinate you, perhaps because you faced adversities growing up, or you never felt as if you fit in. In any case, you have a special gift for taking early adversities and empowering other people to learn from your example. You inspire people to overcome their challenges.

If you were born on November 22nd, you receive the benefits of this master number. Nov 22nd is described both for Sagittarius and Scorpio, so please confirm which sign you are. If you are a Sagittarius number 22, you are a free spirit with a rebellious streak that cannot be pinned down. You feel your life is yours the way you want to live it, and are more likely than others to follow your dreams, regardless of what other people say. Just when someone thinks they know you, you will surprise them with another side to your multifaceted nature! Your brilliance is shown through your aptitude for bringing the truth to light, exposing power abuses, injustices and human rights violations, anywhere people are taking advantage of others for their own gain.

In terms of career, choose positions where your need for freedom, autonomy, variety and intellectual curiosity are satisfied. Ideally you would like a sense of adventure and discovery too. You may enjoy jobs involving a foreign component, public speaking, sports, skilled trades, the occult, metaphysics, astronomy, business management, politics, writing, working with children, working with animals, religion or spirituality.

You may be a perfectionist in some sense, certainly you have an eye for detail and quality. Jobs involving a high degree of attention would be a good use of your skill.

Creatively you may enjoy music, interior decoration, fashion, graphic designing, and painting.

Your talent for digging to the core of the matter may be useful in investigations, research, law, forensics, medicine, psychology, or psychiatry.

Naturally inventive and authoritative, you may start your own business. In whatever you do, your commitment to quality takes you far.

In romance, you are attracted to free spirited people who are eager to explore the world, and make new discoveries. You need a partner who is willing to explore with you, but also reign in your tendency to take too many risks (although they admire your courage to pursue your dreams with everything you have). As a family, you will enjoy constantly trying new things, and socializing with people from all walks of life. They admire your optimism, perseverance, and resiliency.

Celebrities

Charles de Gaulle, 18th French President, recipient of numerous awards and honours including Grand-Croix of the Légion d'honneur and Grand Master of the Ordre de la Libération (Nov 22nd)

Nick Vujicic, Christian evangelist, motivational speaker who was born with tetra-amelia syndrome, winner of the Australian young citizen award for his bravery and perseverance (Dec 4th)

Taylor Swift, multi-award winning and best-selling singer, songwriter, and actress (Dec 13th)

SAGITTARIUS NUMBER 5 (NOV 23RD, DEC 5TH, DEC 14TH)

There is a deep love of travel in you, this is probably one of your main passions in life. Indeed you will most likely have the opportunity to travel far and wide. You also travel via your imagination through books and media that transport you to the most exotic and exciting places. Walt Disney (b. Dec 5th) made it possible for guests to Walt Disney World to travel all over the world and into the future by visiting his theme parks.

Quick-witted, intelligent, and with an endless love of learning, you spend a large amount of your time first acquiring knowledge, and then sharing it with others. You believe that it is better to set the bar high and come close to achieving your goals, rather than setting the bar low and achieving them. This philosophy has allowed you to accomplish things that most people have not been able to do.

It is very hard trying to pin you down because you surprise people with different facets of your nature when they aren't expecting it. The good thing is that you are confident in what makes you different rather than trying to fit into other people's perceptions of who you should be. Similarly, you don't believe something just because the majority believes it or an expert espouses it. You believe things based on your personal analysis and experience.

In terms of career, roles which require imagination, creativity, multitasking, and a sense of humour are well suited to you. You have many talents and interests and can easily adapt to a variety of roles. Sales, marketing, advertising, healing arts, culinary arts, counselling, yoga, law, drama, music, sports, philosophy, filmmaking, entertainment, feng shui, the occult, writing, politics, and music may hold special interest, as will careers involving travel, aviation, the outdoors, or animals.

In romance, you are attracted to people who love learning, exploring and growing. Your partner appreciates your intelligence, sense of humour, and ability to adapt to changing circumstances with grace. You encourage your family to be immune to what other people think of them, and to act authentically from their heart. They love your wild imagination and ability to reach for the stars.

Celebrities

Robin Roberts, multi-award winning TV show host and best-selling author (Nov 23rd)

Walt Disney, multi-award winning entrepreneur, cartoonist, animator, voice actor, and film producer, co-founder of Walt Disney World (Dec 5th)

Nostradamus, poet, apothecary, and prophet (Dec 14th)

SAGITTARIUS NUMBER 6 (NOV 24TH, DEC 6TH, DEC 15TH)

Family and friends are your world. Relationships are sacred, and you spend a lot of time building bonds with those around you. You have high hopes for your loved ones and want to help them do well. Motivating those around you to reach their goals is a strong suit.

Seeing people treated fairly and with dignity is a major concern of yours; you believe in the equality of all people. You may be active in your community trying to help those who are being oppressed or marginalized.

The love of luxuries and beauty is very strong in you, and you are much happier when allowed to treat your mind, body and spirit to a little pampering. Visiting beautiful places and landmarks gives you great pleasure as you admire the aesthetics and cultural significance. At the same time you must be careful not to go overboard with too many indulgences. Similarly, when making promises to other people you sometimes bite off more than you can chew, you have to make sure your promises are realistic enough to keep.

In terms of career, philosophy, law, education, human rights, writing, fitness, wellness, research, healthcare, sales, culinary arts, customer service, administration, medicine, architecture, engineering, politics, counselling, coaching, and working with animals or with plants may be areas of special interest.

Creatively, music, drawing, painting, and acting might be good expressions of your energy.

Because your senses are heightened, a harmonious work environment is key to your success. An environment that has too much negative energy will drain your energy very fast.

In romance, you enjoy indulging all the five senses and appreciate partners who contribute to these memorable experiences. Lovers are attracted to your self-confidence and charm. You do have to try to lessen the tendency to be too competitive, or argumentative with your partner, participating in experiences that are team building helps to create greater intimacy. Your children appreciate your faith in their talents, and that you encourage them to not worry about failing, just to go for it!

Celebrities

Baruch Spinoza, philosopher (Nov 24th)

Byron Katie, motivational speaker and best-selling author (Dec 6th)

Alexander Gustave Eiffel, civil engineer and architect, Eiffel Tower (Dec 15th)

SAGITTARIUS NUMBER 7 (NOV 25TH, DEC 7TH, DEC 16TH)

You are likely a philosophical, reflective, spiritual, or mystical thinker with great powers of intuition and flashes of insight. Highly imaginative, often when you are least expecting it, you get an answer to your problem, or you receive sudden inspirations. Even your dreams are very lucid, and sometimes prophetic, so you would benefit from keeping a dream journal. The deeper and more hidden workings of the universe and people fascinate you, as you seek to uncover the truth. Questions of good and evil, right and wrong, moral and immoral, occupy your mind, although you have to avoid sharing your opinions as a fact on these topics.

Although you can be friendly and enjoy spending time with family and friends, you probably prefer to do more things alone than with others. There is a part of you that may feel a sense of not quite fitting in or having interests that are much different than other people of your age. This may have caused some discomfort growing up. However when you became older, you probably realized that there is a strength in being able to offer what other people can't. You are able to think from non-linear perspectives that add a different insight than the one most people default to.

In terms of career, you are inclined towards change. It may take you a while to really find your passion, but once you find it, you are capable of channeling immense energy into it.

You may gravitate to drawing, healing arts, painting, philosophy, music, writing, interior decoration, graphic design, filmmaking, languages, metaphysics, the occult, religion, and entertainment.

Generally, you excel in roles that allow for a good deal of solitude, reflection and creativity. If you are more left-brained, science, math, engineering, information technology, computer science, dentistry, law, medicine, business management, and research are also good fits.

In romance, you are very idealistic and have high hopes for how you would like your partnership to be. You are attracted to people who display faith and optimism. Lovers are attracted to your passion and empathy. However sometimes you see them through rose-colored glasses, and you need to be more accepting of faults and limitations. Your children admire your generosity and willingness to listen to them.

Celebrities

Andrew Carnegie, business magnate and philanthropist (Nov 25th)

Noam Chomsky, multi-award winning linguist, philosopher, political activist, and writer (Dec 7th)

Ludwig van Beethoven, cultural icon, composer, and pianist (Dec 16th)

SAGITTARIUS NUMBER 8 (NOV 26TH, DEC 8TH, DEC 17TH)

Perhaps more practical and pragmatic than the typical Sagittarian, you nonetheless are capable of being idealistic and philosophical in outlook at certain times. There is a strong drive towards accomplishment, but your idea of success is broader than what is typically defined by society. This would include joy, inner peace and a sense of connection to the Universe or a Higher Power. Ethics and morals weigh heavily on your mind, as you contemplate your actions, the actions of those around you, and current events. You may feel compelled to share your thoughts either orally or in writing.

In terms of career, your conscientiousness, endurance and resiliency ensure that you can reach any goal you are passionate about achieving. Setbacks and disappointments only serve to strengthen your resolve to do better next time.

Areas you may enjoy are international relations, music, dance, international business, social justice, politics, journalism, medicine, healthcare, rehabilitation, accounting, real estate, religion, publishing, languages, speech pathology, audiology, teaching, literature, science, computer science, humanitarian work, or research.

Generally, roles that give you a sense of freedom but that also have a clear sense of expectations are best for you.

In romance, you need a partner with a good sense of humour, and who brings out your imagination. Lovers are attracted to your honesty and fairness. Family members appreciate that they know where they stand with you, and that they are free to also let you know where you stand with them. One thing to keep in mind is because of your sometimes tough exterior, other people may not know how sensitive you really are. Therefore, you must try not to take criticisms too personally. Your children benefit from your broadmindedness and willingness to open up to them.

Celebrities

Tina Turner, Grammy award-winning singer, dancer, actress, and author. She was inducted into the Rock and Roll Hall of Fame in 1991 (Nov 26th)

Sammy Davis Jr., dancer, singer, actor, musician, and impressionist. He was the recipient of the Kennedy Center Honors in 1987 and awarded the Spingarn Medal by the NAACP in 1968 (Dec 8th)

Pope Francis, 266th and current Pope of the Catholic Church, and prolific author (Dec 17th)

SAGITTARIUS NUMBER 9 (NOV 27TH, DEC 9TH, DEC 18TH)

You are concerned with truth in all of its forms, and with your warrior personality, you can be a powerful advocate in causing the change we need to see in the world. Global and humanitarian issues are of particular interest. Because you see yourself as a citizen of the world, your understanding that we are all interconnected helps you bridge the gaps between people who are mentally and/or physically apart. Fortunately you are blessed with courage; you are not afraid to say what needs to be said and do what needs to be done in implementing the change you wish to see. Persistent in whatever activity you commit to, you give it 110%.

In terms of career, you thrive on a sense of challenge, it gets the adrenaline pumping, and gives you something to work towards. Your imagination is capable of producing far-reaching visions, or ideas just waiting to become part of the collective consciousness. While other people may be satisfied with a job to pay the bills, personal meaning in your work is very important to you. You may also spend a significant time volunteering, and are generous with financial donations.

You are able to take the risk of starting your own business, and often are successful due to your vision, effort, and ambition. Working in communications, law, social work, charity work, environmental studies, science, publishing, fundraising, religion, spirituality, or foreign relations may suit you.

Other areas you may enjoy are veterinary care, nursing, sports, athletics, sales, entertainment, astronomy, the occult, yoga, firefighting, law enforcement, the military, comedy, filmmaking, and music.

In romance, lovers appreciate your eagerness for adventure, and courage to take the road less travelled. You are enthusiastic, and wish to explore the full extent of what life has to offer. This applies both in terms of the physical world, and in exploring what lies beneath the world we experience with the five senses. Thus you need a lover who is willing to come along for the ride with you. You also desire someone who is compassionate and cares for people on a global scale. By encouraging your children to speak their truth, they are able to tackle problems that give them a sense of challenge and accomplishment.

Celebrities

Bill Nye the Science Guy, science educator, mechanical engineer, comedian, television host, actor, writer, and scientist (Nov 27th)

Judi Dench, multi-award winning stage and movie actress. She holds the record for most major acting awards across all six American and British events (Dec 9th)

Brad Pitt, multi-award winning actor and producer (Dec 18th)

CHAPTER 16

CAPRICORN NUMBERS 1-9

CAPRICORN NUMBER 1 (DEC 28TH, JAN 1ST, JAN 10TH, JAN 19TH)

You are very determined to succeed, and will work hard in rising to the top of your field. You want to be respected and admired for your contributions, particularly in a professional sense. You particularly detest being in a subordinate position where you must follow the orders of someone else. There is a desire for leadership and you can be an efficient leader, although you must watch for a tendency to be autocratic. High standards are set for yourself and for those you are in care of, or manage.

Sometimes you can be too focused on your own work; you must make a stronger effort to help those who ask, and understand that everyone learns at their own pace. Paying more attention to nonverbal communication will help you cultivate more authentic relationships. Making compromises based on everyone's interests will be a lifelong lesson.

In terms of career, there is definitely entrepreneurial talent. Your talents can also be used in companies, or working for others as long as you have independence and autonomy. For example, management positions in businesses or in the government would be good for you. An admirable trait about you, is your perseverance. Another person may have more natural talent or environmental opportunities than you, but your strength is that you don't give up easily. If you get knocked down, you will brush it off and keep trying. You do well in roles involving problem solving and clearly defined expectations.

Professions capturing your interest may include science, math, martial arts, sports, literature, technology, rehabilitation, medicine, physics, administration, engineering, law, dentistry, healthcare, military, real estate, broadcasting, metaphysics, yoga, comedy, astronomy, landscaping, and architecture.

In romance, you are attracted to self-assured people who have a clear sense of direction about who they are and where they are going in life. Lovers appreciate your honesty and ability to get necessary work done efficiently. Being more willing to lean on them in times of need, or to ask for help as required, develops intimacy. You have a tendency to pay attention to what your family says, but not so much to how they may feel about what you say or do. Greater sensitivity to your children's thoughts and feelings is needed to deepen bonding.

Celebrities

Denzel Washington, multi-award winning actor and filmmaker (Dec 28th)

J. Edgar Hoover, founder of, and first Director of the Federal Bureau of Investigation of the United States and the recipient of numerous distinguished honours. He was presented the honorary knighthood in the Order of the British Empire in 1950 by King George VI of the United Kingdom (Jan 1st)

George Foreman, professional boxer, two-time World Heavyweight Champion, Olympic gold medalist, ordained minister, author, and inventor of the best-selling George Foreman Grill. He was inducted into the International Boxing Hall of Fame in 2003 (Jan 10th)

Dolly Parton, multi-award winning and best-selling country music singer-songwriter, instrumentalist, actress, author, businesswoman, and philanthropist (Jan 19th)

CAPRICORN NUMBER 2 (DEC 29TH, JAN 2ND, JAN 11TH)

You can excel in business because you combine shrewd, logical thinking with diplomacy and listening skills. While you know the value of working hard, you are more genial than the typical Capricorn and enjoy doing team oriented activities. The process of brainstorming with others is something you enjoy.

Responsible to a fault, you have a tendency to take on all the work in your family and other social groups to which you belong. One of your lessons is to delegate responsibility when needed.

Your role models are usually people who may have started modestly but triumphed over early obstacles, and used their ingenuity to make a success for themselves. Perhaps because of this as an adult you so often fit this description yourself.

If you were born on January 11th, you receive the benefit of this master number. You have a unique blend of practicality, responsibility, creativity, and mysticism that can inspire others to carry over their spiritual practice into other areas of their life. Idealistic, but at the same time realistic, you have a vision to create meaningful change, and you develop a workable plan to start doing it. Perhaps you may share these insights through writing, lecturing, or some form of media. You may do well in spiritual, religious, philosophical, and humanitarian organizations in which your organizational talents can be used.

In terms of career, your skills of strategizing, negotiation, tact, and ability to listen can be used in many roles. You can intuitively figure out what people want, and give it to them. You may use your skills in a variety of ways such as teaching, music, psychology, acting, politics, business management, hospitality, tourism, administration, medicine, culinary arts, skilled trades, rehabilitation, yoga, dentistry, comedy, speech pathology, event planning, telecommunications, sports, finance, real estate, the occult, astronomy, and pharmaceuticals.

In romance, you show your lover how much you care with practical acts of service and devotion. Lovers are attracted to your innovative spirit. You need someone who understands that while you can be critical on the outside, you are actually sensitive to criticism from others. With your family, you are warm and generous. Your children respect the fact that you push them to do well, but also appreciate when they have tried their best.

Celebrities

Mary Tyler Moore, multi-award winning actress (Dec 29th)

Christy Turlington, supermodel, film director, and founder of Every Mother Counts (Jan 2nd)

Sir John A. McDonald, First Prime Minister of Canada (Jan 11th)

CAPRICORN NUMBER 3 (DECEMBER 30TH, JAN 3RD, JAN 12TH)

There is a good blend of idealism and realism in you. Hope for the best but be prepared for the unexpected could characterize your approach. On one hand, you can be looking to the future with the glass half full, believing things that aren't going the way as planned have a silver lining. However, you can also look at a good situation and figure out what might go wrong with it. You are one who dares to dream, but realizes that concrete action is needed to make those dreams a reality. Thriving on challenges, you will strive to succeed even if all the cards seem stacked against you, and everyone around you says you can't do it. Success comes to you because you are capable of devoting all your time and energy into the desired goal, without becoming distracted or losing interest.

You enjoy discussing philosophical and religious topics, and spending time involved in discussions about important questions that face the world today. There is an appreciation for other people who are aware of current events, world issues, and the quality of life for people on a global scale. In fact you could do a lot of foreign travelling, seeking to gain a deeper appreciation and understanding of different cultures, belief systems, and ways of living.

In terms of career, politics, social justice, law, media, communications, and humanitarian efforts are good fits. You need a sense of adventure or continuous learning and growing. Roles which offer little change, excitement, or discovery drain your energy.

Projects which involve fixing things and presenting them in a better developed state may capture your interest such as buying old houses, redecorating and then re-selling. Or you may refurbish antique items for collections or sales. This idea may also apply to people and make you adept at coaching, motivation, or counselling people who are at low points to revitalize their life.

There is also a lot of creativity in you which may be expressed through singing, dancing, poetry, and visual arts. Other areas that may interest you include yoga, medicine, healing arts, literature, education, editing, publishing, and languages.

In romance, you are looking for someone who is practical, but also has a sense of adventure and discovery. Your lover appreciates the freedom you give him or her to explore and exchange opinions and ideas freely. Your mix of generosity and frugality is passed on to your children. As a result they have good work ethic and know the value of a dollar, but are also encouraged to be a cheerful giver.

Celebrities

Matt Lauer, multi-award winning TV show host and journalist. He co-hosted the opening ceremonies of several Olympic Games (Dec 30th)

Eli Manning, multi-award winning football player, led the Giants to victory in Super Bowl XLII and Super Bowl XLVI (Jan 3rd)

Jeff Bezos, billionaire, founder of Amazon, and owner of The Washington Post (Jan 12th)

CAPRICORN NUMBER 4 (DEC 22ND, DEC 31ST, JAN 4TH, JAN 13TH)

Practical and logical in your approach to doing things; if others wish to convince you of something, it must make sense. Emotional pleas are less likely to work. You are very good at following through on projects because your hardworking nature will push them to completion. Endurance and persistence are key to your success.

Within you there is also a spirit of invention, future-oriented thinking and exploring the path less travelled.

A natural curiosity and tendency to question things can lead to unusual insights or discoveries.

You have a natural understanding for what is beautiful, elegant and sophisticated, and there is a special appreciation for luxuries and technology that make your life more enjoyable. Often you are noted for your personal sense of style, and skill for beautifying your surroundings.

If you were born on December 22nd, you receive the benefits of this master number. There is a wonderful blend of future oriented thinking, vision and brilliance, with solidity, structure and practicality. These skills allow you to steadily progress towards your aims, and complete work that leaves a lasting legacy. You possess a powerful intuition about people, places and things, which should be relied on a lot more often, for its truth surpasses the linear mind. When you look back on it, you will see that your major successes were when you trusted your gut instinct, despite how things looked at the time. There is entrepreneurial talent, particularly with respect to finance, science, new technology, and electronics.

In terms of career, you need to be original, and are willing to carve out your own niche if the existing ones do not satisfy your need for expression. Not limited by external circumstances or people around you, you firmly believe the only limits, are the ones you set for yourself.

There is an interest in health and the human body that could lead to careers in the medical, science, healing arts, kinesiology, health, nutrition, sports, rehabilitation, diet, wellness or fitness fields. Interestingly, Andreas Vesalius who is known as the founder of modern human anatomy, and Shonda Rhimes, creator, head writer, executive producer, and showrunner of the medical drama TV show Grey's Anatomy, are both Capricorn number 4 people!

You are interested in potential and self-development, ways in which people can constantly grow and improve themselves. Thus careers such as social work, psychology, coaching, counselling, the occult, metaphysics, addictions and mental health, and education are good fits.

There may be a need for self-expression; poetry, dance, writing, and drawing may hold particular appeal.

Your eye for beauty and appreciation for luxury, can be used in the real estate, interior decoration, feng shui, fashion, hairstyling, or cosmetics fields.

Other areas of interest may include math, engineering, journalism, culinary arts, media, and administration.

In romance, you are attracted to unconventional people who are free spirited and innovative. Your partner appreciates your no-limits attitude and determination to achieve your goals. You raise your children with the belief that they can do anything they set their minds to as long as they have the passion for it. As a family you may engage in activities geared towards self-development, discovery, and invention.

Celebrities

Diane Sawyer, multi-award winning TV journalist. She was inducted into the Television Hall of Fame in 1997 (Dec 22nd)

Andreas Vesalius, physician, author, and founder of modern human anatomy (Dec 31st)

Sir Isaac Newton, multi-award winning physicist, mathematician, inventor, and author. The Isaac Newton Medal is given annually to one physicist from around the world for outstanding contributions to physics (Jan 4th)

Shonda Rhimes, multi-award winning screenwriter, director, and producer (Jan 13th)

CAPRICORN NUMBER 5 (DEC 23RD, JAN 5TH, JAN 14TH)

You are well-spoken, and communicate your ideas in a simple way. The need to express yourself is very strong, and you may be compelled to write, speak, broadcast, or put your message out to society in some other form. Regardless of subject, what you talk about is not just abstract musings, but has a lot of real world applicability. For example, even though Paramahansa Yogananda (b. Jan 5th) was intensely spiritual and ethereal, his publications were focused on tangible exercises that the public may engage in to bring more peace into their daily lives.

You love foreign travel and exploration, and you will enjoy learning about foreign people. It is possible that you may permanently move to different countries or at least spend part of your life living in a foreign country.

One of your greatest strengths is that you rarely give up, even after being told the odds are not in your favour, you will forge ahead anyway. Sometimes this doesn't pay off, but your capacity to recover from setbacks is remarkable. When your persistence does pay off, you are able to enjoy large rewards, and the satisfaction of proving the naysayers wrong. Thus your innate ability to turn a setback into a setup for success is a positive feature in any situation.

In terms of career, communication is a strength, so careers involving verbal or written expression are good expressions of your talent.

Your desire to help others may be used in in medicine, psychology, humanitarian work, spiritual advising, and coaching. Sales, advertising, marketing, and telecommunications allow you to use your skill for persuasion.

You may find yourself in the role of helping people manage their money such as financial advising, banking, investing, and real estate.

You could do well when combining business, writing and travel, for example a travel writer, vacation specialist or advertiser for vacations/ hotels.

Your entrepreneurial pursuits are aided by your gift for communicating the advantages of your product or service in a way that captures people's interest. You will probably keep yourself busy well after retirement, either working part-time or keeping current with the latest developments.

In romance, you enjoy conversing with your partner, and crave intellectual stimulation. You desire a lover who is on the same mental wavelength as you, and who challenges you to constantly learn and grow. Your children are inspired by your innate fortitude, and will to keep going in the face of adversity. They also enjoy your straight talk about issues that really matter to them.

Celebrities

Madame C. J Walker, entrepreneur and first female African-American millionaire (Dec 23rd)

Paramahansa Yogananda, Indian yogi, guru, lecturer, and best-selling author (Jan 5th)

Dr. Albert Schweitzer, theologian, organist, philosopher, physician, and medical missionary. He was the winner of the Nobel Peace Prize in 1952 (Jan 14th)

CAPRICORN NUMBER 6 (DEC 24TH, JAN 6TH, JAN 15TH)

You are characterized by responsibility, and can usually be counted on to keep your promises to help those who need it. People who are disadvantaged or disabled in some way earn your empathy, and you seek to advocate on their behalf.

You love beautiful and luxurious things, they indulge your sensual side and make you happy. There is a regular need to pamper yourself with treats like massages, delicious meals, and beautiful clothes; otherwise you find your mental and physical energy being drained.

With a tendency towards introspection, philosophy, metaphysics, ethics, religion, and spirituality might be on your mind. More specifically, it is how to use these ideals and principles in a practical way to improve interpersonal and group relations. You may be compelled to share these thoughts with others through discussion or writing.

In terms of career, you are compassionate and service-oriented so you may do well in the nurturing professions such as nursing, child care, coaching, counselling, rehabilitation, or assisted living fields.

Your desire to own your own business is strong and many people with this combination are successful in small businesses, especially those relating to finance, accounting, real estate, restaurants, entertainment, theatre, music, interior decoration, retail, jewelry, hairstyling, or beauty.

Your interest in human rights or social issues can lead to a career in law or within a non-profit or humanitarian organization.

Your artistic side may be expressed through filmmaking, photography, poetry, or music.

In romance, you are charming, compassionate, and sensual which attracts many suitable partners. You admire people who are idealistic, but are grounded enough to impact change in the world. Your partner enjoys your global outlook and willingness to help others. Participating in luxurious, relaxing activities together builds intimacy. You teach your children to care for those who have less than them, and to treat everyone fairly and with respect.

Celebrities

Howard Hughes, multi-millionaire, investor, aviator, aerospace engineer, inventor, filmmaker and philanthropist (Dec 24th)

Khalil Gibran, artist, writer, and third best-selling poet of all time (Jan 6th)

Martin Luther King Jr, Baptist minister and Civil Rights leader (Jan 15th)

CAPRICORN NUMBER 7 (DEC 25TH, JAN 7TH, JAN 16TH)

You are private and need time to yourself to think and contemplate. Not one for small talk, you may not say a lot unless you are talking about something you are passionate about. In this case your arguments can be detailed and eloquent.

You are more imaginative than other Capricorns, often coming up with creative plans to difficult problems. Your sharp intuition allows you to accurately sense other people's thoughts and feelings. There may be an interest in unconventional topics or people. This is not for a specific purpose but just as a general study stemming from curiosity and fascination.

In terms of career, you have a very analytical mind and like studying subjects in great depth. A career which involves research, problem-solving, strategic thinking, and studying fits well. Careers which allow for independence and creativity are best because otherwise you quickly start to feel smothered.

There are great powers of observation and there is not much that goes under your radar. Roles involving solving mysteries or paying attention to people, places or things can be a good fit.

Because you are very sensitive to and affected by your environment, you should work in places that do not have excessive noises or aggression. Being near the water or in nature helps to soothe and relax you.

Careers that may capture your interest might be nursing, education, humanitarian work, metaphysics, religion, administration, aviation, music, fashion, information technology, sports, math, science, languages, literature, writing, business management, comedy, psychology, the occult, tourism, hospitality, event planning, culinary arts, and broadcasting.

In romance, you are sensitive, and feel very deeply, but can be somewhat slow to give affection. You need a partner who makes you feel secure enough to express your love in the way you are most comfortable. Your strong belief in destiny, synchronicities and that everything happens for a reason, influences your family. Thus they are likely to appreciate that both good and bad events alike are happening for their greater good.

Celebrities

Clara Burton, Civil war nurse and founder of the American Red Cross (Dec 25th)

Christian Louboutin, multi-award winning footwear designer (Jan 7th)

Kate Moss, multi-award winning model and fashion designer (Dec 16th)

CAPRICORN NUMBER 8 (DEC 26TH, JAN 8TH, JAN 17TH)

Out of all Capricorns, you are most conventional of your sign-- ambitious, hardworking and disciplined. Your core strength lies in your ability to persevere despite obstacles placed in your way. This being a karmic combination (Saturn the ruler of Capricorn corresponds to number 8), life continually presents you with challenges but this is to develop your endurance, willpower, and resiliency. You have had to work harder than most people to succeed. Thus you are determined to rise to the top and earn other people's respect. You will not look for shortcuts and get rich quick schemes, rather you lay the proper foundation for gradual success. There may be particular scientific, mathematical, technical or analytical intelligence that you possess that could amount to genius if you apply yourself.

In terms of career, you have good entrepreneurial ability. You can use your inventiveness to design products, and effectively market them to the public. You probably enjoy positions of status, power, and wealth.

Business management, administration, politics, law, justice, publishing, writing, accountancy, medicine, science, politics, real estate, engineering, architecture, technology, aviation, education, government, social work, the skilled trades, sports, or religion may interest you.

Working with the elderly, disabled, or disadvantaged may be a good expression of your talents.

If creatively inclined, fashion, sculpture, painting, and dance may hold special appeal.

In terms of romance, you are attracted to independent and ambitious people. You need a partner who can lighten things up for you, as sometimes you take yourself and the world too seriously. Once committed to someone, you will stick with them through the good and bad times, and are ready to work out difficulties. You are very self-reliant, thus it may be hard for you to lean on others during times of hardship. Although you may present a tough exterior to the outside world, be more willing to be vulnerable with your family to enhance intimacy. You set an excellent example for your children with regards to self-discipline, fulfilling responsibilities, and setting high goals.

Celebrities

Martin Cooper, engineer and inventor of the first handheld mobile phone (Dec 26th)

Stephen Hawking, theoretical physicist, cosmologist, and best-selling author. Director of Research at the Centre for Theoretical Cosmology within the University of Cambridge (Jan 8th)

Benjamin Franklin, one of the Founding Fathers of the United States, author, printer, political theorist, politician, postmaster, scientist, inventor, civic activist, statesman, and diplomat (Jan 17th)

Capricorn Number 9 (Dec 27th, Jan 9th, Jan 18th)

Within you there are very high standards of excellence and a good deal of drive to make things happen. Even if you fail, you will pull yourself back up, time and time again. You can be very disciplined, ambitious, and hardworking when moving towards important goals. Independent and maybe a little rebellious, you don't take well to following orders but do well in positions where you have freedom and control. Dangerous as an enemy, you have a warrior nature and will fight hard against people and obstacles that you think pose a threat.

A natural teacher, your students come from all different walks of life and you will always present things in a way that they see how it is relevant to their life. Naturally compassionate and sacrificing, there may be a humanitarian streak and you could make an excellent advocate for people who are disadvantaged in some way.

In terms of career, you may be attracted to positions which challenge you mentally or physically, such as medicine, science, psychology, the healing arts, public speaking, humanitarian work, foreign relations, international business, law, politics, government, teaching, engineering, social work, the occult, technology, hunting, construction, the military, the Navy, law enforcement, firefighting, high intensity sports, martial arts, kickboxing, and wrestling.

Creatively, you may like fashion, yoga, feng shui, music, drama, or poetry.

Whatever field you get into has to give you variety and excitement, otherwise you lose motivation and concentration. Your desire for change may mean that you switch careers or participate in multiple careers at the same time.

In romance, you like to take charge and are likely the more dominant one, even if it is behind the scenes. The thrill of the chase is exciting, but once settled down you can be faithful and devoted. You need a partner who is gentle and can help you balance various areas of your life. An effective disciplinarian, you give your children proportional rewards but do not spoil them. Your family admires your simple and honest approach to life, and positive encouragement in their endeavours.

Celebrities

Louis Pasteur, multi-award winning chemist, microbiologist, founder of vaccination, microbial fermentation, and pasteurization. The Pasteur Institute in France continues to do ground-breaking research in preventing and treating infectious diseases. (Dec 27th)

Kate Middleton, British royalty (Jan 9th)

Cary Grant, stage and film actor. Recipient of the Academy Honorary Award in 1970 and the Kennedy Center Honours in 1981 (Jan 18th)

CHAPTER 17

AQUARIUS NUMBERS 1-9

AQUARIUS NUMBER 1 (JAN 28TH, FEB 1ST, FEB 10TH)

A true pioneer, you are the symbol of creativity and inventiveness. You boldly blaze new trails. Combining the originality and high vitality of the number 1, with the visionary ideas and unconventionality of Aquarius, you will be a leader in some sphere of your life. You don't seek to fit your ideas into a previously established mold, rather you create your own path with the ideas of tomorrow.

Your will power is very strong, however you can be stubborn once your mind is made up. Inherently rebellious, one of your challenges is to re-evaluate incoming information to see whether the course of action you began is still is the best option. Naturally confident and independent, you work best either alone, or as a leader.

In terms of career, freedom of speech, thought, and action is important and you need to express your individuality and creativity.

Equality is one of your major concerns, so roles in which you can advocate for fair treatment for disadvantaged, oppressed or marginalized people, and motivate them to their highest potential are a good fit for you.

Entrepreneurial pursuits of all kinds are favourable, because even if you fail a few times, you are well able to learn from your mistakes.

You may be attracted to careers in information technology, business management, teaching, science, research, engineering, electricity, pharmaceuticals, astronomy, media, literature, the occult, languages, psychiatry, psychology, yoga, the environment, social work, and communications.

In romance, you need a partner who cherishes your uniqueness, and respects your need for freedom and independence. Your partner appreciates your courage to be yourself, and stay true to your passion under external pressure. Intimacy can be increased by leaning on him or her in times of need, rather than taking all the burden. Your children like the fact that you encourage them to be creative individuals and put authentic work out into the world.

Celebrities

Carlos Slim Helu, billionaire, business magnate, investor, and philanthropist (Jan 28th)

Langston Hughes, multi-award winning poet, social activist, novelist, playwright, and columnist (Feb 1st)

George Stephanopoulos, Emmy Award winning journalist, Democratic political advisor, and TV news anchor (Feb 10th)

AQUARIUS NUMBER 2 (JAN 20TH, JAN 29TH, FEB 2ND, FEB 11TH)

You have an innate understanding of people that transcends all outer circumstances such as race, country, social status, age, or gender. People's lives and stories hold a deep fascination for you, as you are keen to uncover the eternal truths of the human condition. Seeing people treated unfairly strikes a chord, as you seek to bring their stories into a more public awareness so that change can happen. Tolerance and broad-mindedness are two of your biggest strengths and enable you to form meaningful bonds with people extremely different from you. At heart you are a humanitarian, and your compassion shines through like a beam of hope to all those you seek to inspire, motivate, and teach.

If you were born on February 11th, you receive the benefits of this master number. Idealistic, intuitive, and with a strong need for self-expression, you seek to change the world by using your voice as a catalyst for change. The status quo holds no appeal for you because you think in terms of potential. Fortunately, because you are able to envision people living out their dreams, you often inspire them to action. You are able to intuitively see where people can improve, and instinctively seek to help them. Spirituality, philosophy, technology, drama, visual arts, science, veterinary care, inventions, research, literature, and music may hold special interest for you.

In terms of career, you are people-oriented and do well in positions requiring an understanding of human nature, in furthering the interests of a humanitarian organization, and in seeking to improve the overall quality of life for people or animals.

You have great ability to negotiate, resulting in bringing both sides together to compromise for a win-win situation. In business, you have a talent in gauging what your clients want.

You may do well in studies looking at the behaviour of individuals or groups such as psychology, history, labour relations, sociology, social work, or politics.

Other careers that may interest you are broadcasting, communications, public relations, metaphysics, mediation, foreign relations, environmental studies, education, religion, astronomy, and yoga.

In romance, you are a wonderful listener, and your partner appreciates your empathetic ear. You desire a lover who shares your love for helping people and positively changing the world. You teach your kids to make friends with a diverse range of people to expand their awareness of the world around them. As a family, bonding is made more meaningful by participating in activities designed to help those who most need it.

Celebrities

Buzz Aldrin, multi-award winning engineer, astronaut, and former U.S. Air Force Officer and Command Pilot. He was the second person to walk on the Moon. Awarded the Presidential Medal of Freedom with Distinction in 1969 (Jan 20th)

Oprah Winfrey, multi-award winning talk show host, actress, producer, and philanthropist. Recipient of the Presidential Medal of Freedom in 2013 (Jan 29th)

Havelock Ellis, physician, author, and social reformer of human sexuality (Feb 2nd)

Thomas Edison, multi-award winning inventor and businessman. Recipient of the Congressional Gold Medal in 1928. Awarded the Commander of the Legion of Honour in 1889. (Feb 11th)

AQUARIUS NUMBER 3 (JAN 21ST, JAN 30TH, FEB 3RD, FEB 12TH)

Free spirited and with strong opinions, social and global issues-- and how best to deal with them are foremost on your mind. You try to urge people to break free of socially constructed limitations, because you firmly believe anyone can do anything, regardless of what other people say, or circumstances seem to dictate. In fact, you may derive a special pleasure from breaking past a limitation when all the odds are stacked against you, this motivates you all the more. Leadership, coaching, and teaching come naturally, as you encourage people to go after what they want in life. Morals and ethics play a strong role in your life, in fact your defining lessons throughout life will be centered on these issues.

In terms of career, you are drawn towards positions that allow you to exercise your talent for out of the box thinking and allow you a chance to express your ideas. Jobs requiring strong communications skills, persuasive ability, and that offer opportunities to push the limits appeal to you.

Publishing, technology, computers, writing, humanitarian work, the social sciences, extreme sports, the visual and performing arts, nursing, politics, law, medicine, science, fashion, philosophy, religion, metaphysics, and teaching are particularly well-suited.

In romance, you look for a partner who is first your friend and then your lover because you believe friendship is the secret to a meaningful, long-lasting union. You need someone who shares your sense of humour, love of variety, and need for freedom. Your family enjoys your well thought out reasoning in responding to their questions and comments. You teach your children that their only limitations are those they set for themselves, and that they are capable of much more than they ever dreamed possible.

Celebrities

Christian Dior, multi-award winning fashion designer, founder of Christian Dior fashion house, best-selling author (Jan 21st)

Phil Collins, multi-award winning singer, songwriter, multi-instrumentalist, and music producer (Jan 30th)

Dr. Elizabeth Blackwell, first female doctor in the United States. The Elizabeth Blackwell Award is given annually to a female physician for most outstanding contributions in the field of medicine (Feb 3rd)

Abraham Lincoln, lawyer, 16th President of the United States. He led the United States through the Civil War (Feb 12th)

AQUARIUS NUMBER 4 (JAN 22ND, JAN 31ST, FEB 4TH, FEB 13TH)

With this combination, you are sure to be light years ahead of society in some sphere of thought or action. Inventive, original, and offbeat, you are a trendsetter in every sense of the word. People may have trouble understanding your thinking and behaviour, but that is simply because you are ahead of the times. You boldly go where no one has ever gone before, tackling issues that are thought to be off-limit, taboo or too deeply ingrained into society to ever be challenged. You feel that if change is ever going to happen, it starts with one person, and that person might as well be you! You are a no-nonsense type of person, unwilling to make justifications for excuses such as "that is the way it is" or "that is the way it has always been done." Your discipline and work ethic paves the way for much needed change in this world.

If you were born on January 22nd, you receive the benefits of this master number. Uranus, the ruler of Aquarius corresponds to number 22, so you have a double dose of Aquarian innovation. Truly a visionary, you are able to dream great ideas and have the practicality to implement them. There is a natural brilliance, perhaps even amounting to genius, in some area of your life, although you have to be careful to not let other people dissuade you from your vision. Regardless of how your ideas are perceived by today's society, your work always tends to be more appreciated by future generations.

In terms of career, you are excellent at affecting change that you find meaningful. Careers in law, social work, politics, international business, human rights, humanitarian work, social activism, labour relations, education, visual art, design, aviation, technology, computers, drama, writing, music, and science are particularly appealing. In whatever field you are in, it is important to you that you leave your original print on it.

In romance, you are attracted to adventurous, offbeat individuals willing to explore new frontiers. You need a partner who offers a sense of stability, and is open-minded to different ways of thinking. Although appreciative of some of your lovable eccentricities, your family may find it difficult to understand all of them. When doing something that affects them, be sure to give a well-reasoned explanation. You encourage your children, by example, to be unconventional and stand out from the crowd.

Celebrities

Sir Francis Bacon, philosopher, statesman, scientist, jurist, orator, essayist and author. He is thought of as the father of empiricism (Jan 22nd)

Justin Timberlake, multi-award winning and best-selling singer, songwriter, and actor (Jan 31st)

Rosa Parks, multi-award winning Civil Rights activist and author. She was the first woman, and second non-U.S. government official to lie in honor at the Capitol Rotunda (Feb 4th)

Jerry Springer, multi-award winning TV show host, actor, and former politician (Feb 13th)

AQUARIUS NUMBER 5 (JAN 23RD, FEB 5TH, FEB 14TH)

Intelligent, witty, and blessed with great communication skills, you are able to hold your own in a discussion with anyone. Regardless of formal education, social background, or class, you are able to portray an image of sophistication. Others may perceive you as an authoritative or articulate speaker. You love learning, and your curiosity about people and the world around you is endless. Always the eternal student, you can never get enough information and meaningful conversation.

Although you are compassionate and caring, because you have a highly active mind, you tend to use logic in analyzing your emotions and those of others. One of your challenges is to feel your emotions rather than talking yourself out of them.

Careers involving communications, publishing, journalism, literature, languages, politics, government, charity work, teaching, travel, nursing, broadcasting, media, sports, or research are a natural fit for you.

Thriving on intellectual challenge, you may be interested in getting advanced degrees, or continually expanding your knowledge base through your own reading and research.

Excelling at logic, reason, and analysis, careers in science, math, engineering, forensics, medicine, technology, environmental studies, or academia might allow you to express your skills.

In romance, you crave a partner to discuss interesting ideas, and you thrive on intellectual stimulation. Lovers are attracted by your sense of humour and charm. However, with your gift for speech, you do have to keep in mind that your words leave a lasting impression on people, for good or bad. Your children admire your sense of dedication and your faithful loyalty. Participating in activities designed to encourage original thinking and innovation with your family is enjoyable for everyone.

Celebrities

Caroline, Princess of Monaco, princess and philanthropist (Jan 23rd)

Don Cherry, Canadian ice hockey commentator, author, sports writer, retired professional hockey player, and NHL coach (Feb 5th)

François Hollande, 24th and current President of France, recipient of multiple national and foreign honours, including Grand Master & Grand Cross of the National Order of the Legion of Honour (Feb 14th)

AQUARIUS NUMBER 6 (JAN 24TH, FEB 6TH, FEB 15TH)

You are socially conscious, idealistic, and have a profound desire to serve humanity. You crave making a positive, lasting difference in the world, and feeling that you had a personal impact in other people's lives. Empathy is an admirable trait of yours, although you must resist the temptation to give advice to those who don't request it.

Generous with both your time and resources, you are looked on for help by your friends in times of need. Boundary setting may be an issue for you when younger, but as you grow older, you gain wisdom through experience.

Very enterprising and self-motivated, you may have a desire to work for yourself or operate your own business. Blending the Aquarian talent for innovation with the responsibility and business sense of the 6, you could have a career around helping people live up to their highest potential, or perhaps caring for animals.

You have a lot of physical vitality and may wish a more physically based career in sports, dancing, martial arts, a skilled trade or another career allowing you to burn off extra energy.

Other careers you may find interesting are those in business management, education, yoga, social work, psychology, writing, spirituality, law, teaching, healthcare, rehabilitation, or counselling.

In romance, you are a loyal, devoted, and generous partner. Admirers appreciate your willingness to help where there is a need, and your ability to lend a gentle ear. You have a tendency to make many sacrifices for your family which they appreciate more and more as time goes on. Be receptive when they try to reciprocate your love. There is a natural affinity with children, and they respect you for treating them with an equal level of respect shown to adults.

Celebrities

Neil Diamond, multi-award winning and best-selling singer-songwriter. Inducted into the Songwriters Hall of Fame and the Rock and Roll Hall of Fame in 1984 (Jan 24th)

Bob Marley, multi-award winning reggae singer, songwriter, musician, and guitarist. Winner of the Grammy Lifetime Achievement Award in 2001 and awarded the Jamaican Order of Merit in 1981 (Feb 6th)

Galileo Galilei, astronomer, physicist, engineer, philosopher, and mathematician. Father of modern physics (Feb 15th)

AQUARIUS NUMBER 7 (JAN 25TH, FEB 7TH, FEB 16TH)

Thoughtful, independent, and intuitive, you need a lot of time for reflection on the world around you. Prominent social and world issues of the day capture your attention, and you may use your communicative skill to get the point across to others in a meaningful way.

Your curious mind is attracted to subjects off the beaten path, as you try to investigate the deeper truths and mysteries contained within. Imaginative and visionary, ideas and inventions not yet conceived of take birth in your mind. For this reason, you are an especially vivid writer, both of fiction and of non-fiction. You benefit from keeping a dream journal, or a journal just to record your thoughts and feelings.

Naturally creative, professions such as writing, visual and performing arts, photography, fashion design, and music may draw your interest.

Careers such as teaching, public speaking, journalism, literature, broadcasting, religion, counselling, or coaching suit you well. Your sensitivity to inequality and abuse of power may lead you to work in a field related to social justice.

In romance, you are compassionate and sensitive to your lover's needs and desires. You treat them fairly, and expect to be treated fairly in return. Your intuition is your most powerful guide in love-- if something feels right you should just do it. Your children love your ability to tell stories and keep them entertained! They also admire your ability to teach by example, rather than just give lectures or directions.

Celebrities

William Somerset Maugham, playwright, novelist, and short story writer (Jan 25th)

Charles Dickens, popular novelist and cultural icon (Feb 7th)

Eckhart Tolle, leading spiritual figure and public speaker (Feb 16th)

AQUARIUS NUMBER 8 (JAN 26TH, FEB 8TH, FEB 17TH)

Responsible and ambitious, yet with an awesome sense of humour, you are able to make lemonade out of lemons! You believe that the best things in life come after you have worked for them, and triumphed over personal obstacles. Because there were a lot of trials growing up, you gained strength and perspective in dealing with life's difficulties. A gifted motivator, you are able to get people to focus on the upside to their challenges as well.

Noted for your generosity, your friends greatly appreciate your desire to go out of the way to help them, especially in times of need. Your desire to help extends to those in need, and you probably are devoted to at least one charitable cause.

In terms of career, your work ethic, self-discipline, and authoritative presence take you far. Even if starting at the bottom, your ambition and willingness to go the extra mile earns positive recognition. Leadership comes naturally to you, but you must learn the art of compromise to be as effective as you can be.

You do well in business management, comedy, writing, healthcare, media, sales, science, law, politics, government, corrections, accounting, real estate, technology, the skilled trades, math, and sports. If artistically inclined, music and visual arts may hold special appeal.

In romance, you seek to provide your partner with memorable experiences. Small details really do make a difference! Your children are inspired by your positive slant on the tough times, and they try to find a way to use their difficulties to build inner strength and resilience. You don't always give them what they ask for, and as adults they are grateful that you didn't spoil them! With your family, remember to mix in two servings of praise with every dose of criticism. This will go a long way in building mutual trust.

Celebrities

Ellen DeGeneres, multi-award winning comedian, television host, actress, writer, and producer (Jan 26th)

John Grisham, multi-award winning and best-selling novelist, recipient of the Galaxy British Lifetime Achievement Award in 2007 (Feb 8th)

Michael Jordan, basketball player and six time NBA Champion (Feb 17th)

AQUARIUS NUMBER 9 (JAN 27TH, FEB 9TH, FEB 18TH)

A very strong inventive streak runs through you, as you intuitively know how to deliver products and services people desire. Although multitalented, you are capable of singular devotion to an area in which you can make long-lasting contributions. Your passion rather than an external force is the drive behind your ambition.

Creativity runs through your veins and you should find an outlet to express your message to the world. Often the first to embrace new thought or way of doing things, you help set the trend for those around you.

An excellent coach, your skill for positively framing challenging events helps you turn what other people would term negative experiences, into lessons that can be learned from.

In terms of career, you do well in teaching, social work, working with children, medicine, photography, writing, visual arts, drama, technology, health care, psychology, philosophy, music, politics, entertainment, science, yoga, the occult, and writing.

Owning your own business or being in charge of a group of people is also a distinct possibility. Often having risen up through your own effort and having overcome many obstacles, you are able to be an inspiring leader, one who sets a personal example. Your ability to take risks takes you far.

In romance, it is important to you to keep things fresh and exciting, always learning more with your partner day after day. Your spouse values your optimistic outlook, enthusiasm, and sense of humour. Because of your youthful outlook, your kids feel you are able to relate to what they are going through, and because of that are more honest with you about what they are feeling. As a family, activities designed to promote exciting new discoveries and inventions are fruitful to participate in.

Celebrities

Wolfgang Amadeus Mozart, classical composer, and cultural icon (Jan 27th)

Alice Walker, poet, author and Civil Rights activist. Recipient of the National Book Award and the Pulitzer Prize for Fiction in 1983 (Feb 9th)

John Travolta, multi-award winning actor, dancer, producer, singer, and pilot (Feb 18th)

Chapter 18

Pisces Numbers 1-9

Pisces Number 1 (Feb 19th, February 28th, March 1st, March 10th, March 19th)

Combining the charm, intuition, and emotional sensitivity of Pisces, with the confidence and leadership ability of the 1, makes you an emotionally intelligent leader. You know how to guide people into activities that maximize their natural potential. The daydreamer in Pisces meets the action orientation and ambition of the 1, so that the ideas you envision are able to manifest practically. On the one hand you can be mystical, romantic, and idealistic, but on the other you are able to use logic and analysis. These complimentary abilities give you a good internal balance.

In terms of career, you may enjoy visual and performing arts, healing arts, teaching, fashion design, healthcare, medicine, feng shui, rehabilitation, social work, metaphysics, business management, government, politics, pharmaceuticals, entertainment, or humanitarian work.

In entrepreneurial pursuits you are aided by a sixth sense of market trends, this allows you to design products and services uniquely targeted to your audience. In whatever field you choose, you are blessed with an admirable combination of dreaminess and determination that allows you to successfully deliver on the promises you make.

In romance, lovers are attracted to your warm smile and words of encouragement. You need a partner who understands that while you may be tough on the outside, on the inside you feel much more deeply than the average person, and are sensitive to criticism. With family, it is important to encourage open discussion in the case of disagreements, so that misunderstandings do not get a chance to build up. In seeing your ability to take vitality enhancing risks, your children admire your willingness to step out of your comfort zone and try new things.

Celebrities

Cristina Fernández de Kirchner, first elected female President of Argentina, recipient of the World Telecommunication and Information Society Award in 2012 (Feb 19th)

Bernadette Peters, multi-award winning actress, singer, and children's book author (Feb 28th)

Frederic Chopin, pianist and composer, cultural icon (March 1st)

Harriet Tubman, African-American abolitionist, humanitarian and Union Spy, cultural icon (March 10th)

Bruce Willis, multi-award winning actor, producer, and singer (March 19th)

Pisces Number 2 (Feb 20th, Feb 29th, March 2nd, March 11th, March 20th)

There is a sense of innocence and youth that remains with you all through life. Physically, you age gracefully, often looking better with age. Emotionally, you still find wonder in everyday things, and strive to focus on what to be grateful for.

You are intensely human and feel things very deeply. The empathy and compassion you possess for those less fortunate shines through. You believe that it is better to give generously, so you tend to give people the benefit of the doubt. Although some may try to take advantage, because you are so trusting and expect the best of people, you tend to attract people genuinely in need of help.

People are your main focus, and creating intimate, meaningful relationships with family and friends your top priority. Because you are sensitive to other people and your surroundings, you must take care to not allow too much discord and negativity into your life, as it may result in physical and emotional ailments.

If you were born on March 11th, you receive the benefits of this master number. It is harmonious because the number 11 vibrates to Neptune, the ruler of Pisces. To say you are intuitive is a major understatement; having the combination of the most intuitive sign with the most intuitive number, your sixth sense often borders on psychic insights, uncanny hunches, and visions that often come true. When you walk into a room, you can feel what other people feel almost instantly without the need for words.

This insight could also be applied to animals, and you often have a special affinity with them. Your intuitive insight makes you especially suited for the nurturing professions; animal care, child care, nursing, working with the elderly, working with the disabled, counselling, therapy, and motivational work. Spirituality, metaphysics, the occult, and mysticism may also be natural interests.

In terms of career, you may have artistic talent: music, writing, painting, drawing, filmmaking, dance, fashion design, and photography are well-suited. You are able to go deep within yourself to produce work that touches people's hearts and has universal appeal. In launching your own business, your ability to understand changing moods and trends are a definite asset.

Careers involving understanding of human nature, and that require intuition, such as psychology, the healing arts, coaching, advising, and psychiatry are good for you. Humanitarian work and social justice may also interest you.

In love, you are a true romantic! Sentimental and sweet, you love connecting to your lover on a soul to soul level. You desire someone who is sensitive and compassionate. Craving peace and harmony in relationships, when family fights do happen they can be especially upsetting to you. During these times, make sure to reveal your honest feelings rather than bottling them up inside. Although your children or spouse may not always say it, they are very grateful for your ability to listen to them nonjudgmentally, and understand their changing perspectives.

Celebrities

Gloria Vanderbilt, multi-award winning artist, author, actress, heiress, socialite, and pioneer in designer blue jeans (Feb 20th)

Tony Robbins, multi-award winning motivational speaker, personal finance instructor, life coach, and best-selling self-help author (Feb 29th)

Jon Bon Jovi, multi-award winning and best-selling singer-songwriter, record producer, actor, and philanthropist. Recipient of the Common Wealth Award of Distinguished Service in 2015 (March 2nd)

Rupert Murdoch, billionaire and business magnate. Recipient of the Companion of the Order of Australia in 1984 (March 11th)

Kathy Ireland, former supermodel, actress, author, and founder of kathy ireland Worldwide (March 20th)

PISCES NUMBER 3 (FEB 21ST MARCH 3RD, MARCH 12TH)

Philosophical, observant, and contemplative, you are very interested in things much beyond the world we live in. Perhaps this interest manifests in a desire to know what can't be verified through the five senses, and/or an interest in religion, spirituality, esoteric subjects, and metaphysics. In any case, you have a well-developed inner world that is your sanctuary. You know that just because you haven't experienced something, it doesn't mean it is not real. Thus you have respect for other people's seemingly "unreal" experiences. At the same time, you can be incredibly driven and determined in the outside world, as long as the goal captures your passion. Your motto is if at first you don't succeed, try again! A great strength is your faith, you truly believe you can do what you set out to accomplish.

In terms of career, you are creative and do well in art, literature, fashion design, drama and music.

A particularly strong skill of yours is writing; any job that requires good written communication skills suits you.

You may also like to go into a field that allows you to create a sense of justice, such as law, politics, corrections, social work, or labour studies.

Careers involving higher education, science, teaching, travel, religion, spirituality, the outdoors, nature, or the water may appeal.

You are versatile and are well able to do two or more careers at the same time.

In romance, you can be very idealistic, intuitive and empathetic, with an ability to feel what your partner is feeling. Your hunches about your family are usually dead on. However, your sensitivity has one drawback; your tendency to take things too personally.

Pay more attention to the intention of the person giving you criticism than their actual words. As a family, taking trips near the water or places where there is an abundance of natural beauty brings special bonding. Your family appreciates your calm, soothing presence in times of need.

Celebrities

Hubert de Givenchy, French aristocrat and fashion designer. Recipient of the Lifetime Achievement Award from the Council of Fashion Designers of America in 1996 (Feb 21st)

Alexander Graham Bell, multi-award winning scientist, inventor of telephone, engineer, and innovator (March 3rd)

Annette Adams, lawyer, judge, and first female Assistant Attorney General in the United States (March 12th)

PISCES NUMBER 4 (FEB 22ND, MARCH 4TH, MARCH 13TH)

You are one of the most creative, imaginative, and innovative minds of the zodiac. Your mind thinks in non-linear ways to see things from angles no one else had thought of. Both self-discovery and discovery of the world around you is important, you feel there are always new frontiers to explore. Because of this, you end up being a pioneer in at least one area of your life.

You are gifted with an uncanny intuition, possibly bordering on psychic abilities, at least from time to time. You should rely on this gift for it will rarely, if ever let you down. Even the most gregarious among you needs time to be alone, for this is where your best quality work comes out. Let your intuition guide your creative efforts and you will be amazed with the results.

If you were born February 22nd, you receive the benefits of this master number. Frequently there is a sense of destiny with this combination. You are quite happy to devote yourself to

a cause or social issue you really believe in, particularly those
to do with social justice. Even your work transcends personal
recognition, for something that can really improve quality of life,
or add to cultural development. You are both the idealist and
the revolutionary, and are not afraid to be the first one to step
up and make the desired change you wish to see. Because of the
compassion of Pisces, combined with the master builder energy
of the 22, you can build something of tangible value to help
those who are underprivileged.

In terms of career, you have a very strong need to express your
originality in whatever you do. You desire to have a meaningful
impact on society and in the world, so choosing a career that lets
you feel that you are part of something bigger than yourself is
necessary for happiness.

Careers in humanitarian work, sociology, social work, human
rights, writing, publishing, metaphysics, medicine, healing, yoga,
environmental protection, law, politics, pharmaceuticals, or
astronomy may capture your attention.

You are good at investigation, deciphering messages and
problem solving, thus math, engineering, research and science are
also good fits.

You can be quite unconventional in your interests, and perhaps
you may try turning one of your hobbies into a career.

In romance, you can be changeable and need your freedom,
being with a lover who understands your mutable nature is best.
You need someone who understands your talent and encourages
you in your pursuits, because they are likely to be off the beaten
path, or otherwise very idealistic. Partners who cannot understand
your future oriented thinking should be avoided. Naturally
empathetic, your family often comes to you for advice. Trust your
intuition when responding, as you let yourself be inspirationally
guided as to what to say.

Celebrities

George Washington, first President of the United States, one of the Founding Fathers of the United States (Feb 22nd)

Antonio Vivaldi, Baroque composer and virtuoso violinist (March 4th)

Percival Lowell, businessman, author, mathematician, and astronomer. He was a key figure in the subsequent discovery of Pluto (March 13th)

PISCES NUMBER 5 (FEB 23RD, MARCH 5TH, MARCH 14TH)

Flexible and versatile, you adapt gracefully to change, a major theme in your life. Constant change has been foisted on you from a young age and you have learned to roll with the punches. Often your formal education is in a different field from where life takes you later on. Regardless, your positive outlook tends to see the best in every situation.

Communication is one of your major strengths, you can be a motivator of people and groups. Just when it looks like there is no hope, you teach people to believe there can be. Perhaps this is because often in your own life there could be a theme of defeating all the odds and doing things that people never thought you could do. But first you must overcome your tendency to be indecisive.

Foreign travel may be of interest, or at least transporting yourself to different times and places through books and movies.

In terms of career, you have a special affinity for words, and an ability to make a strong impact on those around you. You believe in meaning what you say and saying what you mean. Careers that utilize your natural skill for public speaking-- lecturing, advocacy, negotiations, mediation, advising, teaching, education, sales, and politics-- are good fits for you.

You are imaginative and do well in the arts, but are particularly good at music, filmmaking, dance, and photography.

Other areas of interest may be rehabilitation, fitness, wellness, assisted living, editing, working with animals, science, technology, pharmaceuticals, recreation and parks, and martial arts.

Multitalented and with a love of intellectual stimulation, you are likely to change careers at least once, and might juggle two or more roles at the same time.

In romance, your love for variety and stimulation mean it could take you a while to find that special someone. You need someone who understands that your destiny involves constantly changing your mind, moods, and ideas and is willing to take the ride with you. Partners who are too fixed in their thoughts and behaviours may find you difficult to understand. Among family you are motivating, open-minded, and tolerant. Your talent for pointing out the silver lining in every cloud is of great comfort to them in challenging times.

Celebrities

George Frideric Handel, Baroque composer (Feb 23rd)

Joel Osteen, preacher, televangelist, best-selling author, and Senior Pastor of Lakewood Church (March 5th)

Albert Einstein, multi-award winning theoretical physicist who developed the general theory of relativity. He was awarded the Nobel Prize in Physics in 1921 (March 14th)

PISCES NUMBER 6 (FEB 24TH, MARCH 6TH, MARCH 15TH)

You have a special eye for what is beautiful and instinctively know how to create visual appeal in anything you design. You can take average products and shape them into something stunning. In cooking, you know how to combine ingredients for maximum flavour. Or you may apply yourself in music, blending rhythms and instruments together to create a unique sound.

Appearance is important to you and you take care to be well-groomed and/or physically fit; firmly believing that your outer self is a reflection of your inner self.

Because you are highly aware of your surroundings, an ugly external environment can throw you off balance physically and emotionally. You are service oriented and compassionate, feeling the need to assist in making people's lives better. As a result you may find a lot of satisfaction in positions that engage your nurturing side. You may excel in caring for animals, the elderly, children, or people who are disabled. Consider working in rehabilitation, healthcare, social work, and charitable organizations.

In terms of career, your eye for beauty and sense of symmetry and proportion can be helpful in the beauty/fitness/wellness or fashion industry, or in connection with real estate, interior design, or luxury goods and services.

Creating works of art with your hand may be of interest, or perhaps you may express your artistic side through poetry, landscaping, photography, filmmaking, drama, or music.

In romance, lovers are attracted to your charm, sensuality, and generosity. You are attracted to partners who have a charitable disposition and who seek to make a positive difference in people's lives. One of your challenges is that you have a tendency to put your partner on a pedestal. Do your best to be more understanding of their limitations so that you aren't too disappointed if they fail to live up to your expectations. By example, you show your family how to fully appreciate the things they have and enjoy the natural beauty everywhere around them.

Celebrities

Phil Knight, billionaire and founder of Nike (Feb 24th)

Michelangelo, sculptor, painter, architect, poet, and engineer of the High Renaissance (March 6th)

Eva Longoria, multi award winning actress, producer, director, activist and businesswoman, named as Philanthropist of the Year in 2009 by The Hollywood Reporter (March 15th)

PISCES NUMBER 7 (FEB 25TH, MARCH 7TH, MARCH 16TH)

This combination is most comfortable for Pisces, as its ruler Neptune vibrates to number 7. You are among one of the most creative and mysterious people of the zodiac, with a very rich imagination and inner life. Solitude is a must for you, as it is here that your most profound ideas take root and grow.

Capable of transporting other people into a fantasy world, or another place and time, you are an especially talented storyteller, writer, actor, or filmmaker. Any form of your creative work is able to evoke strong reactions from others, causing them to ponder.

Your style is probably more abstract and non-linear, and you like to discuss ideals and possibilities, not merely what you can experience through the five senses. There is likely to be a strong contemplative, spiritual, religious, or philosophical side to your nature, possibly even mystical.

Generous and empathetic, you are a good shoulder to lean on in times of need, and go out of the way to help people who need it.

In terms of career, you excel in occupations that allow you a certain amount of time to be by yourself, too much interaction with people will drain you. However with your gifts of empathy, intuition, and listening skill, the fields of counselling, therapy, psychology, coaching, and advising are good fits.

Jobs requiring abstract and creative thinking, writing talent, and adaptability are your forte. You may be attracted to careers involving art, music, the healing arts, humanitarian work, the occult, teaching, foreign travel, graphic design, film, or photography.

Careers located near bodies of water or out in nature may interest you.

In romance, you can be very idealistic but it is hard for anyone to get into your inner world. You believe in quality of relationships and give your heart away only when someone has earned your trust. Lovers are attracted by your idealism, empathy, and independence. At the same time, you can be very secretive. You should share your inner thoughts with your family to build more emotional intimacy. They appreciate that you instilled in them the value of critical thinking and silent reflection early on, and this is something they carry with them always.

Celebrities

Meher Baba, Indian spiritual master and author who established the Avatar Meher Baba Charitable Trust (Feb 25th)

E.L. James, Fifty Shades of Grey NYT best-selling novelist, UK National Book Award winner in 2012 (March 7th)

Jerry Lewis, multi-award winning comedian, actor, singer, film producer, screenwriter and film director. Long running host of the Muscular Dystrophy Association's annual Labor Day Telethon. He was the recipient of the Jean Hersholt Humanitarian Award in 2009 (March 16th)

PISCES NUMBER 8 (FEB 26TH, MARCH 8TH, MARCH 17TH)

You are blessed with the complementary gifts of intuition and vision from Pisces, and the determination and ambition of the 8. Putting them together, you are able to turn your dreams into reality. Frequently, you have your finger on the pulse of the trends of society, and can devise products and services designed to make life easier or more enjoyable for a wide range of people.

As gentle or soft-spoken as you may seem on the outside, on the inside is a fiercely independent thinker, and one who is tenacious enough to achieve his or her goals. The only challenge for you, is selecting the goal you wish to pursue and then sticking with it to completion.

In terms of career, you are a great advocate for a cause you believe in, or for promoting the interests of people in need. The way you question authority and traditional thinking may lead to constructive change to favour the needs of those you represent. With your interest in justice, you may like law, politics, social work, charity work, or working with marginalized people.

A strong streak of creativity runs through you, so writing, fashion design, and music may appeal.

Science and technology may satisfy your desire for invention and discovery.

In romance, you are attracted to lovers with a good sense of humour and who have the spirit of exploration and discovery.

Others are attracted to your innovative mind and flexibility. With your children, you have a tendency to make rules or decisions, but then with a little emotional persuasion, can go back on them. You should make sure that you explain to your children the reasoning behind your rules to create a sense of fairness, and help to cultivate discipline. Your family admires your intelligence and that you encourage them to fight for what they believe is right.

Celebrities

Victor Hugo, novelist, poet, novelist, and dramatist of the Romantic Movement (Feb 26th)

Josephine Cochrane, inventor of the dish washing machine (March 8th)

Alexander McQueen, fashion designer and couturier, four-time winner of British Designer of the year (March 17th)

Pisces number 9 (Feb 27th, March 9th, March 18th)

Very attuned to your powerful intuition, your willingness to trust it, even if other people say otherwise, can make a big difference in your overall life success. There is a unique ability to see possibilities not yet apparent in people and situations. This talent can make you great as a motivator towards positive change. It can also be used in discovering the hidden talents in those around you. There is a strong intellectual need to learn new things about this world and possibly worlds beyond; after all Yuri Gagarin born on March 9th, was the first person to travel to outer space!

In terms of career, you would do well in the healing arts, poetry, music, dance, sports, or creative writing fields.

Advocacy for non-profit organizations, those with special needs, or those who have been mistreated are some of your other skills.

Sales, marketing, and advertising, are suited to you due to your blend of charm and self-assertiveness. In fact in many areas of life, you can make a convincing pitch while still remaining likeable.

There is an ability to relate to those younger than you, therefore careers involving children and adolescents may appeal.

Your love of animals, the outdoors, nature, or the water may influence your career.

Idealism, combined with your strength of will, can help you in all careers that seek to make the world a better place to live.

In romance, you are passionate and sensitive. You have great range and depth of emotion, so you need a lover who understands your changing moods and is able to go with the flow. You may be slow to commit, but when you do, you give it your all. Despite your outward appearance of gentleness, there is a fighter in you that is very resilient to the hard knocks of life. You teach your family by example, to not let other people mistake their kindness for weakness.

Celebrities

Henry Wadsworth Longfellow, popular poet, educator, and cultural icon (Feb 27th)

Yuri Gagarin, Soviet pilot and cosmonaut, first person to journey into outer space in 1961 (March 9th)

Vanessa Williams, multi-award winning singer, actress and producer, first African American woman crowned Miss America in 1984 (March 18th)

Appendix 1

Female Heads of State 2015

Astrological Sign	Number of times appearing in the sample /28	Rank
Pisces	6	1
Sagittarius	5	2
Taurus	4	3
Libra	4	3
Aries	3	5
Scorpio	2	6
Cancer	2	6
Virgo	1	8
Aquarius	1	8
Leo	0	10
Capricorn	0	10
Gemini	0	10

Birthday Number	Number of times appearance in sample /28	Added amount (if applicable)	Adjusted number of times in sample	Original Rank	Adjusted rank
2, 11, 20, 29	8			1	1
5, 14, 23	4	1	5	2	2
1, 10, 19, 28	4			2	3
3, 12, 21, 30	3			4	6
7, 16, 25	3	.75	3.75	4	4
8, 17, 26	3	.75	3.75	4	4
6, 15, 24	2	0.5	2.5	7	7
4, 13, 22, 31	1	.10	1.10	8	8
9, 18, 27	0	0	0	9	9

Keep in mind when looking at the table that birthdays 5, 6, 7, 8, 9 only have three dates each whereas 1-4 have four dates each, so we would expect 25% more appearance times from 1-4. To be even more precise, there are 5 months which don't have the 31st. The more dates there are for a given number, the more chances for the number to appear all else being equal. To adjust for these discrepancies, I added 25% to numbers 5-9 to make them equivalent in real terms to numbers 1-3. Also, for number 4, since 5/12= 41.6, I multiplied 25 x 0.416= 10.4, therefore I added 10.4% to number 4 to make it equivalent in real terms to numbers 1-3. It is noted that February lacks the 29th every 4 years and the 30th each year but the discrepancy is too small to make a difference in real terms in the rankings.

Appendix 2

Female Heads of State Since Mid-20th Century

Historical Head of State	Birthday	Sun sign/ birth date combination
Khertek Anchimaa-Toka	January 1st	Capricorn 1
Sükhbaataryn Yanjmaa	February 15th	Aquarius 6
Soong Ching-ling	January 27th	Aquarius 9
Isabel Martínez de Perón	February 4th	Aquarius 4
Lidia Gueiler Tejada	August 28th	Virgo 1
Vigdís Finnbogadóttir	April 15th	Aries 6
Maria Lea Pedini-Angelini	July 15th	Cancer 6
Agatha Barbara	March 11th	Pisces 11/2
Gloriana Ranocchini	No birth data	
Elisabeth Kopp	December 16th	Sagittarius 7
Corazon C. Aquino	January 25th	Aquarius 7
Ertha Pascal-Trouillot	August 13th	Leo 4
Maria Liberia Peters	May 20th	Taurus 2
Sabine Bergmann-Pohl	April 20th	Aries 2
Violeta Chamorro	October 18th	Libra 9
Mary Robinson	May 21st	Unknown time, born on a cusp
Edda Ceccoli	June 26th	Cancer 8
Ruth Dreifuss	January 9th	Capricorn 9
Patrizia Busignani	May 11th	Taurus 11/2
Chandrika Kumaratunga	June 29th	Cancer 2

Ruth Perry	July 16th	Cancer 7
Mary McAleese	June 27th	Cancer 9
Janet Jagan	October 20th	Libra 2
Ruth Metzler-Arnold	May 23rd	Gemini 5
Borjana Krišto	August 13th	Leo 4
Rosa Zafferani	August 16th	Leo 7
Vaira-Freiberga	December 1st	Sagittarius 1
Mireya Moscoso	July 1st	Cancer 1
Tarja Halonen	December 24th	Capricorn 6
Maria Michelotti	October 8th	Libra 8
Gloria Macapagal-Arroyo	April 5th	Aries 5
Megawati Sukarnoputri	January 23rd	Aquarius 5
Micheline Calmy-Rey	July 8th	Cancer 8
Valeria Ciavatta	January 16th	Capricorn 7
Fausta Morganti	August 20th	Leo 2
Ellen Sirleaf	October 29th	Scorpio 2
Michelle Bachelet	September 29th	Libra 2
Doris Leuthard	April 10th	Aries 1
Pratibha Patil	December 19th	Sagittarius 1
Cristina Fernández de Kirchner	February 19th	Pisces 1
Eveline Widmer-Schlumpf	March 16th	Pisces 7
Assunta Meloni	April 21st	Taurus 3
Dalia Grybauskaitė	March 1st	Pisces 1
Roza Otunbayeva	August 23rd	Virgo 5

Laura Chinchilla	March 28th	Aries 1
Simonetta Sommaruga	May 14th	Taurus 5
Dilma Rousseff	December 14th	Sagittarius 5
Maria Berti	October 6th	Libra 6
Atifete Jahjaga	April 20th	Aries 2
Joyce Banda	April 12th	Aries 3
Denise Bronzetti	December 12th	Sagittarius 3
Park Geun-hye	February 2nd	Aquarius 2
Antonella Mularoni	September 27th	Libra 9
Anna Maria Muccioli	August 15th	Leo 6
Catherine Samba-Panza	June 26th	Cancer 8
Marie Louise Coleiro Preca	December 7th	Sagittarius 7
Kolinda Grabar-Kitarović	April 29th	Taurus 2
Sirimavo Ratwatte Dias	April 17th	Aries 8
Indira Gandhi	November 19th	Scorpio 1
Golda Meïr	May 3rd	Taurus 3
Élisabeth Domitién	No birth data	
Margaret Thatcher	October 13th	Libra 4
Nataša Mićić	November 2nd	Scorpio 2
Biljana Plavšić	July 7th	Cancer 7
Dame Mary Eugenia Charles	May 15th	Taurus 6
Gro Harlem Brundtland	April 20th	Aries 2
Milka Planinc	November 21st	Scorpio 3
Benazir Bhutto	June 21st	Unknown time, born on a cusp
Kasimiera Prunskienė	February 26th	Pisces 8

Begum Khaleda Zia	August 15th	Leo 6
Edith Cresson	January 27th	Aquarius 9
Hanna Suchocka	April 3rd	Aries 3
Sylvie Kinigi	No birth data	
Tansu Çiller	May 24th	Gemini 6
Agathe Uwilingiyimana	May 23rd	Gemini 5
Sheikh Hasina Wajed	September 28th	Libra 1
Jenny Shipley	February 4th	Aquarius 4
Helen Clark	February 26th	Pisces 8
Mame Madior Boye	No birth data	
Maria das Neves Ceita Batista de Sousa	No birth data	
Luísa Días Diogo	April 11th	Aries 11/2
Yuliya Tymoshenko	November 27th	Sagittarius 9
Maria do Carmo Trovoada Pires de Carvalho Silveira	No birth data	
Angela Merkel	July 17th	Cancer 8
Portia Simpson-Miller	December 12th	Sagittarius 3
Han Myung-sook	March 24th	Aries 6
Zinaida Grecianîi	February 7th	Aquarius 7
Michèle Pierre-Louis	October 5th	Libra 5
Jóhanna Sigurðardóttir	October 4th	Libra 4
Jadranka Kosor	July 1st	Cancer 1
Kamla Persad-Bissessar	April 22nd	Taurus 22/4
Mari Kiviniemi	September 27th	Libra 9
Julia Gillard	September 29th	Libra 2

Iveta Radičová	December 7th	Sagittarius 7
Cissé Mariam Kaïdama Sidibé	January 4th	Capricorn 4
Yingluck Shinawatra	June 21st	Gemini 3
Helle Thorning-Schmidt	December 14th	Sagittarius 5
Alenka Bratušek	March 31st	Aries 4
Tatyana Turanskaya	November 20th	Scorpio 2
Aminata Touré,	October 12th	Libra 3
Erna Solberg	February 24th	Pisces 6
Laimdota Straujuma	February 24th	Pisces 6
Ana Jara	May 11th	Taurus 11/2
Ewa Kopacz	December 3rd	Sagittarius 3
Saara Kuugongelwa-Amadhila	October 12th	Libra 3

Astrological Sign	Number of times appearing in the sample /97	Rank
Libra	14	1
Aries	13	2
Cancer	11	3
Sagittarius	11	3
Taurus	9	5
Aquarius	9	5
Pisces	8	7
Leo	6	8
Scorpio	5	9
Capricorn	5	9
Gemini	4	11
Virgo	2	12

Birthday Number	Number of times appearance in sample /99	Added amount (if applicable)	Adjusted number of times in sample	Original Rank	Adjusted Rank
2, 11, 20, 29	18			1	1
3, 12, 21, 30	13			2	3
1, 10, 19, 28	12			3	5
6, 15, 24	12	3	15	3	2
7, 16, 25	10	2.5	12.5	5	4
5, 14, 23	9	2.25	11.25	6	6
4, 13, 22, 31	9	0.94	9.94	6	9
8, 17, 26	8	2	10	8	7
9, 18, 27	8	2	10	8	7

Keep in mind when looking at the table above that birthdays 5, 6, 7, 8, 9 only have three dates each whereas 1-4 have four dates each, so we would expect 25% more appearance times from 1-4. To be even more precise, there are five months which don't have the 31st. The more dates there are for a given number, the more chances for the number to appear all else being equal. To adjust for these discrepancies, I added 25% to numbers 5-9 to make them equivalent in real terms to numbers 1-3. Also, for number 4, since 5/12= 41.6, I multiplied 25 x 0.416= 10.4, therefore I added 10.4% to number 4 to make it equivalent in real terms to numbers 1-3. It is noted that February lacks the 29th every 4 years and the 30th each year but the discrepancy is too small to make a difference in real terms in the rankings.

BIBLIOGRAPHY

Abadie, M.J. (2001). *Teen Astrology*. *Rochester,* Vermont: Bindu Books.

Cheung, T. (2007). *The Element Encyclopedia of Birthdays*. Hammersmith, London: HarperCollinsPublishers.

Cheiro. (2011). *Cheiro's Astro-Numerology & Your Star*. New Delhi, India: Diamond Pocket Books.

Cope, L. (1999). *Your Stars are Numbered*. Boston, Massachusetts: Element Books, Inc.

Ducie, S. (2008). *Do it Yourself Numerology*. Edison, New Jersey: Castle Books.

Frankl, V. (2006). *Man's Search for Meaning*. Boston, Massachusetts: Beacon Press.

Goldschneider, G. & Elffers, J. (2013). *The Secret Language of Birthdays*. New York, New York: Penguin Group.

Hand, R. (2002). *Planets in Transit*. Atglen Pennsylvania: Whitford Press.

Ilibagiza I. (2006). *Left to Tell: Discovering God Amidst the Rwandan Holocaust*. Carlsbad, California: Hay House.

Kelleher, J. (2006). *Path of Light Volume 1*. Ahimsa Press.

Kelleher, J. (2006). *Path of Light Volume 2*. Ahimsa Press.

Lewi, G. (1998). *Astrology*. New Delhi, India. B Jain Publishers.

McCants, G. (2005). *Glynis Has Your Number*. New York, New York: Hyperion Books.

Rao, K. N. (2003). *Karma & Rebirth in Hindu Astrology*. New Delhi, India: Vani Publications.

Scott, C. (1991). *The Initiate*. Weiser.

Singer, M. (2007). *The Untethered Soul*. Oakland, California: New Harbinger Publications.

Svoboda, R.E. (1998). *The Greatness of Saturn*. New Delhi, India: Rupa Publications.

Teal, C. (2008). *Lunar Nodes: Discover Your Soul's Karmic Mission*. Woodbury, Minnesota: Llewellyn Publications.

Tompkins, S. (2006). *The Contemporary Astrologer's Handbook*. London, England: Flare Publications.

Yogananda, P. (1946). *Autobiography of a Yogi*. New York, New York: The Philosophical Library.

Notes: Biographical and award related information on all celebrities referred to in this book were taken from their respective profiles on www.biography.com, www.imdb.com, Wikipedia.com, as well as their official professional websites. Sun signs for celebrities born on a cusp were confirmed using birth data taken from Lois Rodden's Astrodata Bank and Solar Fire's v8 public figure database.

ABOUT THE AUTHOR

Samantha I. Samuels holds a B.A in psychology and has studied formally at the International Academy of Astrology and American College of Vedic Astrology. She has lectured for organizations such as Astrology Toronto, the State of the Art Astrological Conference, and Kepler College. A prolific author, she has published articles in Astrology Toronto's Midheaven newsletter, The Weekly Voice, and the Canadian Association for Astrological Education's Ideas newsletter among several others. At the Canadian Association of Astrological Education, she teaches courses on astrology, numerology and astronumerology. "Your Destiny in Numbers," her popular numerology forecast column, is internationally syndicated.

Samantha resides in Mississauga, Ontario, and you can visit her website www.astronumerologywisdom.com to learn more about her classes and readings.

60540777R00192

Made in the USA
Lexington, KY
09 February 2017